Financial Abus
Older Clients.
Law, Practice and Prevention

Financial Abuse of Older Clients:
Law, Practice and Prevention

Ann Stanyer
Partner, Private Client, Wedlake Bell LLP

Bloomsbury Professional

Bloomsbury Professional

An imprint of Bloomsbury Publishing Plc

Bloomsbury Professional Ltd	Bloomsbury Publishing Plc
41–43 Boltro Road	50 Bedford Square
Haywards Heath	London
RH16 1BJ	WC1B 3DP
UK	UK

www.bloomsbury.com

BLOOMSBURY and the Diana logo are trademarks of

Bloomsbury Publishing Plc

British Library Cataloguing-in-Publication Data

A catalogue record for this book is available from the British Library.

ISBN:	PB:	978 1 78451 549 2
	ePDF:	978 1 78451 550 8
	ePub:	978 1 78451 551 5

Typeset by Phoenix Photosetting, Chatham, Kent
Printed and bound by CPI Group (UK) Ltd, Croydon, CR0 4YY

To find out more about our authors and books visit www.bloomsburyprofessional.com. Here you will find extracts, author information, details of forthcoming events and the option to sign up for our newsletters

Foreword

This is a timely book. Its publication coincides with many discussions and reports of inter-generational inequality in the news and current affairs. The premise of many of these discussions is that as a result of falling real incomes, declining home ownership and loss of secure pension expectations for young adults, the wealth of today's 'older' generation, particularly the hundreds of billions of pounds represented by privately owned homes, is likely to matter more to their children and grandchildren than it did to the 'older' generation when they came of age in the middle of the twentieth century. At the same time, a growing population of over-65-year-olds, with increasing life expectancy and increasing costs of care in later life impose a financial burden on the 'older' generation and their families, and diminish the inheritance expectations of their children and grandchildren. This economic and demographic landscape is the background to financial abuse of the elderly. As Ann Stanyer says in her opening chapter, defining financial abuse is not complicated, but it is a term which encompasses not only the crimes of theft and fraud, but improper pressure in relation to money or other property, and its use in ways which the owner does not or cannot fully consent to.

Early in the book, Ann Stanyer identifies some characteristics of an elderly victim of financial abuse. The dominant profile that emerges from her analysis of published judgments of the Court of Protection in 2015 is of a woman between 80 and 95 who has suffered financial abuse at the hands of an adult child she has trusted to manage her property and affairs as her attorney. It is helpful to keep this characteristic figure in mind, for, as the book demonstrates in detail, there is neither a single source of the law and practice in this field, nor a universal recognition of the characteristics of victims and the abuse that they are vulnerable to. This melancholy profile also illustrates one of the intractable problems of prevention of financial abuse: the failure of the trusted family member to act with integrity and in the best interests of the older person, in a private domestic setting from which professional advice or supervision is frequently absent. The loss of capacity to manage property and affairs is a profound and frequently insidious loss. There are no easy answers to achieving a balance between the preservation of personal autonomy and protection from financial abuse. Nor are there easy answers to the problems of protection of adults who are vulnerable, as a consequence of declining capacity and/or other frailties but who do not lack capacity within the meaning of the Mental Capacity Act 2005 (MCA 2005).

The MCA 2005 itself, which enables best interests decisions to be made for adults who lack capacity to make decisions for themselves, covers a range of protective structures: enduring powers of attorney made before 1 October 2007; lasting powers of attorney made after that date; deputyship and best interests decisions taken by the Court, with the Public Guardian also taking an administrative, investigatory and supervisory role in connection with the Court's jurisdiction. All of these structures are clearly explained in this book. Even when such a structure is in place, it cannot guarantee protection from financial abuse, and the remedies for such abuse form pieces of a jigsaw which must be identified and put together in each case. This is well illustrated in the case of *MJ and JM v The Public Guardian* [2013] EWCOP 2966/*Re Meek* [2014] EWCOP 1, one of the cases which is discussed in detail in this book. JM and MJ abused their position as property and affairs deputies for the elderly widow of JM's uncle, by making extravagant and unauthorised gifts with a value of over £250,000 to themselves and others out of GM's estate. The Court of Protection refused to give retrospective approval to the majority of these gifts, and revoked MJ and JM's appointment as deputies. On a further application to deal with a statutory will for GM, described by Senior Judge Denzil Lush as 'the missing piece in the jigsaw', the court authorised a will which excluded JM and MJ from any benefit, and also directed that the £275,000 security bond which they had been required to take out as property and affairs deputies should be called on in order to redress their wrongdoing.

All of these are steps in restitution rather than prevention, and this book deals with both, with entire chapters dedicated respectively to protection of the individual and recovery of assets, and to practical steps to safeguard against abuse. These are discussed with an emphasis on the needs and sensitivities of the older client within the framework of law and practice for those who advise them. Ann Stanyer draws widely on her own professional experience as a private client solicitor; on the current law as it has developed both under the MCA 2005 and the common law in cases where the validity of a will or lifetime gift has been challenged after death; and on research and guidance published by other agencies concerned with older people and their welfare, including a comparative survey of approaches to similar problems in other parts of the UK, the Republic of Ireland and the USA. She deals with every aspect of individuals' property and affairs, from everyday banking transactions to sales and transfers of older clients' homes, and the problems which can arise when an older client moves into property which forms part of another family member's home (a 'granny annex'). The Treasury estimate that over 30,000 such flats or annexes exist, but there are many financial issues to be considered and which give potential for financial abuse, and which are fully discussed here, as are the family care allowances which may be authorised by a deputy or by the Court of Protection.

Although the focus of the book is on the older client of the solicitor practising in civil law, in private client work or specialising in the problems of older clients or clients who lack mental capacity, Ann Stanyer dedicates a chapter to criminal offences associated with financial abuse and involving the police in an investigation, including some guidance on what to do if the police refuse to investigate.

The book concludes with Ann Stanyer's recommendations for reforms which might offer further safeguards against financial abuse of older clients. These include a call for desirable coordination and integration of the work done by various agencies, for standing Parliamentary oversight of legislation that affects the elderly and ultimately for a governmental appointment: a Minister for the Elderly, or at least a Commissioner for the Elderly speaking up for the elderly and overseeing policy. At the date of writing this foreword, a general election has been called – early, under the provisions of the Fixed Term Parliaments Act 2011 – for 8 June 2017, with the consequence that a new government will be formed immediately afterwards. Publication of this book may be timely not only in meeting a need for an accessible and up-to-date guide to the law and practice of financial abuse of the elderly, but in meeting an opportunity to put its call for reform into practice.

Barbara Rich
April 2017

Preface

I have been a private client solicitor for nearly 30 years. Over that time I have observed many elderly clients struggling to secure their finances, often for the benefit of close relatives, at their own expense. We help them as much as they allow us to. Very often we are first approached by the son or daughter who tells us that their parent is struggling with their finances or wants to avoid care home fees or a large inheritance tax bill upon their deaths. Very often none of this is actually for the elderly person's benefit. Our client has very often convinced themselves that they ought to be helping their children out. It is very rarely the case that an elderly person contacts you because they fear that someone is helping themselves to their money. It is usually a concerned third party who contacts us first, or we observe this ourselves. Very often financial abuse only comes to light after the elderly client loses their capacity or dies. We are then able to assess what has happened, but it is often too late for the client themselves. My reason for writing this book is to drive the debate, increase awareness amongst professionals and just perhaps to encourage a more proactive stance on the part of government and all concerned with the care of the elderly to stamp out this abuse before it becomes an epidemic.

Background

At the outset I think it helps to look at some statistics. In 2011, 9.2 million people over 65 years of age were living in England and Wales. This represents 16% of the total population. The reason for an aging population is a combination of reduced smoking rates, medical treatment and healthier diet and lifestyle. It is expected that one in three babies born today in the UK will survive to the age of 100.

According to the Office of National Statistics, 13% of the usually resident population of England and Wales were living alone in 2011. The European average was 14%. Interestingly, the more southern European the country, the more likelihood of not living alone so, for example, in Spain the rate was 9%, whereas in Denmark the rate was 23%.

In England and Wales 59% of that figure were 85 or over and 17% of that figure were in the age range 50–64 years. Older woman were more likely to live alone than older men. This clearly relates to women living longer than men. The majority of those living alone were residing in properties with two or more bedrooms and therefore they could be said to be living in under-utilised accommodation. Furthermore, 54% of those who lived alone owned their own homes.

It is estimated that one in every six persons over the age of 60 will fall victim to some kind of financial abuse. An ageing population is putting pressure on younger care-givers and/or relatives. This leads to pressure on their own finances and those of any family members who live with them. Pressures on accommodation and sharing a home with an elderly person provide opportunities for abuse and also motivation.

There is no doubt that the increasing wealth of the elderly provides a temptation for others. Elderly relatives are likely to be living in mortgage-free properties whilst the younger generation struggles to get a mortgage. The dramatic rise in property prices in recent years enables the elderly to downsize and free up capital. They are then under pressure to pass this on to their children.

Trust

Generally, the older generation has a uniquely trusting nature are are easy prey for sophisticated fraudsters, who may appear to be taking more of an interest in the elderly person than their close family and friends. They will answer the door, engage people on the telephone, trust people with bank cards or make financial or property gifts in return for continued emotional support.

Formerly straightforward financial transactions – for example, dealing with banks – has also become more complex as branches close down, and online or telephone banking require passwords. Handing over finances to another person requires trust, but also a reduction in independence. Elderly people are usually proud and have a desire to keep financial arrangements to themselves. They resent what they see as prying into their affairs. This is a challenge for the professional who suspects abuse is taking place but is bound by confidentiality rules to keep quiet.

What is financial abuse of the elderly?

The Law Society Practice Note in 2013 on Financial Abuse stated:

> 'There is no statutory definition of financial abuse. However, statutory guidance published by the Department of Health entitled "No Secrets" defines financial abuse as follows:
>
>> "Financial or material abuse, including theft, fraud, exploitation, pressure in connection with wills, property or inheritance or financial transactions, or the misuse or misappropriation of property, possessions or benefits. (DH/Home Office, 2000)"'

Action on Elder Abuse defines it as stealing from, defrauding someone of, or coercing someone to part with, goods and/or property.

You can see from these definitions that professionals, whether they are solicitors, accountants or medical professionals, have a front-line role to play in identifying instances of financial abuse. Certain red flags should be at the forefront of our dealings with the elderly. An assessment of financial capacity should accompany a medical or legal assessment carried out by professionals.

Reports

Tthe 2000 Department of Health 'No Secrets' guidance was followed by the Solicitors for the Elderly's report, 'Elder Abuse Strategy 2011'. There has also been the 'UK Study of Abuse and neglect of older people' in June 2007 prepared for Comic Relief and the Department of Health. The charity Action on Elder Abuse is at the forefront of groups trying to raise public awareness to the dangers of abuse in general.

Case law

Practitioners will have seen the recent flurry of cases in the Court of Protection involving what is tantamount to fraud and theft carried out against mentally incapacitated adults. The perpetrators were in positions of trust and supposedly putting the interests of their relatives first. In *Re Buckley: The Public Guardian v C* [2013] EWHC 2965 (COP) a niece had used her aunt's money to set up her own business with consequent losses to the aunt's estate of up to £150,000. In *Re GM: MJ and JM v The Public Guardian* [2013] EWHC 2966 (COP) the court-appointed deputies made gifts from their relative's funds to themselves and others of between £300,000 and £500,000. They did not believe that the patient needed these funds so they left her with just £200,000. They honestly believed that their appointment as deputies gave them carte blanche to do as they liked with the funds. Finally, the case of *Re Joan Treadwell (Deceased); OPG v Colin Lutz* [2013] EWHC 2409 (COP) again illustrated the extent to which access to funds by a resentful deputy can lead to an unauthorised dissipation of the patient's funds.

Challenges for the professional

For the professional advisor these all present challenges of which we must be aware. We must also ensure that the law is adequate and flexible enough to meet these new challenges. In many ways the law shows itself to be a blunt instrument which is inadequate in the face of increasing financial abuse. Cases before the Court of Protection show a litany of ex-post facto attempts to rectify some of the abuse. Surely it is time to put in place adequate statutory protection for the elderly comparable to that now in place to deal with child abuse? The Mental Capacity Act 2005 has at its core the principle that everyone is presumed to be mentally capable unless it is proved that they lack mental capacity. We accept that clients should be allowed to engage in 'foolish' transactions, but surely only after taking independent legal advice? Attorneys or deputies should not be allowed to spend any funds on themselves unless there is pre-authorisation from the court. The court should always call in the security bond whenever a donor's funds have been misused. To most laypeople a misappropriation of funds or property would be seen as theft and reason to call in the police. This is far from what actually happens.

The Office of the Public Guardian has recently changed the procedures and format of lasting powers of attorney (LPA). One of the changes was to remove the requirement to serve notice when the LPA was being registered. This safeguard is no longer mandatory. Similarly, there is no longer a requirement in the forms to state the basis of the certificate provider's qualification. It does seem strange that the few safeguards that were in place and were heralded as improvements on the old EPA system have now been removed.

Other difficulties arise when taking steps to uncover the abuse when the client has lost capacity or has died. In addition, the recovery of assets from the perpetrator is by no means straightforward. The case of *Bashir v Bashir* [2013] EWHC 2572 (QB) is a classic case of the problems faced by the lawyers in recovering assets.

The purpose behind this book is to draw practitioners' attention to the rise in financial abuse, to look out for the warning signs, not take a client's reassurances that everything is fine as the truth, to be aware of what legal protection there is, and above all to demonstrate that change is needed to an imperfect system.

Media reaction

When cases of financial abuse are reported in the press there is an indignant reaction, but very little changes. From the elderly poppy-seller hounded by hundreds of charities who should have known better, to the family who squabbled ceaselessly over their mother's care, accommodation, finances, and pretty much every else. In *Aidiniantz v Riley* [2015] EWCOP 65 the judge declared that 'It is in the public interest for the public ... to see the consequences'. It seems that we are forever playing catch-up with families, carers or institutions abusing vulnerable adults to extract their finances for their own ends. It is clear that we should have far more statutory oversight and tougher rules to combat this growing problem. Increasing digitisation heralded as progress, whether it is LPA online preparation, Land Registry automation or digital banking services does not have sufficient safeguards to protect the most vulnerable but financially independent in society. Progress is slow and, for example, the Solicitors Regulation Authority (SRA) is only now reviewing its guidance on breaching confidentiality rules. At present solicitors are bound by Outcome rule 4.1 where you must keep the affairs of clients confidential unless disclosure is required or permitted by law or the client consents; if abuse is detected the professional ethics helpline forbids you from disclosing suspicions if the client does not consent.

Personal experience

My own experience of nearly 30 years shows how easy it is for the elderly to be taken advantage of by apparently caring individuals. In all the cases I have come across the abuse was perpetrated either by carers employed directly by the family or client, or it involved close family members. The abuse ranged from pretending that large transfers of cash were genuine gifts to a client with severe Alzheimer's being taken to a bank to extract funds for the relative. There are too many instances of emotional bullying of elderly parents to their social isolation from caring members of the family or friends to an increasing dependence on their abuser.

Solicitors, like other professionals, are at the front line and have a duty to protect their clients. The Law Society has recently published further guidance for solicitors in its Practice Note, 'Meeting the needs of vulnerable clients' (July 2015). This followed the guidance 'Making gifts of assets' (October 2011) and 'Financial abuse' (June 2013). In addition, the SRA sets out in Principal 9 of its handbook on the code of conduct that you must run your business or carry out your role in the business in a way that encourages equality of opportunity and respect for diversity; in indicative behaviour rule 1.6 you are bound in taking instructions and during the course of the retainer, to have proper regard to your client's mental capacity or other vulnerability, such as incapacity or duress.

We can also learn from how other countries are dealing with this problem. In the USA there is the Senate Special Committee on Aging, which in 2015 held hearings into 'Combating Financial Exploitation of Vulnerable Seniors'. This was first established in 1961. It would help if we had a permanent body reviewing how we treat and provide for our elderly population. There is nothing comparable in Parliament. Indeed, the elderly hardly get a mention. At the very least we could emulate the Northern Ireland Commissioner for Older People.

I hope that this book will add to the debate about the impact financial abuse is having and how solicitors and others can be proactive in protecting their elderly clients.

Ann Stanyer

Contents

Contents

Table of Cases

Table of Statutes

Table of Statutory Instruments

Table of EU Legislation

Chapter 1

What is Financial Abuse?

Defining financial abuse is not complicated. What seems less clear is why there is a tendency to too easily treat it as something less than a crime. It seems to be more of generic term used to describe any number of situations where one party (the elderly vulnerable person) is relieved of their money, possessions or property by another person, usually a close relative or someone in a 'caring' role. It may be for this reason that there is a certain reluctance on the part of some police forces to properly investigate and prosecute offenders: calling it 'financial abuse' rather than 'theft' or 'fraud' somehow lessens the act.

Section 42(3) of the Care Act 2014 defines financial abuse as follows:

- having money or other property stolen;

- being defrauded;

- being put under pressure in relation to money or other property; and

- having money or other property misused.

The Office of the Public Guardian's (OPG) safeguarding policy document describes it in the following terms:

> 'Abuse can lead to a violation of someone's human and civil rights by another person or persons. Abuse can be physical, financial, verbal or psychological. It can be the result of an act or a failure to act. It can happen when an adult at risk is persuaded into a financial or sexual exchange they have not consented to, or can't consent to. Abuse can occur in any relationship and may result in significant harm or exploitation.'

Indicators and red flags

Financial abuse takes many forms, but common behaviour patterns repeat themselves in the evidence from agencies. For example, the Welsh Government identified the following types of behaviour in its Access to Justice project in 2011:

- being pressurised to lend money to a relative or friends;

- being charged excessive amounts of money for service;

- people frequently requesting small amounts of money from you;

1

- family members moving into your home without your consent and without a prior agreement on sharing costs;

- pressurising you to sign over your house or property;

- taking money, cashing a cheque or using credit or debit cards without your permission;

- pressurising to change a will or sudden or unexpected changes in a will or other financial documents;

- someone else taking charge of your benefits and not giving you all your money;

- a change in living conditions or a lack of heating, clothing or food;

- inability to pay bills/unexplained shortage of money;

- unexplained withdrawals from an account;

- unexplained loss/misplacement of financial documents;

- the recent addition of authorised signers on a client or donor's signature card;

- failure to pay care home fees;

- control of access to the victim or their home.

The OPG explains that whilst such examples may or may not be indicators of actual abuse, they show that further investigation is needed.

As practitioners we see instances of these subtle and not-so-subtle examples. As we have seen above, many of these acts will be perpetrated by close family members, such as the son or daughter who has not left home or has moved back into the family home to live with the elderly parents. There is often an unequal balance of financial power between the adult child with perhaps little or no income and the parent with a home, reasonable pension and savings. The familial and emotional bonds are often too strong to withstand the demands and when the child has succeeded in extracting funds or property from the parent there will then be a reluctance to tell anyone about what has happened and certainly a sense of shame that they have allowed it to happen.

Where might abuse occur?

Home

Abuse, if perpetrated by the close family member, will be carried out in the parent's home. The parent will feel isolated, vulnerable and due to physical frailty perhaps not be able to get out of the home independently to tell a neighbour, GP or other concerned third party about what has happened. At the same time the relative may be controlling and isolating from family friends or professionals who may have concerns.

Care home

Instances of abuse could be perpetrated by staff in care homes. Contracted carers who visit the elderly in their homes will also have opportunities for abuse unless monitored and supervised. Often where temptations and opportunities present themselves then abuse will occur.

Other environments

Abuse could also take place at a bank, or in a solicitor's or investment manager's office.

When might the abuse occur?

There appear to be various trigger points that allow and perhaps facilitate abuse. Often it is a change in circumstances that provide a potential abuser with an opportunity and motivation to carry out the financial abuse. For example:

- sale of the parent's home to fund care home fees;
- moving back into the family home;
- caring for an elderly physically dependent parent;
- parent being dependent and becoming isolated with no contact with others;
- opportunity – giving bank card to another to obtain cash to pay for carers, etc;
- parent wanting to change their will to provide for the caring child;
- parent believing that a gift of their home to the caring child will ensure that they can continue to live in the home and avoid care home fees;
- parent moving in with adult child and their family.

As professionals these trigger events should alert us to the potential for abuse. We need to ask ourselves: what is to happen to the proceeds of sale of the parents' home now they have been moved to a care home? Why might someone not have their care home fees paid when they have seemingly more than sufficient funds to do so? Why is the client being accompanied by the adult child to your office to change their will? Who is instigating the execution of a power of attorney and, if they become the attorney, are they the most suitable candidate to take over management of the client's affairs?

Typical losses

Losses to the victim cannot just be measured in financial terms. They may have lost capital assets but these may also have been income-producing. So the loss has a double effect. The losses often involve instances of the following transactions:

- property – sales or transfer to the abuser, funding abuser's own home purchase or refurbishment;

- savings – abuser using the victim's savings for their own ends;

- chattels – taking possession of treasured possessions without permission and to ensure other members of the family do not receive these on the victim's death;

- mortgage or loan liabilities – pressuring the victim to loan them funds which they have no intention of refunding;

- equity release liabilities – pressuring the client to take out equity release on their home in order to fund substantial gifts for the abuser;

- unexpected tax bills resulting from the loss.

Other losses:

- physical independence;

- financial independence;

- insufficient time to make up the losses;

- loss of family visits;

- loss of their home;

- feelings of shame, embarrassment and foolishness.

Other forms of abuse – physical and mental:

- isolation;

- dependence;

- having their own sanity questioned;

- not reporting the abuse because of retaliation.

Typical actions of the financial abuser

Real situations

My colleagues and I have dealt with clients who have suffered both financial and emotional abuse at the hands of close relatives or non-familial carers. We have seen instances of the following over the last few years:

- Online banking: a carer setting up online banking for an elderly couple who did not have a computer. She transferred significant funds to her own account and then claimed that the transfers were gifts. The police took no action.

- Transfer of investments by investment managers: the elderly person and the perpetrator had a meeting with an investment manager and asked him to transfer all her investments to the perpertrator. She had capacity, but was clearly vulnerable, elderly and recently bereaved.

- Gifts of valuable chattels: the disappearance of valuable items from a collection which the perpetrator claimed were gifts but which had been left to a member of the family in the victim's will. The rest of the collection left when she died was significantly diminished as a result.

- Carer becomes spouse: the seemingly innocent introduction into the elderly parent's home of a live-in carer can lead to significant problems unless monitored closely. It is always sensible to employ such a person through an established agency rather than directly. We have seen how such a situation can turn into what have been described as 'predatory' marriages.

- Gatekeeper roles: Where a live-in carer denies access to the parent to other family members or friends without any good reason. The carer may be another member of the family where again taking court action to enable access is not an ideal solution.

We shall now look at specific problems and common areas of financial abuse. Many of the cases reported in the Court of Protection show that an abuser will very often not just want to control the victim's estate during their lifetime but also put unreasonable pressure on them to alter their will to their benefit. This may take the form of altering the amount of residue that the abuser receives, indirectly effecting the dispositions in the will by selling assets passing to others or by ensuring that other family members are excluded from benefiting.

Wills

As we shall see in the discussion of undue influence, the elderly do come under real pressure to change their wills to benefit particular family members. It is naturally quite often the case that one member of the family will be the principal carer for the parent. Usually it will be an unmarried daughter or son who either lives with the parent or nearby. Or the parent moves in with a married child and their family. Occasionally an annexe will be built or provided by the child to accommodate the parent. The parent then understandably wants to reward that caring child and very often this takes the form of an increased part of the estate to the detriment of the other children who will be completely unaware of what has happened until the parent has died.

In many cases the parent will be fully capable and not entirely a vulnerable person. However, in a significant number of cases questions arise as to how the will was changed, who arranged it, whether the child was present at the meeting with the solicitor and if a full due diligence enquiry was made into the parent's estate and other familial obligations.

As you would expect, the Law Society, Society of Estate and Trust Practitioners and Solicitors for the Elderly have considerable guidance in this area. The Law Society advises that the test of capacity to make a will remains the old common law rule in *Banks v Goodfellow* (1870) LR 5 QB 549.

The High Court in *Walker v Badmin* [2014] All ER (D) 258 reviewed various conflicting decisions on whether the correct test of capacity is the Mental Capacity Act 2005 (MCA 2005) test or that established in the case of *Banks v Goodfellow*. It confirmed that the common law test remains correct test.

This test is that the testator must:

- understand the nature of his act (of making a will) and its effects;
- understand the extent of the property in his estate;
- be able to comprehend and appreciate the claims to which he ought to give effect; and
- with a view to the above point, ensure that no disorder of his mind 'shall poison his affections, perverse his sense of right, or his will in disposing of his property'.

The Law Society's July 2015 paper on financial abuse advises that 'When drafting wills, you should be particularly alert for potential abuse in the following instances:

- where the person making the will is not being allowed individual access to you;
- where instructions come from a third party;
- where instructions are coming from a third party who is to benefit from the will;
- where a third party is always present at an interview with the solicitor;
- where a third party is using their own solicitor to prepare a will for a vulnerable person who has previously had their own solicitor.'

A testator may be led but not driven

An old case distills the essence of what pressure is on a testator. In *Hall v Hall* [1868] LR 1 P&D 481 Sir JP Wilde said:

> 'To make a good will a man must be a free agent. But all influences are not unlawful. Persuasion, appeals to the affection or ties of kindred, to a sentiment of gratitude for past services, or pity for future destitution, or the like – these are all legitimate, and may be fairly pressed on a testator. On the other hand, pressure of whatever character, whether acting on the fears or the hopes, if so exerted as to overpower the volition without convincing the judgement, is a species of restraint under which no valid will can be made. Importunity or threats, such as the testator has not the courage to resist, moral command asserted and yielded to for the sake of peace and quiet, or of escaping distress of mind or social discomfort, these, if carried to a degree in which the freeplay of the testator's judgment, discretion or wishes is overborne will constitute undue influence, though no force is either used or threatened. In a word a testator may be led but not driven and his will must be the off-spring of his own volition and not the record of someone else's.'

The 'golden' rule

The case above has been cited in recent cases and still applies. Similarly the 'golden rule' still has a place here and remains good practice when taking instructions from an elderly person. It was stated in 1975 by Mr Justice Templeman in *Kenward v Adams* [1975] CLY 3591 as follows:

'in the case of an aged testator or a testator who has suffered a serious illness, there is one golden rule which should always be observed, however straightforward matters appear, and however difficult or tactless it may be to suggest that precautions should be taken. The making of a will by such a testator ought to be witnessed or approved by a medical practitioner who satisfies himself of the capacity and understanding of the testator, and records and preserves his examinations and findings. There are other precautions which should be taken. If the testator has made an earlier will this should be considered by the legal and medical advisers of the testator and, if appropriate, discussed with the testator. The instructions of the testator should be taken in the absence of anyone who may stand to benefit, or who may have influence over the testator. These are not counsels of perfection. If proper precautions are not taken injustice may result or be imagined, and great expense and misery may be unnecessarily caused.'

These all seem sensible straightforward steps and will reassure the practitioner that they have done all they can to protect the interests of their client and ensure that both the client's wishes are being carried out and that no undue pressure has been placed on them. Without following these steps a will could be challenged and potentially overturned.

Later-life or predatory marriages

A predatory marriage is described as where one spouse is significantly advanced in age over the other spouse and they may be lonely due to losing a long-term spouse or due to illness or incapacity. The liaison is frequently clandestine, ie kept secret from the adult children and legitimate heirs, and the elderly spouse has brought most of the assets into the marriage (see work by Kimberly Whalen, an estate lawyer who practices in Ontario).

Such later-life marriages can bring much distress to the family of the elderly parent. Often it is the elderly father who has been recently bereaved who is taken under the wing of a much younger partner. If it is a true predatory marriage then the news that the parent has got married in secret with no family present and that suddenly the family home is being shared by a relative stranger can cause much anger and upset. The fault is that the test for marriage is such a low one as compared with the test of capacity to make a will.

The test for capacity to marry in England and Wales was established by the case of *Durham v Durham* (1885) 10 PD 80. Here the Earl of Durham sought a decree of nullity, and claimed his wife had not had the mental capacity needed for marriage. The judge said the contract of marriage is a very simple one, which does not require a high degree of intelligence to comprehend.

Mr Justice Hedley reminded the Court of this in the case of *A, B & C v X & Z* [2012] EWHC 2400 (COP). That case involved an elderly recently bereaved father who had lost his capacity to manage his property and affairs but was found to have capacity to marry. The judge reviewed the authorities and in particular the case of *Sheffield City Council v E* [2005] 2 WLR 953.

> 'The question whether there was capacity to marry was not to be considered by reference to a person's ability to understand or evaluate the characteristics of some particular spouse or intended marriage, but rather it was about the ability to understand the nature of the marriage contract and the duties and responsibilities that attached to marriage, namely that marriage was a contractual agreement between a man and a woman to live together, to love one another to the exclusion of all others in a relationship of mutual and reciprocal obligations involving the sharing of a common home and a common domestic life and the right to enjoy each other's society, comfort and assistance; though the contract of marriage was essentially a simple one which did not require a high degree of intelligence to understand; that the court was only concerned with capacity to marry and it had no jurisdiction to consider whether a particular marriage was in a person's best interests.

> 'The law, as it is set out in these authorities, can be summed up in four propositions:

> (i) It is not enough that someone appreciates that he or she is taking part in a marriage ceremony or understands its words.

> (ii) He or she must understand the nature of the marriage contract.

> (iii) This means that he or she must be mentally capable of understanding the duties and responsibilities that normally attach to marriage.

> (iv) That said, the contract of marriage is in essence a simple one, which does not require a high degree of intelligence to comprehend. The contract of marriage can readily be understood by anyone of normal intelligence.'

Mr Justice Hedley confirmed his agreement with Munby J who said, 'There are many people in our society who may be of limited or borderline capacity but whose lives are immensely enriched by marriage. We must be careful not to set the test of capacity to marry too high, lest it operate as an unfair, unnecessary and indeed discriminatory bar against the mentally disabled.'

Marriage succession rights

Unfortunately, what these cases do not address are the significant succession rights that flow automatically from the act of marriage. Under the intestacy rules a married spouse is entitled to the following:

(1) if estate is over £250,000:

   (a) The husband, wife or civil partner keeps all the assets (including property), up to £250,000, and all the personal possessions, whatever their value.

    (b) The remainder of the estate will be shared as follows:

        (i)   the husband, wife or civil partner gets an absolute interest in half of the remainder;

        (ii) the other half is then divided equally between the surviving children;

        (iii) If a son or daughter (or other child where the deceased had a parental role) has already died, their children will inherit in their place.

(2) If the estate is under £250,000 the spouse receives everything.

It will often be the case that a new will will not have been made to take account of the new spouse: the act of marriage revokes any pre-existing will so a new will would be necessary. If an inadequate will had been made post-marriage then the surviving spouse would be entitled to make a claim for reasonable provision from the estate under the Inheritance (Provision for Family and Dependants) Act 1975. The sadness for the children of the first and long marriage will be that all the family possessions pass automatically to this new spouse and they will not be entitled to any of them without the agreement of the new spouse. This one provision causes so many problems and understandably much upset.

The fault in this area is the low bar for the test of capacity to marry coupled with the significant succession rights that flow from the act of marriage. It is something I would argue needs to be addressed in order to protect an ageing population from abuse. It is all very well to have a rosy-tinted view of the act of marriage, but it may blind the judiciary from seeing the abuse in front of them. If the test is to remain this low then a change to the automatic entitlement to succession rights must be made. If someone is unable to manage their property and affairs it is not logical to allow an automatic granting of succession rights to a new spouse without further consideration. See the author's article with Victoria Mahon de los Palacios in *PS* magazine (September 2013).

Bank accounts

Access to bank accounts is another significant area in which financial abuse takes place. Either an elderly vulnerable adult gives their bank card to another person to retrieve cash for that person or a third party becomes an appointee, attorney or deputy with legal authority to access the other's funds. There have been some extraordinary cases reported in the Court of Protection over the last few years showing how brazen some of the 'looting' by even court-appointed deputies has been.

One such case was *Re GM* [2013] COPLR 290 which highlighted seemingly unlimited spending by the deputies. It shows that even a court order in the hands of untrustworthy individuals can wreak untold damage on a patient's finances. In that case the deputies, MJ and JM, made a series of gifts which were itemised by the court as follows:

Funds disposed of or held by the deputies	£
Charity	57,352.00
Family and friends	62,500.00
MJ	55,856.00
JM	48,396.50
Other	7,155.00
Car for MJ	25,200.00
Car for JM	19,393.21
Computer for MJ	1,299.99
Computer for JM	659.04
Expenditure for GM	4,098.00
Nursing home fees	40,559.94
Assets remaining in GM's estate	177,230.96
Total	**£499,701.54**

The gifts that MJ had received personally were:

Rolex watch	£18,275
Ring	£16,500
Alexander McQueen handbag	£995
Perfume	£86
Cash gift from Barbara's estate	£20,000
	£55,856

As will be seen later in the chapter on gifts, a deputy's powers to make gifts for their patient are extremely limited, but clearly the deputies did not understand this. Their expressed reasons for making these gifts were explained in the court judgement:

> 'Throughout these proceedings MJ and JM described the watches and the rings they had bought as "heirlooms", which they had acquired in memory of GM and Barbara with the intention that they would be passed down through the family from generation to generation.'

MJ's witness statement gave their justification for the gifts:

> 'Having a close relationship with GM and Barbara we feel the gifts and donations made on their behalf are in accordance with their wishes and that they were made as per the C.O.P. given to us 25/8/10 and were reasonable taking into account the size of the estate, and has left her with approx £200,000 and she is 92 yrs old.'

It is clear from this that they regarded the patient's money as theirs with only a derisory concern for the patient, her wishes, her care needs in the future or indeed the ultimate beneficiaries of her estate. What they were not made in were the best interests of GM.

The court clearly had no choice but to revoke their deputyship appointments as they had exceeded their authority and were not acting in the patient's best interests. A panel deputy was appointed who would be under a duty to consider steps towards restitution of the funds.

Very often misuse of funds by deputies comes to light through the annual accounts procedure required of all deputies. Sadly, no such accounting is required by attorneys. Although attorneys are urged to keep accounts by the OPG there is no auditing requirement unless the donor of the power of attorney had included this as an instruction in the body of the instrument when it was signed. As a consequence, attorneys are unsupervised as to their expenditure, gifting and management of the donor's estate. It is only when concerns are raised during the donor's lifetime or funds are found to be missing after the donor's death that action can be taken. It would be so much better if there was mandatory accounting for active attorneyships so that problems can be addressed as soon as possible and attorney's removed where necessary.

Another case illustrates the brazen use of a mother's funds by her attorney son. In *Re ARL* [2015] EWCOP 55 misappropriation of funds included, but was not limited to:

'(a) The purchase of a property in his own name, using £174,950 of his mother's funds. One of my particular concerns is that ICL is currently going through an acrimonious divorce, and there is a possibility that ARL's funds could somehow, inadvertently, become part of the settlement in the matrimonial proceedings.

(b) Pocketing the rental income from the property for the last two years.

(c) The funds referred to in paragraph 16 (a) to (i) above, which by my reckoning amount to £36,524.17.

(d) ICL's admission at paragraph 16(k) that he cannot specifically account for the remainder of the £90,500, "However, I am sure that, save for the £2,500 borrowed by my sister, it would have been used by me in order to cover the living costs of my family.'

The court ordered the revocation of his appointment as attorney and the appointment of joint deputies for property and affairs to act in his place. The Public Guardian was to be left to consider steps to recover the funds removed from the donor's estate.

Once again it shows a wilful disregard for the rights and property of the donor by someone who as his mother clearly believed was the most suitable person to act as her attorney.

Another case that illustrated an attorney's duties was *Re SM (revocation of a Lasting Power of Attorney)* [2015] EWCOP 27. Here the attorney failed to account to the

Public Guardian; failed to pay care fees; the bank statement evidence shows that the attorney had allowed SM's accounts to become overdrawn; and spending from SM's funds had not always been for SM's benefit or in her best interests. The Public Guardian sought an order from the court under MCA 2005, s 22(4) revoking and cancelling the registered lasting power of attorney made by SM.

Scams

Older people are particularly vulnerable to financial abuse by strangers and in particular by organised mass-marketing scams.

Research by the Office of Fair Trading in 2006 estimated that 3.2 million adults in the UK (around 1 in 15 people) collectively lose around £3.5 billion to mass-marketed scams each year. This equates to about £70 per annum for each adult living in the UK. Accordingly, it is estimated that about half the adult population is likely to have been targeted by a scam.

Research for the Office of Fair Trading carried out by the University of Exeter (54/09, 17 May 2009) entitled 'The psychology of scams: Provoking and committing errors of judgement' highlighted the following key findings in relation to victims of scams:

- up to 20% of the UK population could be particularly vulnerable to scams, with previous victims of a scam consistently more likely to show interest in responding again;

- a good background knowledge of the subject of a scam offer, such as experience of investments, may actually increase the risk of becoming a victim through 'over-confidence';

- victims are not in general poor decision-makers; for example, they may have successful business or professional careers, but tend to be unduly open to persuasion by others and less able to control their emotions; and

- victims often keep their decision to respond to a scam offer private and avoid speaking about it with family or friends.

The research included profiles of ten different types of mass-marketed scam: advance fee (419) scams; international sweepstake scams; fake clairvoyants; prize draw pitch scams; 'get rich quick' scams; bogus investment scams; bogus lottery scams; 'miracle' health cures; premium rate prize draw scams; and bogus racing tipsters.

The Little Big Book of Scams (third edition) issued by the Metropolitan Police details all the different scams perpetrated including identity, courier and holiday frauds alongside telephone and investment scams and banking and payment card scams. It details the ten golden rules to help people beat the scammers. It is worth listing these:

(1)   Be suspicious of all 'Too good to be true' offers and deals. There are no guaranteed get-rich-quick schemes.

(2) Do not agree to offers or deals immediately. Insist on time to obtain independent/legal advice before making a decision.

(3) Do not hand over money or sign anything until you have checked the credentials of the company or individual.

(4) Never send money to anyone you do not know or trust, whether in the UK or abroad, or use methods of payment that you are not comfortable with.

(5) Never give banking or personal details to anyone you do not know or trust. This information is valuable so make sure you protect it.

(6) Always log on to a web site directly rather than clicking on links provided in an email.

(7) Do not rely solely on glowing testimonials: find solid independent evidence of a company's success.

(8) Always get independent/legal advice if an offer involves money, time or commitment.

(9) If you spot a scam or have been scammed, report it and get help. Contact ActionFraud on 0300 123 2040 or online at www.actionfraud.police.uk. Contact the police if the suspect is known or still in the area.

(10) Do not be embarrassed to report a scam. Because the scammers are cunning and clever there is no shame in being deceived. By reporting you will make it more difficult for them to deceive others.

As we have seen above, financial abuse comes in many forms. In the next few chapters we will consider some of these in more detail.

Chapter 2

Who is Vulnerable to Financial Abuse?

We may all think that we would know someone who was being abused if we met them. You would think that there would be some indicators that would ring alarm bells and put you on your guard. However, it is likely that those who act for elderly clients have met many such vulnerable people over the course of their work and simply were not aware of that person's vulnerability. It is helpful to consider the various reports from public bodies and research papers in this area to get a better understanding of the problem.

It is hoped that by considering this work it will supply key indicators that we should consider when dealing with elderly clients. We should set aside our pre-existing assumptions about the type of client we have in front of us and consider a checklist of vulnerability that will guide and inform us. There has been considerable research and many reports over the years into who are the vulnerable. A review of these reports and the conclusions they have reached will highlight the issues and guide us to be more informed counsellors in the future.

In the 1997 Consultation Paper 'Who decides?' issued by the Lord Chancellor's Department, a person was considered a vulnerable adult if they are were a person 'who is or may be in need of community care services by reason of mental or other disability, age or illness; and who is or may be unable to take care of him or herself or unable to protect him or herself against significant harm or exploitation'. This is a wide-ranging definition which will encapsulate many of the elderly clients we advise.

'No Secrets'

This definition was also adopted by the Department of Health report, 'No Secrets: Guidance on developing and implementing multi-agency policies and procedures to protect vulnerable adults from abuse' (20 March 2000). (Note that in Wales the guidance was issued as 'In Safe Hands'.)

A report by the House of Commons Health Committee published on 20 April 2004 simply titled 'Elder Abuse' contained the following statement:

'A small, but significant, proportion of older people experience abuse from those who care for them; either in the context of informal care (by family and friends), or health and social care staff. A commonly used definition for elder abuse is: "a single or repeated act or lack of appropriate action occurring within any relationship where there is an expectation of trust which causes harm or distress to an older person.'

The Care Act 2014 and statutory guidance

The 'No Secrets' and 'In Safe Hands' guidance led to new procedures for adult safeguarding, which in turn were repealed by the Care Act 2014 on 1 April 2015. This Act now contains mandatory requirements for adult safeguarding. The Act embodies six key principles: empowerment; prevention; proportionality; protection; partnership; and accoutability. The struggle to resolve conflicts between these principles underlies much of the work in this area. How on the one hand do you empower individuals to maintain their independence whilst at the same time protecting them from abuse? As we shall see later, the case of *DL v A Local Authority* [2012] EWCA Civ 253 is a classic example of this conflict between the rights of the individual and the state's wish to protect.

The Care and Support Statutory Guidance as issued by the Department of Health provides:

Incidents of abuse may be one-off or multiple, and affect one person or more.

Professionals and others should look beyond single incidents or individuals to identify patterns of harm, just as the Care Quality Commission, as the regulator of service quality, does when it looks at the quality of care in health and care services. Repeated instances of poor care maybe an indication of more serious problems and of what we now describe as organisational abuse. In order to see these patterns it is important that information is recorded and appropriately shared.

Patterns of abuse vary and include:
- serial abusing in which the perpetrator seeks out and 'grooms' individuals. Sexual abuse sometimes falls into this pattern as do some forms of financial abuse;
- long-term abuse in the context of an ongoing family relationship such as domestic violence between spouses or generations or persistent psychological abuse; or
- opportunistic abuse such as theft occurring because money or jewellery has been left lying around.

Financial abuse is the main form of abuse recognised by the Office of the Public Guardian (OPG). Financial recorded abuse can occur in isolation, but as research has shown, where there are other forms of abuse, there is likely to be financial abuse occurring. Although this is not always the case, everyone should also be aware of this possibility.

The Statutory Guidance lists potential indicators of financial abuse, including:

- change in living conditions;
- lack of heating, clothing or food;
- inability to pay bills/unexplained shortage of money;
- unexplained withdrawals from an account;
- unexplained loss/misplacement of financial documents;
- the recent addition of authorised signers on a client or donor's signature card; or
- sudden or unexpected changes in a will or other financial documents.

The guidance illustrates this by the following example:

Mrs B is an 88-year-old woman with dementia who was admitted to a care home from hospital following a fall. Mrs B appointed her only daughter, G, to act for her under a Lasting Power of Attorney in relation to her property and financial affairs.

Mrs B's former home was sold and she became liable to pay the full fees of her care home. Mrs B's daughter failed to pay the fees and arrears built up, until the home made a referral to the local authority, who in turn alerted the Office of the Public Guardian (OPG). The OPG carried out an investigation and discovered that G was not providing her mother with any money for clothing or toiletries, which were being provided by the home from their own stocks.

A visit and discussion with Mrs B revealed that she was unable to participate in any activities or outings arranged by the home, which she dearly wished to do. Her room was bare of any personal effects, and she had limited stocks of underwear and nightwear.

The police were alerted and interviewed G, who admitted using the proceeds of the mother's house for her own benefit. The OPG applied to the Court of Protection for suspension of the power of attorney and the appointment of a deputy, who was able to seek recovery of funds and ensure Mrs B's needs were met.

It is clear in this example that an opportunity presented itself by the sale of that property and that the attorney took advantage of that unsupervised situation.

How does this help us to assist our clients? Many of our older and more vulnerable clients may simply present themselves as a client in need of legal advice and assistance. However, we would do well to think further than this. We are not expected to act as a social worker for our client but we are obliged to satisfy ourselves that, for example, the abuser had not brought their victim to the office for the purpose of providing a legal framework and some kind of justification to the underlying abuse.

A simple example will illustrate this: on one occasion I was asked to visit a client in a care home to take instructions for a new will. As I entered the room a member of staff handed to me a piece of paper with a list of names to help the client remember who she should include in her will. It may have seemed innocuous but the list rang alarm bells and even more so when the staff member explained that the relative had given her the list to hand to me and that that relative was now downstairs presumably waiting in eager expectation that her wishes would somehow find their way into the will. I carried out my duty without reference to that list and it soon became clear that the client could not remember any names to put in her will and clearly did not have sufficient capacity to give me instructions. We have to remain alert and ensure that our staff are well trained to spot any unusual circumstances.

How can we identify clients who are at risk of abuse?

It is believed that the reason that financial abuse is so prevalent is that it is not easy to detect unless there is training, reporting and continuing research. As solicitors or other professionals we are on the front line to detect abuse. We are also unwitting enablers to financial abuse. Property transactions would not take place without the input of a solicitor who can explain and advise on the legal documents required. Redrawn wills and powers of attorney may empower an abuser. See the case of *Hart v Burbidge* [2014] EWCA Civ 992 where the solicitor Mr Pick did all he could to protect the the elderly bereaved widow with sound advice but was frustrated in the end by the intervention of the abuser.

The UK Study of Abuse and Neglect of Older People Prevalence Survey Report by the National Centre for Social Research, 2 King's College London (June 2007) found that financial abuse is the second most prevalent type of abuse, affecting roughly one older person in every 150. It increases with age for men but not for women. The survey supports earlier research in finding that financial abuse is significantly more prevalent for people living on their own. Divorced/separated women are also at higher risk. Both men and women in bad/very bad health report rates of financial abuse, but the association does not hold for limiting long-term illness. Women who reported being lonely were more likely to experience financial abuse, but this was not found for men.

Interestingly, it found that where both men and women who were in receipt of home care services or in touch with professionals were more likely to report financial abuse. This is an important finding and surely reinforces the need for more vigilance and more social contact with professionals or care providers. Although, as we shall see, there is recognition that much financial abuse is perpetrated by care workers.

The victims of abuse may often live with the family member who is abusing them or is receiving care from their abuser. This may simply be because of the additional opportunities that present themselves in that environment, but it also can be shown that financial abuse often is accompanied by psychological or emotional abuse by the carer/close relative. They summarised the risk factors as: those living alone, those in receipt of services, those in bad/very bad health, older men, and women who are divorced or separated, or lonely.

In the USA a June 2013 paper entitled 'Understanding Elder Abuse: New Directions for Developing Theories of Elder Abuse Occurring In Domestic Settings' by Shelly L Jackson, PhD and Thomas L Hafemeister, JD, PhD analysed the paucity of research into elder abuse and noted that instances of financial abuse were the fastest growing type of abuse amongst the elderly. The surveys showed 33% more cases involving financial abuse. It is an instructive paper that is worth looking at in detail. The authors considered the existing theories of elder abuse and noted that it lacked one guiding theory: that elder abuse lacked national attention and concern; that it did not attract the same notoriety as other forms of family violence, for example, child abuse and domestic abuse between spouses and partners. It also lacked a powerful advocacy group to speak up on its behalf and above all it did not attract any national data collection system to try to understand its existence and prevalence.

They identified various reasons for this including ageism, negative attitudes to older persons and apathy about mistreatment. It was noted that in the US 97% of federal funding was allocated for child mistreatment cases, 2% for spouse mistreatment and only 1% for elder abuse cases.

They also reported a lack of testing of theories as to why elder abuse takes place. For example, social exchange theory had not been tested to explain the continuation of abuse involving elderly parents and their adult offspring. It is often the case that an imbalance in the relationship leads to discord and then abuse. That theory may have limited application where the victim and the abuser are dependent upon one another. The parent may be providing energy and costs to care for the adult child, who may in turn have a dependence on that parent because of financial need, serious mental illness or substance abuse. The social exchange theory would expect the parent to end the relationship in these circumstances but in fact due to parental attachment, affection and obligation the relationship continues. This attachment is at the heart of much of financial abuse of the elderly. How do we break those strong ties between parent and adult child which has turned abusive?

The research shows that where the abuse only involves family members then physical abuse can occur alongside the financial abuse. Whereas, where the abuse involves both family and non-family members, instances of financial abuse alone occur. For this reason further research would provide statistics on the prevalence of the different types of abuse occurring and then be able to consider how to prevent it.

The researchers concluded with the following points:

- Elder abuse is multidimensional. It involves a number of disparate and unrelated sets of events. It is not suitable to lump all types of elder abuse together.

- Theories should not just focus on the victim. Many cases show that not all elderly people are 'pure victims'. There is often tacit complicity of some victims with their abuser.

- Not all abusers are driven by evil intent. A perpetrator may simply have failed to resist an unexpected opportunity.

- There are often different dynamics at work when a family member abuses and when a stranger does so.

What are the characteristics of an elderly victim?

There has been some research into identifying the types of people most vulnerable to this type of abuse. For example, the Law Society issued a Practice Note of 13 June 2013 on this subject. This identified older people and other vulnerable adults as particularly at risk. It referred to a study by the Solicitors for the Elderly in January 2010 (Strategy for Recognising, Preventing and Dealing with the Abuse of Older and Vulnerable People) which considered the problem and found that the following characteristics predispose older persons to financial abuse:

- advanced age;
- stroke;
- dementia or other cognitive impairment;
- physical, mental or emotional distress;
- depression;
- recent loss of spouse or divorce;
- social isolation;
- middle or upper income bracket;
- taking multiple medications;
- frailty.

The study also recommended that practitioners should consider a client's background in order to assess their capability. For example, some older women may not have had an involvement in the family finances, so a partner's death can have a greater impact on their capability than is immediately evident. See *Hart v Burbidge* [2014] EWCA Civ 992 where the widow, Mrs Hart, had no knowledge of financial affairs before her husband died. He had taken care of all matters. When he died she then relied entirely on her daughter and it appeared that Mrs Hart did not have a full understanding of the value of her assets.

However, as we noted from the US report above, unless we also take into account both the victim and the abuser including their cognitive functioning, the types of abuse, the domestic setting and the nature of their relationship, we will not begin to understand the full implications of the abuse.

Similarly, as there are a number of indicators as to when financial abuse is taking place there should not be too much reliance placed on just one or two indicators of possible abuse, but on a cluster or pattern of signs. It must become evident that without an in-depth knowledge of the victim's financial affairs it would be almost impossible to detect financial abuse taking place. There will be any number of individuals with whom the victim comes across that could inform as to possible abuse taking place – bank staff, solicitors, Land Registry officials and investment managers are all on the front line as they are often unknowing facilitators of the abuse. Then there are family members, carers, neighbours, friends and medical practitioners who, through their interaction with the victim, should look out for warning signs.

We shall return to the financial and other institutions later in this book, but for now the indicators that individuals may detect can be set out as follows:

A. Professionals and others paying a visit to the victim's home may note the following:

   1. Financial irregularities:

       missing belongings or property;

       missing paperwork;

       evasive or implausible explanations;

       unawareness or confusion by the victim of a recent transaction;

       the victim being afraid or worried about talking about finances;

       unpaid bills;

       eviction notices.

   2. Lack of care:

       evidence of lack of care, eg lack of clothing, food other necessities;

       unkempt home where the victim used to be house-proud;

       untreated medical problems;

       provision of unnecessary services.

   3. Social isolation:

       discontinued relationships with friends and family;

       increased dependence on others;

       sudden heavy traffic in and out of the home;

       new acquaintances;

       caregivers or family members having an excessive interest in amount of money being spent on the elderly person.

   4. Family dependence:

       mutual dependence on another member of the family;

       family members addicted to alcohol or drugs.

21

B. Conduct of banking transactions:

unexplained transfers out of or between accounts;

unusual or unexplained sudden activity;

large withdrawals when the elderly person is accompanied by another person;

frequent transfers or ATM withdrawals;

change of address for statements and cheque books;

suspicious signatures;

inclusion of other names on bank card;

suspicious credit card activity;

ATM withdrawals by housebound person;

online banking by person with no internet-enabled device or IT experience;

person with no awareness of personal financial affairs, eg is now in debt but not sure why;

unusual number of cheques written to cash.

C. Legal transactions:

execution of powers of attorney where the client appears confused or does not understand or remember the transaction;

forged signatures;

changes in their property, wills or other documents where the transactions are unexpected, sudden or in favour of new acquaintances;

elderly client coming to a meeting with one adult child with a view to transfer of property to them alone where there are other children to be considered;

sudden appearance of previously uninvolved relatives claiming rights to the victim's affairs and possessions.

D. Visits to health care providers:

unmet physical needs;

missed medical appointments;

dropping out of treatment;

declining physical and psychological health;

defensiveness by caregiver during visits or on telephone, and unwillingness by caregiver to leave the victim alone during appointments.

In particular, older people are extremely vulnerable to financial abuse, whether perpetrated by relatives, carers or strangers. You should not assume that any person accompanying your client has their best interests at heart. You should be alert to the nature of the instructions you receive and the manner or behaviour of someone who accompanies the client.

Different characteristics and real situations

There is some helpful guidance from the Law Society of Scotland for Vulnerable Clients (October 2013). The following possible situations and indicators are offered as examples, not as a comprehensive list, but to make you aware of where there is no abuse, where you should be on your guard and where abuse is clear:

Type A: Capable client making own independent decisions, has justified faith in competence and trustworthiness of proposed appointee (capacity and no undue influence).

Type B: Client dominated by proposed appointee, nevertheless capable and proposed appointee competent and motivated to act properly. (capacity and influence, influence not undue or malign).

Type C: Client capable and not subject to undue influence, but instructions seem unwise. (The solicitor's role is to advise, perhaps in strong terms, but in this situation there are no grounds for refusing to act. It is wise to record concerns, advice given, and reasons for acting

Type D: Client of limited but sufficient capacity, vulnerable to undue influence but not in fact unduly influenced. (The solicitor must respect and if necessary support the client's capacity, without discrimination on grounds of the client's disability).

Type E: Client subject to influence which is undue and malign, not benign, and unable to resist it through incapacity or facility or the dominance of the influencer(s). (Regardless of level of capacity to consult and instruct, the solicitor will not be able to implement instructions.)

Type F: Presents as any of types A–D, but there is in fact undue and malign influence which may be covert or deliberately concealed (including by the person influenced).

The report also supplies helpful tips and levels of difficulty in recognising where you will encounter problems.

It is noted that strong influence is not necessarily undue influence. It may be necessary to try to assess the motives and intentions of an influencer (or influencers) whom the solicitor may not even have met.

Consider who has approached the solicitor ('initiator')

- Client who is well known? Be alert to possible changes in capacity and vulnerability.

- A new client? Be alert to possible incapacity or vulnerability.

- Neutral person on behalf of the client? Be careful – see below if there is possible significant influence.

- Proposed appointee or donee on behalf of the client? Be very careful (but this could still be a type A or B, or even D, situation).

- Initiator reluctant to 'stay completely out of the way' when instructions are taken? Be very careful.

- Initiator resistant to possibility of joint appointment or additional donees? Be very careful.

Other possible indicators

- Any references to family disunity? Be very careful.

- Initiator a dominant personality? Be very careful.

- Client appears to be very influenced by initiator? Be very careful, and if initiator is proposed appointee or donee – danger sign!

- Client 'doesn't want to upset' proposed appointee or donee? Danger sign!

- Client 'doesn't want to upset' family or others? Be very careful.

- Proposed appointee or donee seems largely motivated by need to mitigate tax, avoid means-testing? Danger sign!

- Possibility of some form of 'mental disorder' (broadly defined)? Investigate.

This is helpful and a practical tool to assist legal practitioners, but like all tools there will be cases that do not fit the pattern.

Prevalence of abuse

Some charitable organisations providing services for the elderly in the UK have reported their own research in this area and have set out useful indicators.

Action on Elder Abuse

Action on Elder Abuse is a leading light in campaigning for greater recognition in this area. In December 2014 they launched their Care Providers Campaign to visibly support older people who are being abused or are at a risk of abuse. They report that 67% of abuse occurs within the community and in victims' own homes, and care-providers were concerned that press reports unfairly focus a spotlight on them despite the vast majority being hardworking volunteers and care workers.

AgeUK

In November 2015 Age UK Research published 'Financial Abuse Evidence Review'. This identified various factors that make some elderly persons more vulnerable to financial abuse than others. In particular the following were noted as risk factors:

1. Age-related: dementia and reduced cognitive function, increasing poor health and those at risk of clinical depression.

2. Social risk factors: increasing low levels of social support, needing help with activities of daily living, family problems and being dependent on the abuser.

3. Gender: the Met life study in the US showed that women were twice as likely as men to suffer financial abuse; the majority would be living alone, aged between 80 and 89, and single or widowed.

4. Ethnicity: more financial abuse was also suffered by those of different races, cultures or who spoke different languages.

The Age UK report suggested that further research should be carried out into the usefulness or otherwise of the the Older Adult Financial Exploitation Model and that this should be tested in the UK.

They also discussed the significant impact of financial abuse on older persons. What is often overlooked in this debate is the very real harm and damage that financial abuse inflicts on its victim. It can be catastrophic financially as it will be much more difficult for an elderly person to recover the financial losses at their age. They may lose their home as a result or have to sell their home to fund their later years.

There are also the emotional implications. They will feel betrayed, usually by someone quite close to them. They will be embarrassed that they have allowed it to happen and that they have been fallen for a scam or conned into giving up their life savings. They will be distressed, feel a loss of confidence and may feel socially isolated as they will not want to explain to others what has happened to them. What is worse is that these feelings may make them even more vulnerable to further abuse and exploitation. Lastly, financial abuse leads to further health problems including depression and anxiety.

Alzheimer's Society

The Alzheimer's Society 2001 report, 'Short Changed', noted that persons suffering from mild cognitive decline struggled to manage their finances, felt pressurised, found it difficult talking about finances and struggled with having to shop in unfamiliar places.

Other problems that were noted include where the elderly person feels that that their story is not being believed and so will not report it. They also fear the outcome of reporting it. For example, that their abuser will then move them out of their own home or the shared home and they will be put in a care home. There is also a natural reluctance to bring criminal proceedings against family members. They fear being blamed. There is also a lack of awareness and knowledge of their rights.

25

Measuring financial exploitation

The Older Adult Financial Exploitation Measure mentioned above was a 2014 pilot study to test a measuring tool for appropriateness in an Irish context. Unfortunately the sample surveyed turned out to be quite small in number, reflecting various difficulties in obtaining participation and furthermore in getting buy-in from the professionals involved in the study. One of the key determinants was that all those elderly persons surveyed must have had sufficient mental capacity to take part. Inevitably this meant that none of the test results would have any application to assessing financial abuse in those where cognitive decline had advanced so much as to effect mental capacity. Some felt that the tool was too unwieldy – in some cases it took up to 60 minutes to complete and inevitably then involved large time commitments for the case workers (senior care workers and social workers) on top of their other work obligations.

Some elderly people reported that they had suffered more than nine different instances of financial abuse. What it also showed was the prevalence of not just isolated instances of financial abuse but how numerous were the types of abuse perpetrated against single individuals. These seems to support the point mentioned above that once an elderly person has weakened and been made more vulnerable they are then open to more abuse. It is a vicious cycle. One of the consequences of abuse not being monitored or policed is that perpetrators (and similarly the victims) may feel that financial abuse is somehow tolerated and justified.

It also illustrated that as an older person ages there is an increased reliance on younger members of the family to assist with finances. Throughout the reports there is a theme that suggests a reduced sensitivity to the financial abuse of older persons. The view quite often expressed is 'they don't need it as as much as the young'. The pilot study found that three-quarters of older people in the sample identified more than one potentially abusive experience of financial abuse and 25% had nine or more positive responses.

The AgeUK Factsheet 'Later Life in the United Kingdom' (October 2016) contains some interesting statistics. There are now over 15 million people in the UK aged 60 and above and 1.5 million people are aged 85 or over.

The study reports that 'Approximately 342,000 older people living in private households in the UK are abused each year. We estimate that, taking into account care homes, up to 500,000 older people in the UK are abused each year (roughly 5% of the older population). Every hour, over 50 older people are neglected or abused in their own homes by family members, friends, neighbours or care workers'. In a study based on 10,000 phone calls to a help line in 2004, the proportion of calls concerning financial abuse was 20%.

It also showed that as at December 2015 nearly six million households are headed by a person aged 65 and over in England. By 2021 this is expected to increase to over seven million. Around one-third of all households are older households. Where financial abuse involves property sales, transfers or gifts the potential problems will increase over time unless some significant improvements are put in place to prevent fraud and other financial abuse taking place.

We noted above that the Older Adult Financial Exploitation Measure was designed only for those elderly persons who could pass a cognitive assessment test. Accordingly, this test would be suitable subject to some adaptations for rolling out to a wider population and the test carried out by professionals dealing with the elderly. One can envisage a time when questions about the incidence of financial abuse will be commonplace for professionals. It really should not take too much to organise routine questionnaires and collation of statistics in this area. In the UK we lag behind other countries in our recognition of the extent of this problem, which is very likely to get worse over the next few years. A body comparable to the Eire Government's HSE Elder Abuse Service established in 2007 would assist in this process (see www.hse.ie/eng/services/list/4/olderpeople/elderabuse).

In the cases reported in the English Court of Protection in 2015 the following statistics were noted in respect of financial abuse cases:

Sex of victims:	Male = 25% Female = 75%
Sex of abusers:	Male = 65% Female = 35%
Deputies:	15% of cases
Attorneys:	85% of cases
Age range of victims:	80–95 = 10/18 = 55% Less than 80 = 8/18= 45%
Age range of abusers:	50–60 years = 55% Under 50 years = 45%
Abuser as child of the victim:	95% of cases
Unpaid care home fees:	40% of cases

This pattern is replicated in other years (see the table of statistics in Appendix C). It is possible to extract from these cases a victim archetype: usually an elderly widowed mother with an abusing middle-aged son (and slightly less frequently a daughter). The mother will very often be in a care home and the sale of her home has often been the facilitator of the financial abuse. The perpetrator is often an attorney and as such he or she is not supervised in carrying out financial transactions. There have also been some significant cases involving deputies but the abuse is detected rapidly with the requirement to submit annual deputyship accounts. In the case of the perpetrators their undoing has usually been the unpaid care home fees. The care home or the local authority have then reported this to the OPG who then instigates an investigation.

In conclusion, we can see that there is still much important work to be done in this area: research to really understand the motivations behind the abusers and the vulnerabilities of the victims, and how we can protect them. The research outlined above highlights the types of victims that need that protection, but it also shows that the professional advisor could be a key watchman in this area. More research is necessary as a matter of urgency.

Chapter 3

Vulnerable and Mentally Capable

In considering what protection we can afford to the elderly in the community, the law is clear that certain protections are available to those who fall within the statutory definition of mentally incapable. However, there are many others who do not fall within the statutory definition below but who are nevertheless vulnerable. We shall explore how important it is to differentiate between the two categories.

The MCA 2005 definition of 'mentally incapable'

MCA 2005 provides the framework of protective measures for those who fall within ss 2 and 3 of that Act. These provide that a person lacks capacity in relation to a matter if at the material time he is unable to make a decision for himself in relation to the matter because of an impairment of, or a disturbance in the functioning of, the mind or brain. Section 3 further provides that a person is unable to make a decision for himself if he is unable to complete one or more of the following functional tests.

- understand the information relevant to the decision;

- retain that information;

- use or weigh that information;

- communicate that decision.

The MCA principles

Underlying the rationale of the MCA are the s 1 principles which apply to all matters relating to the Act:

- a person must be assumed to have capacity unless it is established that he lacks capacity;

- a person is not to be treated as unable to make a decision unless all practicable steps to help him to do so have been taken without success;

29

- a person is not to be treated as unable to make a decision merely because he makes an unwise decision;

- an act done, or decision made, under the Act for or on behalf of a person who lacks capacity must be done, or made, in his best interests.

Thus the Act is structured in such a way as to enable the individual to take decisions wherever possible by themselves rather than someone else taking decisions for them. An assessment to establish whether a person lacks capacity should take place whenever there is concern that an individual might lack the mental capacity to make a proposed decision. A person must be assumed to have capacity unless it is shown that they lack capacity.

If, having considered all steps to assist their own decision-making, they are still unable to take a decision within the functional tests above, then and only then will the Act step in to give another the power to take the decision for them. Such third-party decision-making must always be made in the individual's best interests.

If a person falls within the MCA definition then the Act can protect them in a wide range of areas. The only excluded decisions are set out in s 27(1): these relate to family relationship decisions, for example, consenting to marriage, divorce or adoption. All other decisions, whether of a care and welfare nature on the one hand, or which concern finances or property on the other, can be taken on that person's behalf. The Act provides that an attorney, deputy or the Court of Protection itself can act for that person in this regard. That court, as the name suggests, provides a protective shield for those who fall within its remit. It does not, however, have any jurisdiction over those that are not mentally incapable.

Protection of the vulnerable but mentally capable by the Inherent Jurisdiction of the Court

For those vulnerable elderly who are unable to carry out independent decision-making due to reasons other than mental incapacity, a body of cases has been developed by the courts to provide separate protection. The High Court has an inherent jurisdiction to protect adults. This was available long before the MCA was enacted in 2005. Mr Justice Munby was at the forefront of many of these court decisions. As he himself explained in *E v Channel Four News* [2005] 2 FLR 913, para 55, it was 'in substance and reality, a jurisdiction in relation to incompetent adults which for all practical purposes indistinguishable from its well-established parens patriae or wardship in relation to children'.

He expanded on this in his judgement in *A Local Authority v (1) MA (2) NA and (3) SA* [2005] EWHC 2942:

'This case raises novel questions about the court's inherent jurisdiction in relation to vulnerable adults. I have before me a vulnerable young woman who has just turned eighteen and has therefore attained her majority. While she was still a child the court had exercised its inherent parens patriae and wardship jurisdictions to protect her from the risk of an unsuitable arranged marriage. The question is whether I have jurisdiction to continue that protection now she is an adult.

'The question arises because expert evidence establishes that this young woman, although undoubtedly vulnerable, equally undoubtedly has the capacity to marry. In other words the case raises the question of whether the inherent jurisdiction in relation to adults can be exercised for the protection of vulnerable adults who do not, as such, lack capacity. In my judgment, the jurisdiction can be so exercised. And I propose to exercise the jurisdiction in this particular case, so that a young woman who remains just as vulnerable now she is an adult as she did when she was still a child should not suddenly be deprived of the protection which the court has hitherto felt it necessary to afford her and which I believe is still very much required in her best interests.'

At paragraph 77 he stated:

'It would be unwise, and indeed inappropriate, for me even to attempt to define who might fall into this group in relation to whom the court can properly exercise its inherent jurisdiction. I disavow any such intention. It suffices for present purposes to say that, in my judgment, the authorities to which I have referred demonstrate that the inherent jurisdiction can be exercised in relation to a vulnerable adult who, even if not incapacitated by mental disorder or mental illness, is, or is reasonably believed to be, either (i) under constraint or (ii) subject to coercion or undue influence or (iii) for some other reason deprived of the capacity to make the relevant decision, or disabled from making a free choice, or incapacitated or disabled from giving or expressing a real and genuine consent.'

He quoted Lord Eldon LC in *Wellesley v Duke of Beaufort* (1827) 2 Russ 1 at p 20 with the observation that the jurisdiction:

'is founded on the obvious necessity that the law should place somewhere the care of individuals who cannot take care of themselves, particularly in cases where it is clear that some care should be thrown around them.'

What is a vulnerable adult?

Mr Justice Munby further elaborated on what he meant by 'vulnerable adult' at para 82 of that case:

'In the context of the inherent jurisdiction I would treat as a vulnerable adult someone who, whether or not mentally incapacitated, and whether or not suffering from any mental illness or mental disorder, is or may be unable to take care of him or herself, or unable to protect him or herself against significant harm or exploitation, or who is deaf, blind or dumb, or who is

31

substantially handicapped by illness, injury or congenital deformity. This, I emphasise, is not and is not intended to be a definition. It is descriptive, not definitive; indicative rather than prescriptive.

So it appears that the following characteristics are important when establishing whether your client falls within the category of vulnerable but not mentally incapable adults and therefore warrant protection under the inherent jurisdiction of the court:

(1) the definition is descriptive rather than definitive;

(2) it is indicative rather than prescriptive;

(3) the person is an adult who is or is not incapacitated by mental disorder or mental illness; or

(4) is unable to take care or him or herself; or

(5) is unable to protect him or herself against significant harm or exploitation; or

(6) is deaf, blind, dumb; or

(7) is substantially handicapped by illness, injury or congenital deformity; or

(8) is, or is reasonably believed to be, either:

  (a) under constraint; or

  (b) subject to coercion or undue influence; or

  (c) for some other reason deprived of the capacity to make the relevant decision; or

  (d) disabled from making a free choice; or

  (e) incapacitated or disabled from giving or expressing a real and genuine consent.'

His declaration that this applies to all vulnerable adults who are or who are not mentally incapacitated would be questioned now bearing in mind the MCA's jurisdiction over those assessed as mentally incapable within the definition of the Act.

The important case of *DL v A Local Authority* [2012] EWCA Civ 253 has now confirmed the status of the *Re SA* decision. This case concerned a local authority, which sought to invoke the inherent jurisdiction for the protection of two elderly people, GRL and ML, claiming that the couple lacked capacity as a result of undue influence and duress brought to bear upon them by their son, DL. The local authority was concerned about DL's alleged conduct towards his parents, which was said to be aggressive, and on occasions resulted in physical violence by DL towards them. The local authority had documented incidents going back to 2005 which chronicled DL's behaviour and which included physical assaults, verbal threats, controlling where and when his parents could move in the house, preventing them from leaving the house, and controlling who may visit them, and the terms upon which they may visit them, including health and social care professionals providing care and support for Mrs L. There were also consistent reports that DL was seeking to coerce Mr L into transferring the ownership of the house into DL's name and that he has also placed considerable pressure on both his parents to have Mrs L moved into a care home against her wishes.

What was also clear from the case was that neither parent lacked the capacity to take proceedings on behalf of themselves or each other by reason of any impairment of or disturbance in the functioning of the mind or brain. The local authority recognised that Mrs L, in particular, wished to preserve her relationship with DL and did not want any proceedings taken against him. Furthermore, the local authority acknowledged that whilst Mr L was more critical of DL's behaviour, it remained unclear as to whether he, Mr L, would wish to take steps in opposition to his wife's wishes.

The local authority had also considered (and rejected) using the following other routes to resolving the problems:

- the criminal law;

- an application to the Court of Protection under MCA 2005;

- an application for an an anti-social behaviour order (ASBO) under the Crime and Disorder Act 1998;

- an application under the Housing Act 1996, s 153A.

Procedure adopted

The following steps were taken by the court:

(1) **Interim injunctions** were made ex parte and without notice, restraining the first defendant from:

    (i) assaulting or threatening to assault GRL and ML;

    (ii) preventing GRL or ML from having contact with friends and family members;

    (iii) seeking to persuade or coerce GRL into transferring ownership of the current family home;

    (iv) seeking to persuade or coerce ML into moving into a care home or nursing home;

    (v) engaging in behaviour towards GRL or ML that is otherwise degrading or coercive, including (but not limited to): stipulating which rooms in the house GRL or ML can use; preventing GRL or ML from using household appliances, including the washing machine; 'punishing' GRL or ML, for example, by making GRL write 'lines'; shouting or otherwise behaving in an aggressive or intimidating manner towards them.

(vi) giving orders to care staff;

(vii) interfering in the provision of care and support to ML;

(viii)refusing access to health and social care professionals;

(ix) behaving in an aggressive and/or confrontational manner to care staff and care managers.

2. The Court made a **Harbin v Masterman order** inviting the Official Solicitor to investigate ML and GRL's true wishes and to ascertain whether they were operating under the influence of DL in relation to the contact that they have with him.

3. An **independent social work expert** visited and interviewed GRL and ML and produced a written report

In the context of financial abuse of an elderly client the jurisdiction is more than important. It is a crucial part of the panoply of tools that practitioners must employ to protect their vulnerable clients.

The great safety net

As Dame Elizabeth Butler-Sloss P said in *Re Local Authority (Inquiry: Restraint on Publication)* [2003] EWHC 2746 (Fam), [2004] 1 FLR 541, at para [96]:

> 'It is a flexible remedy and adaptable to ensure the protection of a person who is under a disability ... Until there is legislation passed which will protect and oversee the welfare of those under a permanent disability the courts have a duty to continue, as Lord Donaldson of Lymington MR said in *In re F (Mental Patient: Sterilisation)*, to use the common law as the great safety net to fill gaps where it is clearly necessary to do so.'

There was some concern that with the introduction of MCA 2005 that this body of cases would be redundant and that protection of the mentally capable but vulnerable would be overshadowed by the Act. The Court of Appeal case of *A Local Authority v DL* [2012] EWCA Civ 253 confirmed that this was not the case and the inherent jurisdiction of the High Court continues to protect that category of vulnerable adults. It would have been strange if it had been otherwise. As Lord Justice Kay said in his judgement: 'Where a person lacks capacity in the sense of S 2(1) of the MCA 2005, he has the protection provided by that statute. A person at the other end of the scale, who has that capacity and is not otherwise vulnerable, is able to protect himself against unscrupulous manipulation, if necessary by obtaining an injunction against his oppressor. This case is concerned with a category of people who in reality have neither of these remedies available for their protection. It would be most unfortunate if by reference to their personal autonomy they were beyond the reach of judicial protection'.

Breach of Article 8 ECHR?

There is a risk that Article 8 of the European Convention on Human Rights ('ECHR') ('right to respect for private and family life') would be breached if the inherent jurisdiction of the court is employed too widely.

However, at the same time, so-called 'positive obligations' to protect an individual's rights under the EHCR may require the courts to intervene by exercising its inherent jurisdiction. This implies that in appropriate cases, local authorities should also be asking the courts to consider exercising its inherent jurisdiction on human rights grounds.

According to the courts, the inherent jurisdiction can be exercised for vulnerable adults, with or without capacity, who are 'reasonably believed' to be 'under constraint' or 'subject to coercion or undue influence', or for another reason 'deprived of the capacity to make the relevant decision', or prevented from making a free choice, or from 'giving or expressing a real and genuine consent'.

Power of arrest?

Note the case of *Re FD (Inherent Jurisdiction: Power of Arrest)* [2016] EWHC 2358 (Fam). The issue was whether a power of arrest may be attached to an injunction granted by the High Court under its inherent jurisdiction in the case of a vulnerable adult who has capacity.

A local authority applied to the High Court because of concerns about the risk to FD, aged 18, arising from her relationships with AD (her father) and GH (a male friend). It sought an injunction to prevent AD and GH from having contact with her and going to her home. It also sought an order attaching a power of arrest to the injunction. Judge Bellamy said: 'It is clear that under its inherent jurisdiction the High Court has a wide and largely unfettered discretion to grant injunctive relief to protect vulnerable adults. That discretionary power is at least as wide as its powers in wardship. In *Re G* the Court of Appeal was in no doubt that under its inherent jurisdiction in wardship the High Court has no power to attach a power of arrest to an injunction. I am in no doubt that the position is exactly the same so far as concerns the inherent jurisdiction to protect vulnerable adults.'

Initial assessment problems and gaining access

It is possible under MCA 2005, s 16(2) for the court to issue an interim order or directions. The court can make an order, make a decision(s) on P's behalf in relation to the matter(s) or appoint a person (a deputy) to make decisions on P's behalf. The Act says that it is preferable for a decision of the court to be made rather than the appointment of a deputy, but if a deputy is to be appointed their appointment and powers should be limited in scope and duration as is reasonably practical in the circumstances.

Where there are problems in obtaining an assessment the court can act, as was illustrated by the case of *Re SA; FA v Mr A* [2010] EWCA Civ 1128. This was an application for permission to appeal from a decision given by Roderic Wood J, sitting as a judge of the Court of Protection on 20 May 2010. The proceedings related to a young woman, SA, who was born in December 1989. It is said, although this is vigorously disputed both by SA and by her mother FA, that SA was not merely vulnerable but that she lacked capacity, in particular capacity to litigate the current proceedings, capacity to decide whether or not to participate in the process of a statutory assessment by the local authority in accordance with the National Health Service and Community Care Act 1990, s 47 and, in the event that the outcome of such an assessment is a determination by the local authority that she should be offered services, capacity to decide whether or not to accept those services.

The girl and her mother both denied that she lacked capacity. There were great difficulties in communicating with and obtaining the engagement, assistance and cooperation of both daughter and mother.

Under MCA 2005, s 48 the court may, pending the determination of an application in relation to a person, make an order or give directions in respect of any matter if:

- there is reason to believe that P lacks capacity in relation to a matter;

- the matter is one to which its powers under the Act extend; and

- it is in P's best interests to make the order, or give directions without delay.

In this case an interim order was made by the court against both, with a penal notice attached to it. In essence, the judge determined that it was in SA's best interests that there should be not merely a further assessment as to her capacity to accept or decline community services, but also an assessment as to her eligibility for such services. He gave consequential directions with a view to facilitating each of those two assessments, including a mandatory order requiring the mother to take certain identified steps to facilitate the undertaking of the assessments.

Such a direction can be to obtain the expert specialist evidence required so that P's capacity can be determined. Such directions and orders would not be required if the third party against whom they could made gives an appropriate undertaking to cooperate.

Regulating third parties' behaviour to protect the vulnerable adult

The case of *Re G (an adult) (mental capacity: court's jurisdiction)* [2004] EWHC 2222 (Fam) illustrates how this jurisdiction can be used to good effect.

G was a woman aged 29 with a history of mental illness. Proceedings under the inherent jurisdiction were commenced and it was subsequently established that G lacked capacity. What Bennett J described as a 'protective framework' for G, regulating her parents' contact with her, was put and maintained in place by interlocutory orders made, renewed, and extended.

By the time of the final hearing on 26 July 2004 G no longer lacked capacity. The reason for this was to the effect that G's capacity had been severely compromised by her will being overborne by her father's powerful character; that prior to the protective framework being put in place the father's ability to overbear G's decision-making processes was very significant; that by contrast the protective regime, which limited the father's access to G, had reduced the impact of his power over her decision-making processes; but that if the protective framework was removed, so that G had unrestricted contact with her parents, this would probably lead to disturbance and a significant deterioration in G's mental state, adversely affecting her capacity.

Bennett J's conclusion at para [86] was that: 'If the restrictions were lifted ... it is probable that the situation would revert to what it was prior to March 2004. G's mental health would deteriorate to such an extent that she would again become incapacitated to take decisions about the matters referred to. Such a reversion would be disastrous for G.'

In those circumstances it was argued that because G currently had capacity, the court had no jurisdiction to grant any relief. Bennett J rejected the argument and made orders, the effect of which was to retain the protective framework.

Conclusion

All this will be balanced against the restriction of the adult's decision-making being kept to a minimum, consistent with his best interests.

This widening of the protection for adults has been criticised by some (see, for example, Barbara Hewson, '"Neither Midwives Nor Rainmakers"—why DL is wrong' (Thomson Reuters, July 2013). She states that 'The Act [the Human Rights Act 1998] does not give local authorities a right to regulate the lives of eccentric or wayward adults. It is unfortunate that DL did not appeal to the Supreme Court: the issues raised by his case are of constitutional importance'.

The MCA 2005 was supposed to be a comprehensive solution to protect the mentally incapable. The Act and the Code of Practice recognises that there are situations where mental capacity fluctuates and it could be said that anyone who falls outside the statutory definition of mentally incapable should be able to order their affairs and seek help independently of the Court of Protection and the Office of the Public Guardian. It can, however, be argued that there is a case for maintaining this protective shield or safety net around those often elderly persons who through no fault of their own are in a vulnerable state whether temporary or permanent. We have often been told that we are permitted foolish behaviour, but where a person's will has been overborne by another person or through disability then this powerful tool should remain to protect this important section of the community.

Chapter 4

Who are the Perpetrators of Financial Abuse?

It is often said that those who are in a position of trust carry out most financial abuse. This is undoubtedly the case, but it is also acknowledged that these same individuals also have the most opportunities to carry it out. For example, the family member caring for the elderly parent, or the unsupervised paid carer who sees the victim's purse on a table and helps themselves. Research suggests that financial abuse is most frequently perpetrated by a person acting in a trusted capacity, for example, a family member or, to a lesser extent, friends, neighbours or care workers/other professionals.

Motivation and justification

Some perpetrators, especially those in positions of trust, may also fail to appreciate that their actions amount to a crime. Families in particular may not perceive financial abuse or crime as harmful and think it acceptable to take money from their vulnerable relative – especially if inheritance of the money is likely anyway.

Studies show that the motivation is clearly financial gain with high rewards and minimal risk of detection. For example, where a trusted family member is helping to manage a parent's finances they may feel that using some of those finances to benefit themselves is perfectly acceptable. They will feel almost affronted if you suggest to them that this is theft or fraud. There will be suggestions that the money is coming to them at a later date under the relative's will and therefore there is nothing wrong in what they have been doing. See, for example, *Re GM, MJ, and JM v The Public Guardian* [2013] EWHC 2966 (COP), [2013] MHLO 44 where it was reported that: 'Throughout these proceedings MJ and JM described the watches and the rings they had bought as "heirlooms", which they had acquired in memory of GM and Barbara with the intention that they would be passed down through the family from generation to generation.'

Money removed from the patient's estate is often described by an abuser as an inheritance, an heirloom, gifts or loans. There is clearly a disconnect between the reality of the crime being committed and the perpetrators' perception of that act. The perpetrator will justify their action with statements such as: 'it will be mine soon anyway', 'she would want me to have it', 'it's payment for all the care I'm giving her', 'it's payment for the granny annexe we've had built to accommodate her', 'all the family's money should be pooled', or that it will mean that the local authority can't take her home away from her.

Limited data on perpetrators suggest that the driving force in much financial abuse may be the problems that the perpetrator suffers from. As we will see below, it is estimated 33% of perpetrators have financial, relationship, alcohol or gambling problems.

Strangers

Adults with higher levels of dependency on others may assign higher levels of trust. There may be more scope for abuse against people with higher levels of independence by people unknown to them, such as rogue traders or organised criminals involved in mass-marketing fraud. Individuals knocking on an elderly person's door may represent the first social contact they have had for some time and understandably they will treat a sympathetic voice as evidence that the person is there to help them rather than commit a crime.

Several organisations outside traditional adult safeguarding (OFT, Royal Mail, Serious Organised Crime Agency (SOCA), Trading Standards, Think Jessica) describe examples of these financial crimes, more commonly perpetrated by a stranger, such as mass-marketing fraud, identity theft or rogue trading. These may be just as common as those crimes perpetrated by a person occupying a position of trust, but the adult may be less likely to be recognised as being vulnerable.

One type of abuse may involve other types of abuse

There is also research that suggests that financial abuse is often accompanied by other forms of abuse, including physical abuse and neglect (Help the Aged, 2008). This may lead to stress, anxiety and depression as the realisation dawns that the person they had trusted to take care of their property and finances has been secretly defrauding them.

In an AgeUK study in 2007, 2.6% of people aged 66 and over living in private households reported that they had experienced mistreatment involving a family member, close friend or care worker (ie those in a traditional expectation of trust relationship) during the past year. This equated to about 227,000 people aged 66 and over in the UK. When the one-year prevalence of mistreatment was broadened to include incidents involving neighbours and acquaintances, the overall prevalence increased to 4.0% (approximately 342,400 people). Overall, 53% of perpetrators were found to have been living in the respondent's household at the time of the abuse.

Characteristics of perpetrators

The UK Study of Abuse and Neglect of Older People Prevalence Survey Report (June 2007), although it worked on relatively few numbers, found that financial abuse also displays a quite different pattern in relation to what was then known about perpetrators.

The survey confirmed other research findings that family, other than partners, are the most common perpetrators. The survey results also suggest the following:

- Care workers may be committing around 30% of financial abuse. Note though if neighbours and acquaintances are included, they are equal to other family members as the most common perpetrators of financial abuse.

- Perpetrators of financial abuse tended to be in the 16–64 age range.

- Perpetrators tended to be in paid employment.

- 25% of victims lived with the perpetrator.

- 25% of victims received care from the perpetrator.

- 33% had financial, relationship, alcohol or gambling problems.

The risk factors for the elderly were identified as living alone, in receipt of services, suffering from bad or very bad health, older men, and women who are divorced or separated, or the lonely elderly.

'No Secrets' report

This report (see **Chapter 2**) analysed who may be an abuser. Vulnerable adults may be abused by a wide range of people including relatives and family members, professional staff, paid care workers, volunteers, other service users, neighbours, friends and associates, people who deliberately exploit vulnerable people and strangers. Importantly, the report acknowledged that agencies not only have a responsibility to all vulnerable adults who have been abused, but may also have responsibilities in relation to some perpetrators of abuse.

The roles, powers and duties of the various agencies in relation to the perpetrator will vary depending on whether the perpetrator is:

- member of staff, proprietor or service manager;

- a member of a recognised professional group;

- a volunteer or member of a community group such as place of worship or social club;

- another service user;

- a spouse, relative or member of the person's social network;

- a carer, that is, someone who is eligible for an assessment under the Carers (Recognition and Services) Act 1996;

- a neighbour, member of the public or stranger; or a person who deliberately targets vulnerable people in order to exploit them.

The report also noted that stranger abuse requires a different kind of response from that, appropriate to abuse in an ongoing relationship or in a care setting. Nevertheless, in some instances it may be appropriate to use the locally agreed inter-agency adult protection procedures to ensure that the vulnerable person receives the services and support that they need. Such procedures may also be used when there is the potential for harm to other vulnerable people.

Abuse can occur in any setting where an elderly person resides, whether that is where they live alone or with a relative; it may also occur within a care home or day care settings, in hospitals, custodial situations, support services into people's own homes, and other places previously assumed safe, or in public places. The necessary intervention will then be determined by the environment in which the abuse has occurred. Nursing, residential care homes and placement schemes are subject to regulatory controls set out in legislation and relevant guidance. Day care settings are not currently regulated in this way and require different kinds of monitoring and intervention to address similar risks.

The report commented that paid care staff in domiciliary services may work with little or no supervision or scrutiny. This is clearly a continuing problem. Families have often resorted to covert surveillance techniques to watch over their elderly relatives where they have concerns about care provision.

Assessment of the environment, or context, is relevant, because exploitation, deception, misuse of authority, intimidation or coercion may render a vulnerable adult incapable of making his own decisions. Thus, it may be important for the vulnerable adult to be away from the sphere of influence of the abusive person or the setting in order to be able to make a free choice about how to proceed. An initial rejection of help should not always be taken at face value.

Other types of abuse may also be present

It is noticeable from experience in practice and from the long line of published cases that financial abuse is often coupled with other types of abuse. There is no doubt that an elderly parent sharing their home with an abusing relative will show elements of psychological and emotional abuse. Examples of controlling behaviour are often present. These take the form of the abuser controlling who the parent can see, who they can talk to on the telephone freely, or even when they can purchase new clothes. The following are other forms that may be present:

- Serial abusing in which the perpetrator seeks out and 'grooms' vulnerable individuals – for example, the 'carer' who seeks out elderly vulnerable people and moves in with them as the live-in carer.

42

- In families long-term abuse may have built up over many years. The parent may not have a particularly good relationship with the self-appointed caring relative, but is seemingly powerless to choose an alternative carer from the family.

- Opportunistic abuse such as theft occurring because money has been left around.

- Situational abuse which arises because pressures have built up and/or because of difficult or challenging behaviour – there may be someone in the family who is sharing the home who has addiction or mental health problems who has become dependent on the parent for financial support.

What amount of abuse justifies state intervention?

Inn *DL v A Local Authority* [2012] EWCA Civ 253, the abuser's mother did not want the courts to intervene to protect her and her husband from her son's abuse. The local authority was concerned about DL's alleged conduct towards his parents, which was said to be aggressive and result on occasions in physical violence by DL towards his parents. The local authority had documented incidents going back to 2005 chronicling DL's behaviour, including physical assaults, verbal threats, controlling where and when his parents may move in the house, preventing them from leaving the house, and controlling who may visit them, and the terms upon which they may visit them, including health and social care professionals providing care and support for the mother. There had also been consistent reports that DL was trying to coerce Mr L into transferring the ownership of the house into DL's name. He had also placed considerable pressure on both his parents to have his mother moved into a care home against her wishes.

Seriousness and extent of harm to justify intervention

The No Secrets report can be used as a starting point here to determine the extent and seriousness the abuse has to reach to justify intervention. It uses the definition of 'harm' from the 'Who decides' consultation paper issued by the Law Commission in 1997:

'Harm should be taken to include not only ill treatment (including sexual abuse and forms of ill treatment which are not physical), but also the impairment of, or an avoidable deterioration in, physical or mental health; and the impairment of physical, intellectual, emotional, social or behavioural development.'

It was acknowledged that the seriousness or extent of abuse is often not clear when anxiety is first expressed. It is important, therefore, when considering the appropriateness of intervention, to look at the allegations with an open mind. In making any assessment of seriousness the following factors need to be considered:

- the vulnerability of the individual;

- the nature and extent of the abuse;

- the length of time it has been occurring;

- the impact on the individual; and

- the risk of repeated or increasingly serious acts involving this or other vulnerable adults.

What this means in practice is working through a process of assessment to evaluate:

- Is the person suffering harm or exploitation?

- Does the person suffering or causing harm/exploitation meet the NHS and Community Care Act 1990 eligibility criteria?

- Is the intervention in the best interests of the vulnerable adult fitting the criteria and/or in the public interest?

- Does the assessment account for the depth and conviction of the feelings of the person alleging the abuse?

American research

It is interesting to note that other countries show a similar pattern of characteristics of perpetrators and victims. A research report by Shelly Jackson and Thomas Hafemeister entitled 'Financial Abuse of Elderly People v. Other Forms of Elder Abuse: Assessing Their Dynamics, Risk Factors, and Society's Response' (February 2011) analysed samples of participants in abuse and identified the following types of perpetrators:

- usually male (62%);

- usually related (68%);

- unmarried (70%);

- unemployed (54%);

- in good health but suffering from an unusual life event at the time of the offence (56%);

- ability to drive (85%);

- suffering from alcohol or drug problems (50%);

- no criminal record but may have had an adult history of violence;

- financially dependent on their victim (43%);

- dependent on their victim for their residential needs (37%);

- dependent on their victim for their emotional needs (29%).

These statistics appear to be borne out by experience and reported case law. It should be relatively straightforward on the basis of such figures to compile a checklist of details showing where an elderly person is more at risk of financial abuse. If this was coupled with mandatory reporting and intervention there may be more hope of real improvement in resolving this ongoing problem and imposing deterrent penalties on the abusers.

In the UK context we can look at the cases that have come before the Court of Protection and illustrate the very real problems that the elderly are encountering. This is of course just a snap-shot of the actual situation. Not all victims will report problems of abuse, and not all perpetrators will be caught. Likewise, there will be some cases which are resolved without the need for the involvement of the court. The problem is detection and putting in place sufficient safeguards to protect the most vulnerable in the community. The table of statistics of the Court of Protection cases in Appendix C illustrates the financial abuse cases that have been reported in the years 2014–2016. They are just a snap-shot of the work undertaken by the OPG and the court in dealing with financial abuse cases. They reinforce the statistics reported above as to the type of perpetrators involved.

Understanding and explaining financial abuse

In the US the National Institute of Justice has tried to uncover an explanation for this abuse. In their paper 'Understanding the Causes of Elder Abuse' they identified an adequate guiding theory to explain the range of causes behind elder abuse and have sought to promote systematic data collection. They summarised some of the researchers range of explanations as the following in respect of abuse generally, but there are elements that overlap into financial abuse, in particular:

- abusers have learned from the behaviour of others around them that violence is a way to solve problems or obtain a desired outcome;

- abusers feel they don't receive enough benefit or recognition from their relationship with the elderly person, so they resort to violence in an effort to obtain their 'fair share';

- a combination of background and current factors, such as recent conflicts and a family history of 'solving' problems through violence, influences the relationship;

- abusers use a pattern of coercive tactics to gain and maintain power and control in a relationship;

- many factors in elder abuse arise through individual, relationship, community and societal influences;

- elder abuse can be attributed to both the victim's and the abuser's social and biomedical characteristics, the nature of their relationship, and power dynamics, within their shared environment of family and friends.

Clearly, they conclude that much more detailed and focused research into the victim and the abuser, including their cognitive functioning, the types of abuse, the domestic setting, and the nature of their relationship will help us understand and explain why this is occurring and what preventive measures can be adopted.

Multidimensional abuse cases

It is important to understand that many cases of cases of abuse in domestic settings can be multidimensional. The recent American National Institute of Justice research ('Causes and Characteristics of elder abuse) has shed some light on case characteristics common to different types of elder abuse. They summarised this as follows:

Physical abuse

Contrary to common belief, many elderly victims of physical abuse are high-functioning. The abuser is typically a family member, often the adult offspring of the victim. The abuser may be a long-term dependent of the victim because of health or financial issues and may take out resentment for this dependence on the elderly victim. These victims are generally aware that they are being mistreated, but their sense of parental or family obligation makes them reluctant to cut off the abuser.

Neglect

In cases of elder neglect, the victim may be physically frail or cognitively vulnerable. The caregiver does not take adequate care of the victim, who may acknowledge his own shortcomings as a parent and conclude that the tables are being turned – and that he deserves no better.

Financial exploitation

Victims of financial exploitation often lack someone with whom they can discuss and monitor financial issues. They may have an emerging, unrecognised cognitive impairment; worry about a future loss of independence; and be overly trusting of a caregiver capable of theft, fraud and misuse of assets.

Hybrid cases

Cases where financial exploitation is combined with physical abuse or neglect typically involve financially dependent family members, particularly adult offspring, who have been cared for by the elderly person. As the elderly person declines in health and becomes more socially isolated, he relies more on the abuser for care, resulting in a mutual dependency. Such hybrid cases are unique in many ways and tend to have worse outcomes for victims than other kinds of elder abuse, perhaps because the abuse is accompanied by the stress of financial loss.

They also analysed the type of independence enjoyed by the elderly person. These were either physical or financial.

Physically independent elders were able to care for themselves, could drive, and were cognitively intact and physically healthy. Financially independent elders had the financial assets to cover their needs and often owned their homes.

Elderly victims who were physically and financially independent were more likely to experience pure financial exploitation.

Elderly victims experiencing hybrid financial exploitation tended to be financially independent but physically dependent. They had significant health problems, were unable to drive and were to some degree dependent on others for assistance.

Victims of hybrid financial exploitation were more likely than victims of pure financial exploitation to have:

- been victimised by a relative;

- experienced abuse multiple times over a longer period of time;

- suffered a negative health consequence, financial loss, a disruption in social relationships, or some combination of these as a consequence of their victimisation.

Lessons to be learnt

We can see from the above research clear patterns of abuse and exploitation. What can we draw from this that will enable us as practitioners and advisers to assist potentially vulnerable clients?

- We have now seen clear characteristics of likely perpetrators. An understanding of the family dynamics will assist us in identifying if there is a problem developing and indicate whether there is someone who is taking advantage of the client.

- Early warning of potential problems is important as the client's cognitive powers will decrease over time and our ability to connect with them will diminish as well.

- The importance of staying in touch with your client as they get older: it is not sufficient to just wait for the client to be in touch. Proactive communication and visits will be increasingly important. There is so much more to be learnt from visiting clients in their own homes. It takes time, but the rewards are significant.

- Clearly we do not want to label a member of the family a potential abuser but it is better to be able to offer early guidance to the client and to reassure them as to our ability to help should they need us.

- Written guidance on financial abuse that we can give to the clients will alert them to possible problems. They need to know that certain behaviour is not acceptable and that there are sanctions and procedures that can be adopted to prevent abuse from escalating and repeating. It is often the case that an abuser will start at a low level and if there is no possibility of detection or obstacle in their way then it will develop. As the victim's dependence on the abuser increases so potentially will the abuser's resentment and control over the victim.

- Finally, the more daylight that is shone on this problem the more aware and alert to the signposts we can make our clients.

Chapter 5

What Form does Financial Abuse take?

5A

Unauthorised Gifts

We will see later in this book how attorneys and deputies can assist the elderly in making authorised gifts. However, the majority of gift cases that reach the Court of Protection are where the Office of the Public Guardian (OPG) has had to launch an investigation and has determined that the deputy or attorney has been engaged in making unauthorised gifts. In recent years there have been some exceptional examples and set out below are some of the cases that demonstrate what can go wrong. It will also touch on those cases where the Deputy or Attorney has become out of their depth and retrospective approval of gifts is required and further supervision ordered to assist them in carrying on the financial management of the client's affairs.

In brief, MCA 2005, s 12 provides that:

The attorney may make gifts for the donor on the following occasions

(a) on customary occasions to persons (including himself) who are related to or connected with the donor; or

(b) to any charity to whom the donor made or might have been expected to make gifts, if the value of each such gift is not unreasonable having regard to all the circumstances and, in particular, the size of the donor's estate.

(3) 'Customary occasion' means—

(a) the occasion or anniversary of a birth, a marriage or the formation of a civil partnership; or

(b) any other occasion on which presents are customarily given within families or among friends or associates.

(4) Subsection (2) is subject to any conditions or restrictions in the instrument.

If an attorney wishes to make more extensive gifts than permitted by s 12 they must apply for an order under s 23(4), which provides that, 'The court may authorize the making of gifts which are not within section 12(2) (permitted gifts)'.

As we shall see later, the above rules have been ignored in some cases and misinterpreted in others.

Cases involving attorneys

In *Re OL* [2015] EWCOP 41, OL's property in South Norwood was sold for £730,000 on 23 May 2014. The property in which she then lived with her daughter (DA) in Croydon was bought on 13 June 2014 for £430,000 entirely with OL's funds. OL and the two attorneys had subsequently executed a declaration of trust stating that OL had only a 20% share in the property (worth £86,000), whereas the attorneys, neither of whom had contributed anything towards the purchase price, had a 40% share each. This represented an outright gift of £172,000 to each of the attorneys.

The OPG wrote to the two attorneys on 22 July and 5 August 2014 asking them to produce a full account of their dealings, but had still not received any accounts from them. £127,885 of OL's money was used to pay off DA's mortgage on her former home in South Norwood, which she still owns. It was divided into two flats, one of which is let at a rent of £850 a month. A further £80,000 of OL's money was spent on building work and a loft conversion at DA's property in South Norwood. In a period of six months OL had gone from having a property worth £730,000 to having only £7,000 in her bank account plus, of course, a 20% share of the house in Croydon.

The court revoked the lasting power of attorney and proposed appointing a panel deputy authorised to take such steps as are necessary or expedient to restore OL's estate so far as possible to the position in which it would have been before the attorneys began helping themselves to her money.

Cases involving deputies

The year 2013 saw two cases brought before the Court of Protection which shone light on financial abuse perpetrated by court-appointed deputies. This first case is dealt with in detail as it shows what can happen when those empowered, whether as attorneys or deputies, are left unrestrained.

In the matter of GM, between MJ and JM and the Public Guardian [2013] EWHC 2966

This case was first reported in April 2013. The patient here was Gladys Meek (GM), whose only child, Barbara, had predeceased her. Her daughter's estate passed to Gladys by intestacy and together the assets subject to the court amounted to £500,000. The application was for retrospective approval of gifts made by her deputies, MJ and JM. In the order appointing the deputies the following authority was given:

'The deputies may jointly and severally (without obtaining any further authority from the court) dispose of money or property of GM by way of gift to any charity to which she made or might have been expected to make gifts and on customary occasions to persons who are related to or connected with her, provided that the value of each such gift is not unreasonable having regard to all the circumstances and, in particular, the size of her estate.'

What the OPG had discovered by virtue of a section 49 report was that the deputies were seeking approval of gifts totaling £231,259 and expenses of £46,552. The list of gifts was as follows:

1   Charitable gifts

Christadelphian Church	£20,000
Scottish National Trust	£6,852
Derbyshire Wildlife	£5,000
Guide Dogs for the Blind	£5,000
RSPB	£5,000
Codnor Castle	£5,000
Nottingham University	£5,000
Derby Hospital	£5,000
Air Ambulance	£500
Total	**£57,352**

Comment

Note that MCA 2005, s 12 provides that a donee of an LPA may make gifts to any charity to whom the donor made or might have been expected to make gifts, provided that the value of each such gift is not unreasonable having regard to all the circumstances and, in particular, the size of the donor's estate. The court heard that the Court of Protection's General Visitor had spoken to the patient and the following report was made:

'The Visitor advised that "*GM has no awareness that she or anyone acting on her behalf has made any gifts*" … *She was puzzled by my suggestion that people sometimes gave to charities and I noted her reactions to a sample I listed:*

(a)   Guide Dogs, '*I don't think so.*'

(b)   Eye Hospital, '*My eyes are all right.*'

(c)   Air Ambulance, '*I don't know.*'

(d)   National Trust for Scotland, enthusiastic, '*I love Scotland, so yes.*'

(e)   RSPB/Scottish Birds, '*I like birds but I couldn't support them.*'

(f)   Derbyshire Wildlife, '*No.*'

(g)   Christadelphian Church, '*Yes, they're very good*'."

This illustrates how important it is to involve the patient in accordance with the principles of MCA 2005. Even if it is thought that the patient may be unable to manage their property and affairs it is quite clear from the above comments that hearing GM's wishes and feelings expressed so clearly helped the court in resolving the issue.

2 The gifts that MJ had received personally were:

Rolex watch	£18,275
Ring	£16,500
Alexander McQueen handbag	£995
Perfume	£86
Cash gift from Barbara's estate	£20,000
Total	**£55,856**

Comment

In Tables 2 and 3 the deputies are abusing their position of trust, benefiting personally from that position, and contravening the authority given to them by the court. The deputies were clearly profiting from their position.

3 The gifts that JM had received personally were:

Omega watch	£17,000
Ring	£3,575
Ring	£6,736
Two Mulberry handbags	£1,085
Perfume	£86.00
Cash gift from Barbara's estate	£20,000
Total	**£48,396**

Throughout the proceedings MJ and JM described the watches and the rings they had bought as 'heirlooms', which they had acquired in memory of GM and Barbara with the intention that they would be passed down through the family from generation to generation.

4 The larger cash gifts made to family and friends were:

MJ's daughter, RJ	£10,000
MJ's daughter, KT	£10,000
MJ's husband	£10,000
JM's daughter, SB	£10,000
JM's granddaughter, DB	£10,000

JM's grandson, JB	£10,000
Barbara's friend, SG	£1,000
SG's daughter	£500
SG's granddaughter	£500
SG's other granddaughter	£500
Total	**£62,500**

5   Other smaller gifts that were made to deputies' families:

MJ's daughter, RJ	Vivienne Westwood handbag	£170
	Birthday present	£500
	Christmas present	£500
MJ's daughter, KT	Vivienne Westwood handbag	£135
	Birthday present	£500
	Christmas present	£500
MJ's husband	Derby County season ticket	£510
	Christmas present	£1,000
JM's daughter, SB	Vivienne Westwood handbag	£170
	Christmas present	£1,000
JM's granddaughter, DB	Vivienne Westwood handbag	£170
	Birthday present	£500
	Christmas present	£500
JM's grandson, JB	Birthday present	£500
	Christmas present	£500
Total		**£7,155**

6   Expenses claim

In addition to the gifts they had received, MJ and JM also claimed and sought the court's blessing for the deputyship expenses they had incurred.

Each of them had bought a car and a computer.

- MJ purchased a Mini Countryman for £25,200.
- JM bought a Ford Fiesta for £19,393.21.
- MJ had purchased an Apple MBPRO, which together with the software, came to £1,299.99.
- JM opted for a Sony laptop and an Epson printer, the combined cost of which was £659.04.

They claimed that they had bought the cars so that they could visit GM and the computers so that they could keep any eye on her investments online.

Comment

Lay deputies are only allowed reasonable expenses. In April 2016 the OPG issued a practice note (SD1) outlining their approach to family care payments. This sets out when deputies should seek approval to such payments and when the Public Guardian will consider applying to the court concerning unauthorised payments. Before a deputy can make any family payments they must consider firstly whether the proposed payment is in the client's best interests and secondly, whether the decision to make a payment conflicts with the deputy's duty not to take advantage of their position.

As a consequence of these transactions Gladys' estate was depleted and she was left with only £177,230. The Public Guardian rightly concluded that the gifts were excessive, not in Gladys' best interests and inconsistent with the deputies' fiduciary duty of care to her. Furthermore, he found that they had exceeded their authority given to them in the Order appointing them as deputies and that they exposed themselves to accusations of self-dealing. Forty-four per cent of Gladys' estate had been disposed of by way of these gifts.

The deputies were related to Gladys only by marriage and not by blood and therefore were not going to benefit under her intestacy as she had not made a will. The number and value of the gifts only transpired when the deputies had applied for retrospective approval of gifts made and intended future gifts.

What is interesting about this case is the defence raised by the deputies to try and justify these activities. In particular, they argued that:

> 'We have acted as we thought the COP order granted us, enabling us to gift and donate in relation to the size of the estate. As GM is 92 years old we believe approx £200,000 to be adequate and if this is not enough [for her to live on], there is no way she will go short.'

It is a quite shocking assertion and rightly the court removed them as deputies and subsequently ordered a statutory will to be prepared.

The deputies agreed that they had:

- signed the deputy's declaration when applying to be appointed in which they made various undertakings;

- not read the MCA 2005 Code of Practice;

- not discussed any of the gift proposals with Gladys;

- no evidence as to the extent to which Gladys had made gifts to them in the past when she had capacity to do so. If cash gifts had been made by her they had tended to be in the region of £20 only;

- invested the rest of her money in bank accounts and premium bonds in their own names.

In short, these deputies were clearly unsuited to the role and the question remains as to why stronger action was not taken by the authorities, including the police, who could have charged them with criminal offences.

Summary of considerations

Senior Judge Lush set out a useful summary (at para 67) of the considerations to be taken into account when the court approves gifts:

- whether the gift is in the patient's (P)'s best interests;
- the size of P's estate;
- the extent to which P was in the habit of making gifts or loans of a particular size or nature before the onset of incapacity;
- P's anticipated life expectancy;
- the possibility that P may require residential or nursing care and the projected cost of such care;
- whether P is in receipt of aftercare pursuant to the Mental Health Act 1983, s 117 or NHS Continuing Healthcare;
- the extent to which any gifts may interfere with the devolution of P's estate under his will or intestacy; and
- the impact of inheritance tax on P's death

In the matter of Joan Treadwell, deceased 2013: The Public Guardian and Colin Lutz, Stuart McNeil, Derek Brown and Joanna Wildgoose [2013] EWHC 2409 (COP)

This case concerned the enforcement of a security bond where unauthorised gifts had been made by the deputy, Colin Lutz, who was Mrs Treadwell's son from her first marriage. The OPG was concerned about the level of gifting by the deputy. In the first year of his appointment he made 30 gifts totalling in value £34,800. These included sums of £9,000 to set up trust funds for each of his two children, a £2,500 graduation gift and a £2,500 housewarming gift. None of these gifts benefited the children of Mrs Treadwell's second marriage. In the second year of his deputyship he made gifts of £9,450 and in the next year gifts totalling £15,125. Mrs Treadwell's income was then £10,000 per year and her estate was then worth £150,000. He applied for retrospective approval for these gifts. She was fully funded for her care home fees by the NHS. The Public Guardian requested the Court of Protection to call in the security bond for £44,300 (that is to a value equal to the majority of the gifts made).

The deputy's response to this application was as follows:

'I refer to a copy of the OPG's newsletter for deputies, summer 2009. This reports Lewison J. referring to the "best interests" test, explaining that an important factor was that "what will live on after the person's death is his memory; and for many people it is in their best interests that they be remembered with affection by their family as having done "the right thing" in their will." Although the judge was referring to a will in the quotation, the article goes on to say that the principles apply to other situations in which the court is asked to make a decision on behalf of someone who lacks capacity.

'Joan Treadwell will be remembered with affection in any case, but the long term benefit of providing a financial foundation for her great-grandchildren will enable her memory to be held in even greater regard in the future. This is of greater importance due to the fact that Joan will not have the chance to interact with her great grandchildren as they grow up. They will only have tales and photographs of her.

'Taking this money back would be in effect giving it to two already well-off recipients of the totality of their father's will. During the statutory will application Bill Treadwell's daughters have been deeply insulting to all members of Joan's family. By their own father's admission they did not have a friendly relationship with Joan. This diversion of Joan's funds would be so offensive to Joan's memory that a more grievous insult could hardly be imagined, and directly contrary to Joan's best interests.'

Again, this illustrates the problem that the OPG has with lay deputies (and attorneys) who regard the patient's estate and income has theirs to do what they will. A more vigorous assessment of a deputy's qualities and experience before they are appointed must be considered. Not every candidate who puts themselves forward will be suitable for the role. Their motives should be explored. Why is it that they want to take on this role? Are they being a caring relative acting altruistically for the patient? Or is there some financial motive involved?

Banking

The banks are the frontline of financial abuse, both in respect of access to accounts and in so far they should be the first wall of defence against abuse. There is still evidence of the casual treatment by banks of access to another's bank account. One only has to look at the way accounts are closed after a customer dies with minimal checking or verification of the claimant's authority. Instances where funds up to £50,000 are handed over by banks to beneficiaries rather than executors are commonplace. Training and rigorous systems should prevent this, but should also prevent cash funds being transferred to unauthorised individuals by elderly vulnerable customers.

What types of situations arise?

- A client hands over his bank card and PIN to a third party to buy goods or obtain cash for the client. The third party uses it for their own purposes and leaves the client without the goods or cash.

- A third party sets up new internet accounts for an elderly client and transfers funds to their own account even where the client has no computer or internet connection.

- A third party forges the client's signatures to withdraw or transfer funds to the third party's account.

- A third party incorrectly informs the bank that an elderly client has moved addresses and new bank cards are sent to the new address.

- An elderly customer being accompanied to the bank by a third party.

- Signatures becoming illegible due to poor eye sight and arthritic fingers.

- Mobility issues prevent an elderly person collecting cash.

- Poor financial management by attorneys or nominees by running up overdrafts and comingling of their own and the donor's money. (See *AB (Revocation of Enduring Power of Attorney)* [2014] EWCOP 12 where 'the attorneys treated AB's funds as their own private bank and doled them out to members of the family, until they reached the point where she was unable to pay for the care she needs. This was not in AB's best interest.')

- An attorney adding his name to the elderly person's bank account without giving notice to the co-attorneys (see *Re DWA* [2015] EWCOP 72).

- An attorney signing cheques for substantial gifts to the patient's children, leaving her potentially with insufficient funds to pay her care home fees (see *Re EG* [2015] EWCOP 6).

When the Draft Mental Capacity Bill was being scrutinised in the joint committee of Parliament, the British Bankers' Association submitted written evidence on two significant points. Firstly, that the change in date of registration of powers of attorney should be kept to that point when mental capacity is beginning to be lost or has been lost (as was the case with enduring powers of attorney) and secondly, that consideration should be given to establishing a threshold amount for withdrawals by a third party appointee. In such a way the appointee could only access limited funds. This seemed a sensible proposal, but sadly no such thresholds were imposed.

Protective steps to put in place

It is worth considering how your clients can protect themselves when they reach the point when they need another person to help them with their finances. As we know, there is a stage of vulnerability before loss of mental capacity becomes evident. This is the most critical point and the stage when clients are particularly vulnerable to abuse. It is the time when they will recognise that they need help and will perhaps find someone to help who is not the most appropriate person.

Some banks will have a dedicated team who are well trained to answer specific queries on appointee and attorney banking arrangements. It may be that the bank could be asked to limit access to the account to a certain threshold for withdrawals and transfers. The better way to deal with this is a well-prepared lasting power of attorney appointing two attorneys and limiting their powers or having an audit requirement for transactions over a certain value.

Financial management skills of attorneys

Many of the above steps require careful thought and advice. Time is often limited when discussing lasting powers of attorney with clients. Unfortunately, problems arise because financial abuse is never anticipated. Statutory limits on withdrawals where there are no oversight arrangements in place would be a tough requirement. However, some simple manoeuvres may prevent much abuse. It is therefore recommended that practitioners think about the following when advising their clients:

- Ask the clients how well they know the appointee/proposed attorney and how they rate those appointees' financial management skills.

- Has the proposed appointee ever been bankrupt? Should you carry out a bankruptcy search?

- Discuss how the client manages their finances at present. How many accounts do they have and where are they? What funds do they maintain in those accounts?

- What is their policy on cash gifts?

- Would they expect their attorneys to make substantial gifts, and to whom?

- Would they expect that their attorneys would have power to take out equity release if funds ran low?

- Would they trust the appointee/attorney with their bank card?

- Would they want to put a limit on fund transfers?

- Would they approve payments to recompense their appointee/attorney for the work carried out on their behalf?

- Would they want an audit of their bank accounts carried out annually (if at all) or only in respect of certain special or large value transactions?

- Would they approve of their sole accounts being transferred into joint names with the appointee/attorney?

- Would they expect their attorneys to fund house renovations for the attorneys' own home or to 'borrow' money from the donor?

What practical steps do the banks use to ensure that the correct individuals access bank accounts?

In November 2015 the British Banking Association, the Building Societies Association and the Office of the Public Guardian together issued guidance for 'people wanting to manage a bank account for someone else'. This set out an explanation of what this means and listed the documents that would be required to do this. It is at the point when an attorney or deputy is being registered on the account that thought should be given to the practical implications of managing a donor's bank accounts. If there is more than one attorney or deputy, should both be registered with the bank and given signing rights over the account? Will this cause confusion? If the appointment is on a joint and several basis then is this a sensible arrangement?

If there are concerns about financial mismanagement by one attorney then it would be sensible to put limits on the banking authority. For example, insisting that both attorneys should sign all cheques and authorise all withdrawals. This may be impractical on a day-to-day basis. Careful thought needs to be given here. An unrestricted lasting power of attorney appointing two or more attorneys on a joint and several basis will allow each of those attorneys to act for the donor. However, practically speaking this would make the management of the donor's financial affairs difficult and unwieldy. Usually there is one attorney who manages finances with the others being involved as required. It makes sense in such a situation for the attorneys to sit down every six months and check through the accounts with the 'managing' attorney, remembering that all attorneys remain responsible for the overall management.

Technological advances and fraud prevention

The big challenge for the banks is how they can provide regular banking services for an increasingly elderly population who may have certain disabilities that restrict their ability to access normal traditional banking services. There is still a generation that does not have access to the internet and therefore internet banking services. In addition, they may be subject to more restrictions due to a number of disabilities including mobility, hearing, eyesight and writing difficulties. The able-bodied take it for granted that they can get to a cash machine, or a bank branch, write a cheque on occasion, speak to their bank for telephone banking or view their bank statements clearly. What should also be remembered is that the older population like to have cash on them. So many clients still like to go the post office and collect their pension in cash. The vulnerability that arises here is obvious. Similarly, they do not feel comfortable with getting cashback from their supermarket when paying for the groceries. They want to be able to account for their cash withdrawals easily and this does not lend itself to easy accounting.

Surveys also show that the older population, especially women, are more wary of bank debit or credit cards. This again encourages them to use cash when shopping or paying for services or at the very least writing out a cheque. The younger generation hardly know how to write cheques even if they did have a cheque book.

So the dilemma for the banks is how they provide safe and secure banking services for an increasingly elderly population. If the customer retains their capacity then the bank needs to be able to accommodate their needs and cope with their disabilities. Internet banking is fine provided they are internet-savvy. Otherwise they are dependent on others to show them how it works. Remembering passwords and procedures can be a challenge at the best of times, but it can make an elderly, vulnerable person fearful and distressed if they cannot easily access their money.

The AGE UK report ('The Way We Pay: Payments, Systems and Financial Inclusion', 2011) reported that almost one-fifth of people aged 65 and over ask others to withdraw cash for them. Clearly this involves the disclosure of PINs to third parties. What is also clear is that this age group has grown up in a cash-based era and the idea of using digital payments is by no means straightforward nor necessarily a trusted method to carry out day-to-day transactions.

The Eighty Something project report 'New Approaches to Banking for the Older Old' (February 2012) explored new ways to assist the elderly in using banking services. The older old were those aged 80–85 who were regarded in a 2002 United Nations report as the fastest growing section of the world population. Interesting results showed that those regarded as the 'older old' were used to using cheques. Cheques provided flexibility, record-keeping and familiarity. Conversely, cash withdrawals either required PINs and passwords or personal attendance at a bank or ATM machine. They discussed whether technological advances could provide assistance including secure PIN reminders and a possible 'Guardian Angel Card'. Such a card could be set with geographical, temporal and monetary boundaries – for example, only specific shops or ATMs could be used by the third party user. This would give the elderly more reassurance, and one can only hope that this is being developed.

It is also possible to have what is known as a 'chip and signature' card. This is a good alternative to a 'PIN' bank card. However, the downside to this may be that the card is not accepted in all shops. It is worth exploring what shops would take this as it would be sensible alternative for the client who is finding it increasingly difficult to remember their PIN.

Benefit payments

The Department for Work and Pensions now operates a system whereby benefit payments are paid direct into a bank or building society. However, this does assume that all elderly people have bank accounts. The Post Office has what is known as a Post Office card account, which is designed specifically for receiving benefit payments. It is possible for a third party to be nominated to have access to that account as a 'permanent agent'. However, this can only continue provided the main account-holder has capacity to consent to that appointment.

Banks as the frontline for noticing abuse

Practitioners will know from their experiences of trying to resolve financial abuse issues that quite often the traditional banking arrangements of attending at a branch to effect financial transactions provides a first opportunity for financial abuse to be noticed; for example, the elderly client struggling to remember PINs and being helped by a third party who is unknown to the branch. The retention of local branches for the elderly to attend and where they and their attorneys/ appointees are known are an important key to preventing abuse. Well-trained bank staff can really help to spot the signs that abuse may be taking place.

Reporting abuse

If the banks are at the frontline for spotting abuse, how do they do this? Experience suggests that at present eagle-eyed staff who are trained well will have the best chance of noticing when a customer is in difficulty. There should be a watch or flagging system introduced so that any anomalies can then be identified before significant problems arise. At this point it seems sensible for the bank staff to have a conversation with the customer to try and identify whether there is someone who can assist them, give them guidance and make sure that they are not taken advantage of.

Attorney/deputyship appointments and bank accounts

Attorneys

An attorney appointed under a power of attorney may have full and unrestricted power to manage bank accounts for the donor. It is important to check the terms of the power. It may contain restrictions as to how it is to operate. It may require all attorneys to sign cheques and authorise transfers. It may be unrestricted and simply set out guidance which is not legally binding on the attorneys. This means that they do not need to take account of the advice if they believe they can otherwise act in the donor's best interests.

However the power is termed, the attorneys will only be able to operate the account if they have complied with the particular bank's procedures. Each attorney will need to have produced their power of attorney to the bank, their identity documents and also to have given a specimen signature to the bank to enable them to sign cheques and other bank documents on the donor's behalf. It is imperative that the account remains in the name of the account-holder and not transferred into the name of the attorney or deputy. At all times it is essential to be able to identify that the account belongs to the donor and not the attorney. There are other issues if the account is transferred from the donor's name. The bank may then wrongly defer to the attorney as the customer rather than the donor with all the reduction in customer rights that that would entail.

If the donor retains their mental capacity but would like the attorney/attorneys to assist them with the banking arrangements then they can do so. However, as soon as capacity begins to be lost then other rules apply. In respect of an enduring power of attorney, the attorney is under an obligation to register the enduring power of attorney when the donor is losing or has lost their mental capacity. If the bank has suspicions that this has arisen then they could freeze the account until the enduring power of attorney has been registered and the registered enduring power of attorney has been produced to them showing that the attorney is authorised again to act for the donor.

In respect of general powers of attorney, executed in accordance with the Powers of Attorney Act 1971, s 9 or 10, and unregistered enduring powers of attorney and lasting powers of attorney, each bank will have their own requirements as to the attorney's ability to operate the donor's account. If a donor is physically unable to effect transactions due to physical incapacity rather than mental incapacity, or is away abroad, then an arrangement can be made with the bank so that that attorney can operate the account in those circumstances.

If, however, mental capacity has been lost then the enduring power of attorney or lasting power of attorney for property and financial affairs must be registered before it can be used. The original registered document must then be produced to the bank or a properly certified copy (a copy that the Office of the Public Guardian has stamped on every page or signed on every page by the donor, solicitor or notary public to confirm that it is a true copy of the original).

Deputyship appointments

The order appointing a deputy will provide authority to the bank or building society that the person named as the deputy can operate the accounts for the patient. The order must be checked to ensure it does do so and is not restricted. As above, the account must remain in the name of the patient and not be transferred into the deputy's name. The deputy can be named on the account, but only with reference to their appointment for the patient/account-holder.

Joint accounts

Opening an account in the joint names of the client and a close relative appears at first sight to be a simple solution to managing the elderly client's account. But it is sensible to be aware of the following:

- A joint account can only operate with the consent of the main account-holder. Once capacity has been lost, to the extent that that consent can no longer be given, the bank should freeze the account until such a time as a power of attorney or other authority is produced to allow the joint owner to continue to operate the account.

- The client must ensure that they trust the joint account-holder. They will be entrusting them with access to their funds and that they will account to them for any purchases or cash withdrawals.

- The death of one of the account-holders will ordinarily result in the account passing by survivorship to the survivor. Is this what the deceased would have wanted? An alternative would be to have notice severing that joint tenancy and setting out the shares in which the funds are to be shared.

- The Alzheimer's Society has suggested that when the client has to go into a care home the accounts should be split into sole accounts. This is usually the case where there has been an existing joint account between spouses or partners. If a local authority means assessment is required then only the client's funds will be taken into account.

- Finally, it is important to remember the tax implications of joint accounts. Any bank interest will have to be split between the account-holders for income tax purposes. Similarly, for inheritance tax purposes it is important to remember about the seven-year gift rule in respect of transferring an account into joint names. It is worth being absolutely clear as to whether funds are only to be used for the benefit of the original account-holder or to be used jointly for both account-holders' benefit. If the latter, then a gift of a half of the balance will have to be reported for inheritance tax purposes.

FCA and 'Consumer Vulnerability'

The Financial Conduct Authority (FCA) issued a paper in February 2015 entitled 'Consumer Vulnerability', in which they identified the following practical tips for the banks to adopt:

- having clear and easy-to-understand financial products;
- having a choice of ways to communicate with the customer;
- treating the customer as an individual;
- having a tailored response;
- being able to talk to someone who will take time to listen;
- banks who will spot suspicious activities which may signal abuse or fraud and take appropriate action;
- that carers will be listened to concerns noted, even information cannot be divulged to them;
- consistent advice and treatment should be given to the recently bereaved, those with a power of attorney or third-party mandate.

The paper also included a discussion of innovative tools to assist accessibility in banking, such as talking cash machines and high-visibility debit cards for those who have restricted vision. All these steps show that the banks and the FCA are trying to find solutions. Much more innovative work needs to be developed and tested with the ageing population. Certainly, contactless payment cards for small purchases help this process but do not assist with cash withdrawals, paying the cleaner or gardener, or birthday presents for grandchildren.

Bank branch closures

It is noticeable how many bank branches have been closed in the last few years. The Campaign for Community Banking Services reported in November 2007 that some 40% of branches had closed in Great Britain since 1990. In addition, the Post Office network has been heavily scaled back. In larger conurbations this might not be so noticeable, but in towns and villages the closure of this traditional community lifeline impacts on the most vulnerable in the community. The elderly, disabled, carers, those on low incomes and others with no access to public transport suffer from this disproportionately.

A bank or a post office keeps communities together and also helps small businesses to function. The loss of local access to banking does not favour these communities. It is recognised that traditional methods of banking are changing rapidly, but it should be remembered that recent technological advances do not necessarily help the most needy in the community. This may well change over time, but only if the banks take steps to provide services to all rather than just the young, able-bodied and employed.

There seems to be such a call for some kind of community-based banking service funded by the major clearing banks – perhaps some kind of mobile banking facility visiting villages once a week. It would make such a difference to keeping the elderly independent and village businesses alive. It is not just the provision of ATMs but some kind of counter service where banking services can be discussed with informed bank staff.

Internet banking

The young will grow up knowing only an internet-based world where everything is available at the touch of key stroke. A Eurostat report states that 18% of internet users between the ages of 55 to 74 use online banking. For the age range 25 to 34 this increases to 47%. The message is clear from this that online banking desperately needs to be adapted for an ageing population. For example, for those who can get to an ATM these should be in secure locations, they should be convenient, the system adopted should be user-friendly and the ATM functions should be as broad as possible.

5C

Investments and the Incapacitated Client

Under general law, attorneys' powers depend on the terms of the power of attorney appointing them and the principles in the MCA 2005. Attorneys are empowered to make financial decisions for their donors. This includes buying and selling investments. Any decision taken on behalf of another must be taken in accordance with the terms of the power of attorney and the MCA principles. If, for example, the lasting power of attorney (LPA) is only to take effect when the donor has lost capacity, as is now provided in section 5 of the LPA, then up until that point the donor will have to take those investment decisions themselves. Once it has been shown (through an appropriate certificate confirming) that capacity has been lost then the attorney can then take over management of the investments.

Management of investments must be carried out in the donor's best interests in accordance with the principles in MCA 2005, s 1. By way of reminder these principles are as follows:

- A person must be assumed to have capacity unless it is established that he lacks capacity.

- A person is not to be treated as unable to make a decision unless all practicable steps to help him to do so have been taken without success.

- A person is not to be treated as unable to make a decision merely because he makes an unwise decision.

- An act done, or decision made, under this Act for or on behalf of a person who lacks capacity must be done, or made, in his best interests.

- Before the act is done, or the decision is made, regard must be had to whether the purpose for which it is needed can be as effectively achieved in a way that is less restrictive of the person's rights and freedom of action.

The donor must therefore be consulted about the investment decisions required. They must be helped to understand if this is possible. In the context of best interests what does this mean for an elderly person? It will be difficult for an inexperienced attorney to manage investments without seeking appropriate investment advice. There is an argument to say that the terms of the Trustee Act 2000 in respect of the duties of trustees equally apply to an attorney who is in a fiduciary position with regards to the donor. It is not so apparent that the powers as opposed to the duties under the Act apply in the same way.

The Trustee Act 2000 (TA 2000), s 4 provides for the standard investment criteria. This says that a trustee must from time to time review the investments of the trust and consider whether, having regard to the standard investment criteria, they should be varied.

The standard investment criteria, in relation to a trust, are:

- suitability to the trust of investments of the same kind as any particular investment proposed to be made or retained and of that particular investment as an investment of that kind; and

- the need for diversification of investments of the trust, in so far as is appropriate to the circumstances of the trust.

TA 2000, s 15 provides for asset management functions to be carried out by an agent on their behalf. They can do so provided there is a written agreement with the agent and a policy statement setting out the trustees' guidance. Under s 16 they can appoint a nominee or a custodian to hold the investments.

It is understood that the Office of the Public Guardian (OPG) is considering guidance for attorneys on this issue.

If there is no written instruction in the power of attorney and the investment manager requires this then the only alternative is for an application to the Court of Protection for a specific order that a discretionary investment management agreement can be entered into by the attorney. This seems an unnecessarily cumbersome way to deal with a very common problem. It is hoped that the OPG will take a pragmatic view here and so attorneys can avoid the delay and expense of a court application.

If there is no extra provision in the power of attorney

If the appointing enduring power of attorney (EPA) or LPA is silent on investment management powers then the attorneys will be in some difficulty. The attorneys will have to manage the investments themselves without the benefit of discretionary investment management. The reason is that an attorney cannot delegate his own functions to another person. It may be that the donor had a discretionary management agreement in place with an investment manager before they lost their capacity. Without a specific authority in the power of attorney the attorney will have to rely on the goodwill of the investment manager accepting their authority as a continuance of the donor's instructions. This may lead to problems in the future and it is not a strategy that can be relied on. Alternatively, they will be able to request an advisory management service only from the investment manager. Again, this will cause problems. It may be difficult to find a manager prepared to take on management in this way. The charges may be higher. As we know, investment managers have to react without delay to investment market changes and acting on an advisory basis only where they have to consult the attorney for each investment decision will not be in the best interests of the donor.

It is believed that until the OPG issued their guidance on this point in September 2015 the argument was not a live one. It is debatable as to whether powers of attorney signed before that date will be recognised as empowering the attorneys to at the very least continue an existing management agreement with investment managers. It is likely, however, that a manager could take the point that the previous agreement has now come to an end due to the donor's incapacity.

Recommended action for new LPAs

It is advisable to follow the guidance issued by the OPG in form LP12 (September 2015) at A7, 'Preferences and Instructions'. This provides as follows:

'The only circumstances in which you must write an instruction is in a financial LPA if:

- you have investments managed by a bank and want that to continue

- you want to allow your attorneys to let a bank manage your investments

'In these cases you could use wording like this:

"My attorney(s) may transfer my investments into a discretionary management scheme. Or, if I already had investments in a discretionary management scheme before I lost capacity to make financial decisions, I want the scheme to continue. I understand in both cases that managers of the scheme will make investment decisions and my investments will be held in their names or the names of their nominees."

'However, OPG can't guarantee that your bank will accept this wording. You must ask your bank to confirm in writing that they'll accept the wording before you register your LPA. That will minimise any difficulties in using the LPA if you lose mental capacity.

'You may also want to seek legal advice before you approach the bank.

'If the LPA has already been registered, the attorney(s) will have to apply to the Court of Protection to allow them to use a discretionary fund manager.'

It is important that this clause is entered in the instruction box of the LPA and not the preference box. Instructions are legally binding, but preferences are not. The clause as drafted gives the attorney(s) the power to use a discretionary management scheme, but they are not bound to do so if it is not appropriate. It is clear that this guidance will have a far-reaching effect on those who have already signed and registered their powers of attorney. The words employed in the OPG's guidance suggest that up to the date of the guidance this clause was not essential. It might therefore suggest that there are the following categories of powers of attorney that need to checked over:

- All pre-September 2015 EPAs and LPAs where the donor has investments or is likely to have investments when the power of attorney needs to be used: if the donor has capacity then the options are for the donor to sign a new LPA to ensure compliance. Alternatively, discuss it with the donor and if they are happy not to sign a new LPA then ask them to have a separate sheet of guidance for their attorneys on this point.

- Post-September 2015 LPAs where the donor has capacity: discuss the options with them and consider a new LPA if no clause is inserted.

- Post-September 2015 LPAs where donor has now lost their capacity: consider with the investment manager whether they will agree to continue management. If not, then a court application will be required to remedy the problem.

Interestingly, there is some comment on the problem in the Law Society's response to the 'Enabling Digital by Default' paper issued by the OPG in November 2013:

'One such tick box option which would be very important would be one authorising the use of third party discretionary fund. The prevailing view is that attorneys cannot use discretionary investment management unless authorised. It is, however, very difficult (and likely to be expensive and slow in response times) these days to get investment management on any other basis. This is not just an issue for the wealthy: many older people have saved sufficient to have modest investment portfolios, and this can be a serious practical problem.

'Failure to cover basic additional clauses such as those relating to the Will and investment management are a particular issue if a donor decides to not have their LPA registered until they lose capacity, as any problems in drafting will not be brought to light until it is too late.'

Practical steps

When taking instructions from your client ensure that you have a full discussion with them about their investments. If they do not have investments under management at present consider with them the investment of property sale proceeds if they have to go into a care home. At that point fund management will be important to ensure that the donor's assets are producing income and capital growth for the client.

Insert the standard clause in the 'instruction' box in any new LPA as above. Alternatively discuss the issue with the current fund manager and find out whether the standard clause will be sufficient for their purposes. If necessary, adapt the clause as appropriate. There may be situations where the donor who has appointed his attorneys on a joint and several basis that he wants them to act jointly in respect of a high value transaction (see, for example, *Re XZ* [2015] EWCOP 35).

Deputyship and investment powers

When an application for a deputy to be appointed is being completed, form COP1A must contain full details of the patient's investments. The form asks:

- Does the person to whom the application relates own any investments such as stocks and shares, unit trusts, bonds etc?

- If yes, please provide an approximate value of the investments held and the name of the fund manager (if applicable).

The court order appointing the deputy will then provide the following powers:

'If the deputy considers it in P's best interests to do so, the deputy may appoint an investment manager, who is regulated and authorized to undertake investment business, to manage his assets on a discretionary basis under the standard terms and conditions applicable to such service from time to time, and to permit the investments to be held in the name of the investment manager nominee company.'

Problems

As we shall see below, problems arise when attorneys and deputies forget that the investments and funds they manage are not their own but the donor's or patient's. In respect of attorneys appointed under an EPA or LPA, problems only come to light when someone realises that the attorney is not acting properly – either they are gifting the donor's funds to themselves or others, or they are using the funds in ways which are clearly not in the donor's best interests. In respect of a deputy, a problem is more likely to come to light at a much earlier stage as they must submit annual reports and accounts to the OPG for approval. In this way the OPG can on behalf of the court supervise the deputies and ensure that any problems are resolved at a relatively early stage.

A couple of cases illustrate the problems that can arise in practice:

Firstly, as regards unauthorised investments made by an attorney under a LPA, see the case of *Re Buckley; The Public Guardian v C* [2013] COPLR 39, where the attorney used £87,682 of the donor's funds to set up a reptile-breeding business and then helped herself to a further £43,317. The court heard from an OPG investigations officer, who reported the following findings:

'In April 2011 Miss Buckley's house had been sold for £279,000. Between 17 January 2011 and June 2012 the attorney had withdrawn £72,000 from Miss Buckley's funds to set up a reptile breeding business. The attorney claimed that this was a short-term investment which would generate a 20% return over a two-year period.

'From the evidence gathered so far, I estimate that Miss Buckley has contributed at least £87,682.53 towards the reptile investment venture described by C. In the absence of any contrary evidence, the Public Guardian maintains that Miss Buckley's finances may have been used to heavily subsidize what appears to be a reptile breeding business, without any formal guarantee or security or her share of the alleged investment returns. C also appears to have misappropriated £43,317.47 of her aunt's estate without obtaining consent, contrary to what she had told the police. I have therefore re-referred this matter back to the police to conduct further enquiries.'

The attorney tried to justify the investment as follows:

- 'I was advised by Shirley that I should invest some of her money.'

- 'I investigated this and found a company which specialises in breeding reptiles. I dealt with [*name*] who runs the company and felt that this would be a good investment for my aunt and was told that this would return her money plus 20% interest within two years. My aunt loves animals and I felt that this would be an investment which she would be happy with.'

- 'It is stated that I did not provide evidence that the investment was made in the name of my aunt. I would like to state that I was not aware that the investment had to be made in her name and was concerned about signing on her behalf. I agree that perhaps I should have opened the investment in her name, but my intention has always been that the returns from the investment will go back to my aunt. The only reason that I transferred any money to my son's account was because I did not know how to transfer money abroad using "CHAPS" and he did. I kept receipts for the transfers and provided these to the OPG.'

The comments by Judge Denzil Lush on the investment of funds by an attorney were a reminder of the rules applicable and often ignored, or to which attorneys seem oblivious. He said:

'There are two common misconceptions when it comes to investments. The first is that attorneys acting under an LPA can do whatever they like with the donors' funds. And the second is that attorneys can do whatever the donors could – or would – have done personally, if they had the capacity to manage their property and financial affairs.

'Managing your own money is one thing. Managing someone else's money is an entirely different matter.

'People who have the capacity to manage their own financial affairs are generally not accountable to anyone and don't need to keep accounts or records of their income and expenditure. They can do whatever they like with their money, and this includes doing nothing at all. They can stash their cash under the mattress, if they wish and, of course, they are entitled to make unwise decisions.

'None of these options are open to an attorney acting for an incapacitated donor, partly because of their fiduciary obligations and partly because an attorney is required to act in the donor's best interests. The Mental Capacity Act 2005, section 1(5), states that, "an act done, or decision made, under this Act for or on behalf of a person who lacks capacity must be done, or made, in his best interests".'

The LPA was revoked as the attorney was not acting in the donor's best interests.

A second case concerned an attorney using the donor's money to invest in his own business. In *Re CMW Public Guardian AM* [2015] EWCOP 86 concerns were raised on 15 March 2015 by Surrey County Council Social Services that there had been a deliberate deprivation of assets following sale of donor's house in Weybridge in 2013.

The house was sold on 1 October 2013 for £395,000 and the amount required to redeem her mortgage was £206,815.47. The net proceeds of sale of £186,021.53 were credited immediately to the donor's account and on the following day the respondent withdrew £160,927.42 for his own purposes.

On 18 March 2015 the OPG wrote to the respondent asking him to file a full set of accounts of his dealings since the LPA was registered, but received no response.

The OPG obtained copies of the donor's bank statements, and these revealed that substantial sums of money had been transferred to the respondent long before the house was sold. For example, between December 2010 and October 2013 he had received £76,900 from one account and between March 2010 and July 2011 he had taken £21,000 from another account. In addition, a sum of £38,790 had been transferred to several companies in which he has an interest.

The attorney claimed in his defence:

'that, were my mother in condition to do so and speak, that she would promptly confirm her decision and instruction. Other than her oft-repeated verbal wishes in this regard, there was no documentary evidence of this agreement between a mother and her only child. Because of the trust between us we never perceived there to be any need to put this in writing. It never occurred to us that this might one day be a problem. I am my mother's only child and both executor and sole beneficiary of her estate. She completed her last will and testament when of sound mind, with her local solicitor and in my absence. A copy is attached. Had I elected not to sell the property when I did, I would still be in receipt of all the net funds from it upon her death.

'I do not contradict the documentary evidence supplied for the payments I made from her account. All those payments that were not made to myself were merely payments which, for the sake of simplicity, I did not pass through my own account. The total of the sums disbursed should be taken as if paid to me personally. In most cases these were payments to cover arrears in rent (advanced by others on my behalf), the return of personal loans I had taken out, and long overdue professional fees that needed to be paid to my accountants and suppliers. This also included disbursements to companies in which I have an interest, one of which I was, and still am, building up in an attempt to secure a more regular and constant income in the future. I felt justified in making these payments with what I legitimately considered to be my money on her bank account.

'My own financial situation is not now cash positive. In 2008 my consulting business [*name of company*] went into decline as part of the crash. Competition in the consulting business and fees plummeted and in May of 2009 I was obliged to sell my only personal property. With the proceeds I sustained my own life and paid rent. By necessity I started, and invested in, a new company, [*name of new company*], which continues to be my primary focus and which is not yet profitable nor able to pay me a salary. I am largely supported by my wife until this new business takes off. I no longer own any properties and have no personal assets.'

The court revoked the LPA and appointed a deputy to act in his place as he had contravened the authority granted to him in the LPA.

The investment of funds by an attorney

In *Re Buckley* (see above), Senior Judge Lush set out the principles applicable to attorneys holding investments for their donor. In particular, he reminded the court that managing your own money is one thing; managing someone else's is an entirely different matter. He quoted Mr Justice Lewison on this point in *Re P (Statutory Will)* [2009] EWHC 163 (Ch), [2009] COPLR Con Vol 906. At para 42 he said:

'I would add that although the fact that P makes an unwise decision does not on its own give rise to any inference of incapacity (section 1 (4)), once the decision making power shifts to a third party (whether carer, deputy or the court) I cannot see that it would be a proper exercise for a third party decision maker consciously to make an unwise decision merely because P would have done so. A consciously unwise decision will rarely if ever be made in P's best interests.'

Attorneys hold a fiduciary position, which imposes a number of duties on them. Like trustees and other fiduciaries, they must exercise such care and skill as is reasonable in the circumstances when investing the donor's assets and this duty of care is even greater where attorneys hold themselves out as having specialist knowledge or experience.

Although it does not expressly apply to attorneys, the Trustee Act 2000, s 4 requires trustees to have regard to what are known as the 'standard investment criteria' when exercising any power of investment.

The last edition of *Investing for Patients* was drawn up in 1998 following the decision of the House of Lords in *Wells v Wells* [1999] 1 AC 345. Circumstances have changed since then and the investment codes need to be revised. It also considered other factors:

- Whether any gifts or payments to dependants are likely to be made. This will usually involve an application to the Court of Protection for authorisation to make gifts in excess of the limits imposed by MCA 2005, s 12 in order to reduce the impact of inheritance tax.

- The type of return required; for example, whether a high income is needed from the investments, or whether the capital can be left to grow, or whether a mixture of the two would be more appropriate.

- Risk: whether absolute safety is required for the investment or whether some risk is acceptable in exchange for the possibility of getting a better return.

- Whether there is an existing portfolio and, if so, the tax and cost considerations that may affect decisions about whether to change it and how quickly.

The guidance also considered the interests of beneficiaries under the patient's will or intestacy, but only if the capital available for investment was over £100,000; there is no reason to believe that the patient's state of health is life-threatening; and the capital, when invested, will adequately satisfy the patient's current and future income and capital requirements.

Judge Lush went on to recommend that:

> 'Until such time as the Office of the Public Guardian issues its own guidance to attorneys and deputies on the investment of funds, I would suggest that, as they have fiduciary obligations that are similar to those of trustees, attorneys should comply with the provisions of the Trustee Act as regards the standard investment criteria and the requirement to obtain and consider proper advice. I would also recommend that attorneys and their financial advisers have regard to the criteria that were historically approved by the court and the antecedents of the OPG in *Investing for Patients*, albeit with some allowance for updating, as suggested in paragraph 37 above.'

He also reiterated sensible advice that attorneys should keep the donor's money and property separate from their own or anyone else's, including all investments which must be kept in the donor's name. This applies to investments and, wherever possible, all investments should be made in the donor's name. If this is not possible then a declaration of trust should be executed recording the position. He also advised that an application to court must be made when:

- gifts that exceed the limited scope of the authority conferred on attorneys by MCA 2005, s 12;

- loans to the attorney or to members of the attorney's family;

- any investment in the attorney's own business;

- sales or purchases at an undervalue; and

- any other transactions in which there is a conflict between the interests of the donor and the interests of the attorney.

It is clear that attorneys would benefit from updated guidance on how to make investment decisions. In the majority of cases attorneys have to sell the family home in order to fund the care home fees of their donor. Investment decisions are crucial at this stage to protect the donor's estate and to ensure that the funds are well invested for the remaining years of the donor's life.

5D

Property Transactions

The client's property and transactions relating to it can become emotive, not only because the property is usually the main family home, but also the source of much of their wealth. We are faced with not only the financial side of dealing with the home, but also the care and welfare issues relating to how long the patient can continue to live there independently, and what their wishes are regarding having carers come into the home rather than moving to a care home. If such a move to care home is considered, where should that be? Should it be near their old home, or near to their attorney/family carer. What are their expressed wishes about this?

Aidiniantz v Riley [2015] EWCOP 65 illustrates how such issues can tear a family apart. Here Mr Justice Peter Jackson commented:

> 'Turning to the issues and taking account of all the circumstances, I conclude that it would not be in Mrs Aidiniantz's interests to return to 1 Parkgate Road. In the first place, I accept the evidence of Ms G that she needs the care package that is on offer at the nursing home. Two medically qualified staff are needed at all times. Ms AH and those she enlists to help her are unqualified and unsuited to demonstrating the necessary professional standards. Secondly, and more decisively, it is impossible to approve an arrangement that returns Mrs Aidiniantz to her home when her children have turned it into a warzone. If John took over 1 Parkgate Road, things would be no better. Mrs Aidiniantz needs a safe haven from her children's activities, and that is what she has found in the nursing home. She would not have this respite in a setting that was controlled by either camp.'

The series of cases involving that family was an extreme example of what can go wrong and how an elderly relative can find themselves poorly treated by their children rather than as an elderly vulnerable parent who needs loving care and attention. Their needs and best interests should be uppermost in the minds of their children and attorneys at all times.

A property, whether it is the patient's home or a second property, should only be dealt with in accordance with the rules as to the transfer of properties and after receiving independent legal advice.

Transfers and sales

Transfers and sales of property provide ample opportunity for potential abusers to divest their relatives of estate assets. With the majority of properties registered at a Land Registry there are certain procedures that must be followed.

Does your client have capacity to carry out the transaction?

First of all, does your client have sufficient mental capacity to execute the transfer? The ability of a person to manage their property and affairs is set out in MCA 2005, s 3. It must relate to the particular person and their unique circumstances, and in relation to each decision to be made.

Section 3 provides that a person is unable to make a decision for himself if he is unable to:

- understand the information relevant to the decision;

- retain that information;

- use or weigh that information as part of the process of making the decision; or

- communicate his decision (whether by talking, using sign language or any other means).

A person is not to be regarded as unable to understand the information relevant to a decision if he is able to understand an explanation of it given to him in a way that is appropriate to his circumstances (using simple language, visual aids or any other means).

The fact that a person is able to retain the information relevant to a decision for a short period only does not prevent him from being regarded as able to make the decision.

The information relevant to a decision includes information about the reasonably foreseeable consequences of (a) deciding one way or another, or (b) failing to make the decision.

Assessing the client's capacity for the specific transaction requires careful, patient advice, listening to the client, hearing what they have to say and helping them to communicate if required. Only if you are satisfied can you then proceed with the transaction. If you are in any doubt then a capacity assessment should be recommended to the client. This will be a safeguard both for the client and for you as the professional advisor. A contemporaneous medical certificate confirming that the client has or has not the requisite capacity will protect you from claims at a later date.

Gifts of property

Making a gift of a property or a share of a property should be carried out only with special care and understanding of the motives, objectives and estate and family background of the donor. The Law Society's practice note, 'Making Gifts of Assets' (2011) sets out the good practice that is required when advising a client who wants to make such a gift.

You should be aware that there is often much misunderstanding about the effects of a transfer of a property and what effect this can have on an elderly person. There is no doubt that most practitioners have had clients or children of clients contact them about an expressed wish on the part of the elderly client to transfer the family home to an adult child. There are a number of reasons, but the main ones are for tax, care home fees, and to secure the home for the child after the parent has died.

You therefore need to follow the guidance note and find out:

- what they are seeking to achieve;
- who is to receive the gift;
- what types of assets are involved?

You should spend time with your client to enable you to:

- evaluate their instructions;
- clarify their domestic and financial circumstances;
- establish that they own the assets they wish to dispose of; and
- assess whether they have the mental capacity to make the gift.

Changes of professional advisors

Where you have acted for the same client and the family for some years, you know the family dynamics and the estate assets there should be less concern than when a new client has previously instructed another firm of solicitors. You need to question the reason for the change. There have been cases where attorneys arranging transfers of donor's property have changed solicitors in order frustrate the attempts of the family solicitor to stop financial abuse occurring. See, for example, *Hart v Burbidge* [2014] EWCA Civ 992 and also *The Public Guardian v SR* [2015] EWCOP 32. In the latter case, a solicitor in Reading witnessed the donor's signature to an lasting power of attorney (LPG) in September 2009. In October 2011, she made a will with a firm of solicitors in Yateley, Hampshire and in March 2013 the attorney placed the donor's house in Camberley on the market and instructed yet another firm of solicitors in Stockport, Cheshire to act for her in connection with the sale. A careful analysis of recent transactions should alert you to potential indications of abuse. There may of course be sound reasons for changing solicitors, but it is worth asking the question about the reasons for such a change.

Re Beaney Test

You should also take note of the recommendations from the case of *Re Beaney (Deceased)* [1978] 1 WLR 770, which sets out the test of capacity to make a gift. In particular, it provides that that capacity to make a gift will vary depending on the size, nature and circumstances of the gift. So, for example, the gift of £5,000 of cash is very different from the gift of the family home. The larger the gift as a proportion of the donor's estate, the more advice and investigation required.

The elderly person may be confused as to the consequences of transferring the legal title of their home to another person. They no longer have any right to live in the property. They have lost their home and can only remain in the home with the permission of the new owner. If they have to move to a care home then they cannot sell the home to pay for those care fees. If the transferee themselves get divorced, become bankrupt or die then again the elderly transferor has no rights to stay in the property. The consequences will be catastrophic for them. Furthermore, when the elderly person dies this will very often be the when the rest of their family realises that the house is not part of their estate.

Tax consequences

The consequences may be even more far-reaching. For inheritance tax, a gift of the family home, when the transferor continues to live in the property, will be treated as a 'reservation of benefit'. Their estate will still be charged as though they still own the property and inheritance tax charged on the value. If the transferor had taken proper advice before the transfer they could have arranged to pay a full market rent for their occupation as consideration for their continued occupation of their home.

Local authority powers

If an elderly person makes a transfer of property with a view to avoiding care home fees then the local authority could have the right to set aside the transaction as one designed to avoid potential creditors.

As the Law Society's note states. 'If a local authority believes that an asset has been given away with the intention of creating or increasing entitlement to means tested benefits, it may decide that the donor has notional capital of equivalent value to that of the asset given away.'

One way to establish the intention is the foreseeability or immediacy of the need for care. Any decision to reject or accept the evidence requires an overall assessment of that evidence by the local authority – see *Beeson v Dorset County Council* [2002] HRHR 15. If, for example, your client was fit and healthy and could not have foreseen the need for residential care, it would be unreasonable for the local authority to treat the transfer of assets as deliberate deprivation. However, *Yule v South Lanarkshire Council* [1999] 1 CCLR 546 states that there was no time limit on local authorities when deciding whether a person had deprived themselves of assets for the purposes of avoiding residential care fees.

Annex E to the Care Act 2014 statutory guidance sets out the rules concerning the deprivation of assets. Deprivation of assets arises where a person has intentionally deprived or decreased their overall assets in order to reduce the amount they are charged towards their care. It is up to the person to prove to the local authority that they no longer have the asset. If they are not able to, the local authority must assess them as if they still had the asset. For capital assets, acceptable evidence of their disposal would be: (a) a trust deed; (b) deed of gift; (c) receipts for expenditure; (d) proof that debts have been repaid.

As the guidance explains, there may be many reasons for a person depriving themselves of an asset. A local authority should therefore consider the following before deciding whether deprivation for the purpose of avoiding care and support charges has occurred: (a) whether avoiding the care and support charge was a significant motivation; (b) the timing of the disposal of the asset – at the point the capital was disposed of could the person have a reasonable expectation of the need for care and support?; and (c) did the person have a reasonable expectation of needing to contribute to the cost of their eligible care needs? For example, it would be unreasonable to decide that a person had disposed of an asset in order to reduce the level of charges for their care and support needs if at the time the disposal took place they were fit and healthy and could not have foreseen the need for care and support.

Even if they meet the test above are they under undue pressure from another person to transfer the property or a share in it? There is further discussion on this in the next chapter.

Transfers into sole or joint names

A gift of a property may be of the whole legal title or just a share. If the property is to be held as between joint owners there should be declaration of trust detailing the shares owned by each co-owner and the terms under which the property will be dealt with on the first co-owner's death. Clearly there are tax, management, and survivorship issues to be considered. If a perpertrator has arranged a unauthorised transfer of the property then they may very well not have considered these implications.

As is seen from the case of *Hammond v Osborn* [2002] EWCA Civ 885 the tax effect of an unauthorised gift can have disastrous consequences for the unwitting transferor. In that case the perpetrator Mrs Osborn arranged a sale of Mr Pritler's share portfolio without any consideration of the significant capital gains tax implications of doing so. Mr Pritler was left with such a depleted estate of £30,000 that he would have been unable to pay the resulting capital gains tax liability of £50,000.

Consider also the case of *The Public Guardian v AW (Application to revoke Lasting Power of Attorney)* [2014] EWCOP 28. Here a total of £250,000 has been spent from the donor's capital on one of her attorney's property to which she had moved. There was no declaration of trust showing the donor's contribution to the attorney's property. The court revoked the LPA.

In *The Public Guardian v Marvin* [2014] EWCOP 47 the Office of the Public Guardian (OPG) discovered that the donor's property had been reregistered at the Land Registry into the name of his partner and the partner's son's joint names. The court revoked the LPA for property and financial affairs and appointed deputies for property and affairs; they also authorised them to apply to the Land Registry for a restriction to be entered on the proprietorship register to prevent dealings with the property.

A transfer into joint names may have other unintended consequences. If the transferee dies, becomes bankrupt or divorced then their share of the property will fall to be administered by their executors, trustee in bankruptcy or pass to an estranged spouse.

Transfers under a power of attorney

A transfer by an attorney can be made under a Powers of Attorney Act 1971 power, an unregistered EPA or a registered LPA. However, the donor must consent to the transaction and if necessary their capacity, if in doubt, must be proved.

A power of attorney will either be for a specific purpose or general. If it is for a specific purpose you will need to ensure that it contains clear authority to enter into the transaction in question, as powers of attorney are interpreted strictly. A general power of attorney must follow the form set out in the Powers of Attorney Act 1971 or be in a form to the like effect and expressed to be made under the Powers of Attorney Act 1971, Sch 1, s 10(1). The prescribed form describes itself as a general power of attorney and states that the donor appoints the donee or the donees jointly or jointly and severally to be their attorney or attorneys in accordance with the s 10. An attorney under an EPA or LPA has full powers to sell or transfer a property without there being a need to spell this out specifically in the power.

Deputyship

As regards sales by a deputy, it is important that the applicant for the deputyship requests a power to sell a property when making the first application for their appointment. In this case the first general order can provide the necessary power. In addition, the value of the security bond will have to be increased to cover the likely receipt of proceeds of sale.

House renovation costs

Unless specifically provided for in a power of attorney or a deputyship order, it is not within an attorney or deputy's power to authorise renovation costs for a patient's property. However, even if an EPA or LPA provides for such costs the OPG can apply for the instruction to pay such costs to be removed if it is considered beyond the attorney's power.

In the case of *Re HC* [2015] EWCOP 29 the court found that:

> 'CC has committed a significant amount of expenditure on the renovation of the property in Bristol, exceeding in the Public Guardian's opinion, the scope of the deputyship order, and for which he has declined to request retrospective court approval. The Public Guardian would ask the court to determine whether the £46,646.76 spent to date is reasonable and in the best interests of HC and whether any further costs arising from the renovation, notably in relation to potential significant sums to address the problem of wet rot, will require advance approval of the court.'

Having considered the details, the court did give retrospective approval to those costs, but it is far better to obtain that authority in advance to save the cost of court proceedings.

As can be seen from *The Public Guardian v AW (Application to revoke Lasting Power of Attorney)* [2014] EWCOP 28 the court will not hesitate to revoke a LPA where the donor's funds are being spent on a home in which they live, but for which they have not been given a reciprocal interest in that property.

Charges and equity release in relation to the client's property

It is not just transfers of the legal title that adversely affect the victim, but also where a perpetrator has taken out loans secured on the victim's property which are not in the best interests of the patient.

Capacitated elderly person

If your client has full mental capacity then they are free to charge their property. The finance company will want to ensure that that person has independent advice on the transaction. Taking instructions in such a matter must take time and care. They may still be vulnerable to pressure from family members to take up loans or equity release in order to finance gifts rather than for their own long-term benefit. They need careful independent advice before committing to any such arrangement.

Attorneys

There are two separate points here that need consideration. Firstly, does an attorney under a registered EPA or LPA have the power to arrange a charge or mortgage secured on the patient's property without specific approval from the court? The answer is that such an attorney has extensive powers to deal with the donor's finances and property provided that it is in the donor's best interests and in accordance with the MCA 2005.

Secondly, it appears that equity release companies are content to accept the instructions of attorneys under registered enduring or LPAs to obtain an equity release mortgage for their principal. This is provided the mortgage is for the benefit of the donor and in their best interests.

It could be argued that this is beyond the ambit of a power of attorney unless it was specifically authorised by the donor when the power was set up. I think that most donors would be surprised to be told that their attorneys could take such a step. Surely it would be sensible for new court rules to be applied specifically requiring attorneys to obtain a court order permitting such a mortgage. In my experience, the opportunity to release funds from the equity of an elderly person's house allows for unsupervised attorneys to use the resulting funds for expenditure for themselves and not in the donor's best interests. Most donors would not expect their attorneys to release equity from their home without a rigorous examination of the motives and reasons for this. Understandably, if it is to enable the donor to continue to live in their own home for much longer than their current income permits and this would be in the donor's best interests then this could be justified. But if it enables attorneys to make unauthorised gifts or use the donor's funds inappropriately then oversight of this area should be increased.

Deputies

If there is a deputy appointed then an application to the Court using a form COP9 would be required in order to obtain the necessary authority. Alternatively, this may already have been anticipated in your application for the order appointing the deputy.

Co-ownership

A problem arises where the property is jointly owned and one of the co-owners has lost their capacity and the other is their attorney. In such cases the equity release company will require the attorney to obtain a specific court order appointing someone else to act for the incapacitated principal.

Safe home income plans (SHIP)

Practitioners should be aware of the SHIP code of conduct provided by the members of the Equity Release Council (www.equityreleasecouncil.com). They quote their standards as follows:

'For lifetime mortgages, interest rates must be fixed or, if they are variable, there must be a "cap" (upper limit) which is fixed for the life of the loan.

'You must have the right to remain in your property for life or until you need to move into long-term care, provided the property remains your main residence and you abide by the terms and conditions of your contract.

'You have the right to move to another property subject to the new property being acceptable to your product provider as continuing security for your equity release loan.

'The product must have a "no negative equity guarantee". This means that when your property is sold, and agents' *and solicitors' fees have been paid, even if the amount left is not enough to repay the outstanding loan to your provider, neither you nor your estate will be liable to pay any more.'*

Granny annexes

It would seem surprising to think that providing a home for an elderly relative at their child's home should provide any opportunities for financial abuse. Sadly, this is not the case. There are significant pitfalls that can be avoided with proper advice and understanding on both sides of the transaction. It is estimated by the Treasury that some 31,000 such granny flats or annexes exist. There are possible council tax, stamp duty and CGT issues that need consideration, but clients also need to consider the following:

Objectives

At the outset it would seem that providing a home for an elderly relative is a sensible solution to long-term care needs. It keeps the relative living relatively independently. There is help at hand if problems arise. The home and home life of the adult child is not compromised but enhanced by having their relative living close by. Always bear in mind that the arrangement may not last as long as you anticipate. A change of living environment may not suit an elderly parent and ultimately they may have to move to a care home or require full time home care.

Pitfalls

Potential problems that need to be anticipated by the various parties are as follows:

Elderly relative:

- Will they be asked to contribute to the capital costs of the annex?
- If so how will this be reflected in the ownership of the property?
- What happens if they need to go into a care home?
- Should they amend their will?
- How will other children of the family be protected?

- Will the other children still be able to visit as much as possible?

- Emotionally will the elderly relative feel obliged to the adult child providing the home and feel that they must be compensated?

- Keep the whole family informed of the plans and ensure everyone is involved and approves the plan.

Adult child providing the home:

- Will an annex be built or will the relative move into their home?

- What contribution will they make to the running costs?

- Can the adult child be compensated?

- What happens if the adult child's marriage or partnership breaks up?

- What happens if the adult child loses their home?

Rights of the other children of the family?

- Access rights.

- Ensuring elderly relative is protected from undue pressure.

- Should another member of the family also be attorney for the elderly relative so that there is some independent oversight of financial arrangements?

What advice is required to ensure that problems do not arise?

- Consider who is to pay for the annex: Should it be a purchase of a share in the whole home, a loan of money or a cash gift? It is advisable for each party to take separate independent advice on the proposed transaction and work out what is the most suitable arrangement to protect both parties.

- It is sensible to protect the elderly relative by either a share in the legal title commensurate to the amount contributed to the building/renovation or other costs of the annex. Otherwise a loan agreement should be prepared with a charge on the property to secure that loan.

- What will happen if the relative moves out permanently into a care home? Are they protected because they own a share of the property? Have they made a substantial cash gift to their child from which they will now no longer benefit? If they made a loan, is it in writing, when is it repayable and is interest running?

- What happens if the adult child loses their home? An elderly relative moving to a home of an adult child is subject to any financial problems that that child may have as regards retention of their home. The child may become divorced, bankrupt or die. In any of these situations the elderly relative's continued occupation of the home may be at risk. If the child's home was subject to an existing mortgage, did they obtain the consent of the mortgagee for the relative to become another occupier in the property?

Other property issues

Unauthorised loans secured on client's property

Loans must be taken out only if they are in the best interests of the donor or patient. The case of *Public Guardian v DH* [2014] EWCOP 15 illustrated where this was not the case. In 2011, DH decided that his mother, who was becoming increasingly frail and forgetful, would move in with him and his partner. They would then take out a loan on her property renovate it, and let it to generate an income. Barclays Bank made the loan on 21 October 2011 and it was secured on the donor's property. The loan was for £72,000. Her son, who was her sole attorney, claimed that he spent the entire loan on renovating his partner's late mother's property in Wakefield. The court revoked the LPA and invited the Public Guardian to cancel its registration. The attorney had not acted in the donor's best interests as required by the MCA 2005. The funds had been used for his mother's benefit.

Ongoing home costs once the client has moved to a care home

In *Re RG* [2015] EWCOP 2 the donor of an EPA went into a care home. Their property was subject to a mortgage, which was in their sole name and was being paid solely from their funds, even though he lived in a nursing home. The attorney was living in the property and should have paid the rent and utility bills.

Property rents

It is important to ensure that any rental income from the client's property is being paid at a market rent. In addition, the rent itself must be paid into an account in the client's name.

See also the following cases:

- *BIM v MD* [2014] EWCOP 39, where it was discovered that the applicants had granted an assured shorthold tenancy of the patient's property to their son and daughter-in-law at a rent significantly below the open market rent. A new deputy was appointed.

- *DT, Re* [2015] EWCOP 10 – DT and his wife were the joint owners of the former matrimonial home which was let out at a rent of £550 per month. The rent was being paid directly into his wife's account rather than any of it being paid into the patient's bank account.

Careful planning and open discussion in the family should protect all the parties. The overriding concern, though, should be the elderly vulnerable adult and their best interests. Above all, communication with all members of the family can avoid costly misunderstanding at a later date.

5E

Undue Influence

Financial abuse takes many forms. In this chapter we consider those transactions that have been brought about by the pressure and influence of another.

The ideal for making wills and effecting transfers of property during lifetime is that a client does so of their own volition without pressure, influence or by fraud. It is important that care is taken to ensure that the individual is able to carry out such transactions when they are fully mentally capable, with a good memory and independent of any member of the family, friends or other third parties trying to persuade them to do something other than what they want to achieve. It does not matter if what they want to do is regarded as foolish or not in their best interests if they are of sound mind and free of influence. As professional advisors, this last point sometimes causes difficulties. However, irrational decisions by our clients should be allowed and we should do all we can to assist them after fully advising them of the consequences.

In this chapter we shall look at how cases of actual and presumed undue influence have been dealt with by the courts. There are differences between the amount of influence required where a will is involved as compared to the influence required on other occasions, for example, lifetime gifts.

Wills

Theobald on Wills (Sweet & Maxwell, 2010, 17th edn, para 3-033) explains that a will must not be made as a result of either the undue influence or the fraud of another person. The leading case here is of *Hall v Hall* (1868) I P&D 481, in which undue influence was described as 'pressure so exerted as to overpower the volition without convincing the judgment'. The reality is that the testator is coerced into making a will or part of a will which he does not want to make.

Actual undue influence

This has to amount to some form of coercion. This may be real acts of violence, or imprisonment of the testator. It has also been suggested that talking incessantly to the testator on their death bed so that they feel induced to succumb to pressure just to achieve some peace and quiet may also qualify.

It is clear that gentle persuasion or advice is legitimate and permissible, but coercion is not. A testator may be led but not driven. However, each case turns on its own facts.

A comparison can be made with instances of fraud. Fraud misleads a testator whereas undue influence coerces them.

Lord Hobhouse in *Royal Bank of Scotland v Etridge (AP)* [2001] UKHL 44 said at 103:

> 'Actual undue influence presents no relevant problem. It is an equitable wrong committed by the dominant party against the other which makes it unconscionable for the dominant party to enforce his legal rights against the other. It is typically some express conduct overbearing the other party's will. It is capable of including conduct which might give a defence at law, for example, duress and misrepresentation ... Actual undue influence does not depend upon some preexisting relationship between the two parties though it is most commonly associated with and derives from such a relationship. He who alleges actual undue influence must prove it.'

Burden of proof

The burden lies with the party alleging the undue influence or fraud. They need to show that the will was made as a result of the undue influence or fraud of another person. It is not sufficient to show that simply the particular circumstances surrounding the transaction were consistent with it having been obtained by undue influence.

In *Killick v Pountney* [2000] WTLR 41 the victim changed his mind about the terms of his will as a result of undue influence. His nephew successfully argued that the beneficiaries had used their position to influence him to make the will in their favour. The testator was suffering from some form of dementia. It was for a party who asserted undue influence to prove it. Where there was evidence of improper influence, the additional presence of some enfeeblement in the testator would make it easier to find that such influence was 'undue', but evidence of such infirmity does not itself establish undue influence. The facts allowed for an inference of undue influence.

See also *Re Edwards* [2007] EWHC 1119, which decided that there has to be no other reason for the change of the testator's mind. It must be consistent with no other explanation. It should be coercion and not just persuasion, appeals to ties of affection or pity for future destitution, all of which are legitimate.

If actual undue influence is proved then the transaction will be set aside even if it does not result in a disadvantage to the victim of that influence. There is no application of the presumption of undue influence that can be used to set aside lifetime transactions.

Lifetime gifts

In order to prove undue influence in respect of lifetime gifts it is necessary to prove either actual undue influence or by application of the doctrine of presumed undue influence.

Actual undue influence

This must amount to proving acts of coercion. Each victim of undue influence will have different tolerance levels and it is therefore necessary to look at the particular victim and their own strength of will. Did they easily succumb to the pressure? In *Hall v Hall* (1865–1869) LR 1 P&D 481 the coercion was defined as 'pressure ... so exerted as to overpower the volition without convincing the judgement'. If a person is mentally or physically frail then less force is required than with a victim who is much stronger.

The Judge in *Wingrove v Wingrove* [1885] 11 PD 81 said:

> 'Coercion may be ... of different kinds, it may be in the grossest forms, such as actual confinement or violence, or a person in the last days or hours of life may become so weak and feeble that a very little pressure may be sufficient to bring about the desired result.'

Presumed undue influence

This arises from the presumption of undue influence which has been applied only to lifetime transactions and not to testamentary dispositions. It usually arises in situations where there are relationships between two individuals and one of them has influence over the other.

The leading case here is *Royal Bank of Scotland plc v Etridge (No 2)* [2002] 2 AC 773.

Factors that must be present to allow the presumption to arise:

- relationship of influence between the parties;
- where there is a series of facts that require an explanation;
- a disadvantage to the donor is not essential;
- the burden of proof lies with the person alleging it has taken place.

What kind of relationship is required? Examples often quoted are relationships between parent and child, trustee and beneficiary, priest and member of the congregation, solicitor and client, or doctor and patient.

Lord Hobhouse again in *Royal Bank of Scotland v Etridge (AP)* [2001] UKHL 44 summarised this at 104:

'it necessarily involves some legally recognised relationship between the two parties. As a result of that relationship one party is treated as owing a special duty to deal fairly with the other. It is not necessary for present purposes to define the limits of the relationships which give rise to this duty. Typically they are fiduciary or closely analogous relationships. A solicitor owes a legal duty to deal fairly with his client and he must, if challenged, be prepared to show that he has done so.'

In *Pitt* at p209, Lord Browne-Wilkinson referred to:

'the long-standing principle laid down in the abuse of confidence cases viz the law requires those in a fiduciary position who enter into transactions with those to whom they owe fiduciary duties to establish affirmatively that the transaction was a fair one.'

The transaction must be one that calls for an explanation

So, for example:

- *Hammond v Osborn* [2002] WTLR 1225: a substantial gift that gifted a high proportion of the donor's estate to the done and the tax implications of the gift were such that the donor would not have effected the gift if he had not been under significant pressure.

- *Hewett v First Plus Financial Group plc* [2010] EWCA Civ 312: where the court showed that other factors could be equally significant. In this case the concealment of an affair by the husband was held to 'amount to' an exercise of undue influence.

- *London Borough of Redbridge v G* [2014] EWCOP 485 shows the fine line between a vulnerable elderly person being intimidated by her carer and isolated and a person lacking mental capacity and therefore within the jurisdiction of the Court of Protection. Here the court had to decide the question of her capacity before the case could proceed:

  (1) did she lack capacity; and

  (2) if she did, whether it is because of mental impairment within the meaning of the MCA sections 2 and 3; or

  (3) if not, whether she is a vulnerable adult deprived of capacity by constraint, coercion or undue influence and so entitled to the protection of the court under its inherent jurisdiction.

Standard of proof

This is the civil standard and on a balance of probabilities:

In *Carapeto v Good* [2002] WTLR 801 the facts were that Mrs Carapeto and her husband were the principal beneficiaries under a last will made in May 1999. Neither was a relative of Miss Good, and the only provision Miss Good made in her will for her family was the gift of some specific legacies. Mrs Carapeto was engaged as Miss Good's housekeeper for the last 20 years of her life and Mrs Carapeto and members of her family lived in Miss Good's house during that time. The defendants were the members of Miss Good's family who would take under the intestacy which would arise if, as they claimed, the May will was invalid. Miss Good was quite a prolific will-maker and had made several wills prior to the May will, of which the last was in April 1999. The validity of the April will was not in question and it revoked all previous wills. However, within hours of making it, Miss Good revoked it by destroying it. The result was that, if the May will was invalid, she died intestate.

It was agreed that Miss Good had testamentary capacity when she made the May will. The only issues were whether:

- she knew and approved its contents; and

- it was induced by the undue influence of the Carapeto family.

Mr Chapman accepted that the Carapetos were sufficiently implicated in the events leading to the May will to raise a suspicion as to whether Miss Good knew and approved its contents. He accepted, therefore, that the burden of proving that she did is cast on Mrs Carapeto. It was accepted that the burden of proving undue influence lay with the defendants. Considerable evidence was adduced, comprising statements from about 60 witnesses, of whom 38 were cross-examined.

Mr Justice Rimer said here:

'126. Turning to the facts, I regard the defendants claim that the Carapetos coerced Miss Good into making the May will as weak. There is, in my view, no direct evidence of any conduct which might be regarded as amounting to coercion. The absence of any such direct evidence is of course not surprising, because it will be a rare case in which there will be such evidence. Usually, if a case of coercion is to be found, it will involve the court in drawing inferences from the general circumstances which have been proved in the particular case. But in this case I feel quite unable to draw any such inference.

'I do find that Mrs Carapeto took a greater interest in Miss Good's proposed testamentary activities than she was disposed to admit to in her evidence. She was present at at least two important meetings – the second meeting with Mr Ess on 15 April and the meeting with Mr Frankum on 19 April. I think it likely that it was she who asked Mr Brennan to come up with the name of another solicitor in place of Mr Ess, although I also regard it as probable that she would first have obtained Miss Good's authority to do this. She was at Miss Good's side when Miss Good left the message on Mr Ess's voicemail on 15 April and when she left a like message for Bill Good on 23 April. She may perhaps have engaged in what can be regarded as in the nature of prompting in relation to these calls, and I have referred in my account of the facts to other instances where she became involved in the will-making process. Miss Good's call to Mr Raggett on 19 March 1999 is another instance where Mrs Carapeto appears to have been playing a part in the conversation. I certainly find that that there was no question of her simply toiling quietly away at her duties in the background, ignorant of the somewhat protracted testamentary activities of her employer. She may even, although I make no finding to this effect since it is unsupported by any clear evidence, have made some appeal to Miss Good to provide for her in her will.

'127. But none of this satisfies me that there are sufficient grounds for inferring that she coerced Miss Good into making the May will. I do not ignore that Miss Good was an elderly, vulnerable woman, who was substantially dependent on the Carapetos for her continued enjoyment of life at the house. This scenario no doubt provides a background against which there would or might have been scope for the exercise of some subtle, and undue, influence by the Carapetos over Miss Good. The matters to which I have referred no doubt give rise to a legitimate suspicion that this may have been what was happening, and I can well understand how the family's suspicions have been aroused by them. They have concerned me too, and I have given anxious consideration to them. They are, however, also consistent with a perfectly innocent explanation. It must not be overlooked that the Carapeto family had by 1999 played a central and close role in Miss Good's life for some 20 years. I have found, and have no doubt, that she was genuinely very fond of them. They were on hand day and night, and it is by no means unlikely that over the years she would have built up a sufficient relationship of confidence with them such she would or might wish to discuss her affairs with them. Ultimately, all I have heard and read about Miss Good -in particular from the various solicitors who attended on her during 1999 – satisfies me that, at the time of the May will, she was still a very intelligent, sensitive and independent-minded woman, who was capable of making her own decisions. She had been wrestling with herself as to how best to dispose of a substantial estate, and had come to the conclusion that the calls of the Carapetos on her bounty outweighed those of the family. In those circumstances, she decided to make the May will. I ought only to make a finding of undue influence against the Carapetos if I am satisfied according to the standard of proof to which I have referred that such a case is made out. I am not so satisfied. I reject the claim that Miss Good made the May will as the result of the exercise upon her of coercion by any member of the Carapeto family.'

In *Killick v Pountney; Re Killick Dec'd* [1999] All ER (D) 365, undue influence was found where the testator, who was in a confused state, seemed to fear the defendant, who had banned others from visiting the testator and had also been involved in giving instructions to the solicitors who drew up the will. His nephew alleged that the beneficiaries had influenced him in to making the will in their favour.

In that case James Munby QC said. 'the more serious the allegation, the more cogent is the evidence required to overcome the unlikelihood of what is alleged and thus prove it.'

Another recent case in the Court of Protection illustrates the continuing problem of undue influence in lifetime giving. In *Re EG* [2015] EWCOP 6 concerns had been raised by the London Borough of Bromley because there had been gifting from EG's accounts totalling £75,000; EG had appointed her son and daughter as her attorneys. One of them had made gifts of £15,000 to herself and £20,000 to each of her three brothers. EG had only £17,465.54 left; and the attorney GB's response had been, 'If EG doesn't mind and she is well cared for, what's the harm?'

The court said that even if the donor did have capacity to make gifts totalling £75,000 on 9 April 2014, undue influence would be presumed because:

- the gift was so substantial that it could not be accounted for by ordinary motives;

- there was a relationship of trust between the donor and the attorneys such as to place them in a position to exercise undue influence over her in making the gift; and

- the attorneys failed to ensure that independent advice was made available to the donor.

Chapter 6

How to Prevent Financial Abuse and What Steps to Take when it is Discovered

6A

The Office of the Public Guardian and Supervisory and Investigatory Powers

Where there are concerns about a person who has lost mental capacity or about the person who is managing that person's affairs, then it is important to consider how the Office of the Public Guardian (OPG) can help to investigate those concerns.

The Public Guardian was established by MCA 2005, s 57. He is appointed by the Lord Chancellor. The OPG is the office that works for him in carrying out their functions under the Act.

His functions are a mixture of administrative, supervisory and investigatory. In s 58 they are identified as:

- establishing and maintaining a register of lasting powers of attorney and a register of orders appointing deputies;

- supervising deputies appointed by the court;

- directing a Court of Protection Visitor to visit;

    ○ a donee of a lasting power of attorney;

    ○ a deputy appointed by the court; or

    ○ the person granting the power of attorney or for whom the deputy is appointed;

- make reports to the Public Guardian on such matters as he may direct;

- receiving security which the court requires a person to give for the discharge of his functions;

- receiving reports from donees of lasting powers of attorney and deputies appointed by the court;

- reporting to the court on such matters relating to proceedings under this Act as the court requires;

- dealing with representations (including complaints) about the way in which a donee of a lasting power of attorney or a deputy appointed by the court is exercising his powers;

- publishing, in any manner the Public Guardian thinks appropriate, any information he thinks appropriate about the discharge of his functions.

In addition, under the Lasting Power of Attorney, Enduring Power of Attorney and Public Guardian Regulations 2007, SI 2007/1253, regs 47 and 48:

47

(1) This regulation applies where it appears to the Public Guardian that there are circumstances suggesting that, having regard to all the circumstances (and in particular the attorney's relationship to or connection with the donor) the attorney under a registered enduring power of attorney may be unsuitable to be the donor's attorney.

(2) The Public Guardian may require the attorney—

(a) to provide specified information or information of a specified description; or

(b) to produce specified documents or documents of a specified description.

(3) The information or documents must be provided or produced—

(a) before the end of such reasonable period as may be specified; and

(b) at such place as may be specified.

(4) The Public Guardian may require—

(a) any information provided to be verified in such manner, or

(b) any document produced to be authenticated in such manner, as he may reasonably require.

(5) "Specified" means specified in a notice in writing given to the attorney by the Public Guardian.

48

The Public Guardian has the following functions—

(a) directing a Court of Protection Visitor—

    (i) to visit an attorney under a registered enduring power of attorney, or

    (ii) to visit the donor of a registered enduring power of attorney, and to make a report to the Public Guardian on such matters as he may direct;

(b) dealing with representations (including complaints) about the way in which an attorney under a registered enduring power of attorney is exercising his powers.

Their role is extensive in respect of the affairs of the mentally incapable. As you would expect different rules apply depending on whether the person has someone managing their property and finances or not.

No one appointed

If there are suspicions that financial abuse is taking place against an elderly person the first step is to establish whether they have capacity or not. A capacity assessment must be carried out. As a professional you should be familiar with the test of capacity in MCA 2005, s 3:

> A person is unable to make a decision for himself if he is unable:

- to understand the information relevant to the decision,

- to retain that information,

- to use or weigh that information as part of the process of making the decision, or

- to communicate his decision (whether by talking, using sign language or any other means).

Usually, the individual's GP should be contacted. It may well be (as is often the case) that the GP will decline to carry out such an assessment especially where it is for assessing capacity to carry out a legal transaction. In such cases they ought to be asked for a recommendation to a psycho-geriatrician who will be familiar with carrying out such an assessment and, equally importantly, writing the report which would stand up to scrutiny in court if required.

If the person is found not to have capacity then that person comes within the jurisdiction of the Court of Protection and accordingly an application to that court to appoint a deputy should be considered. The person cannot now sign a lasting power of attorney and the appointment of a deputy is the only option for the management of their finances and protecting them from abuse.

The OPG's supervisory functions

As we shall see, there are some important differences between the supervisory functions of the OPG in relation to attorneys appointed under registered enduring power of attorneys (EPAs) and lasting power of attorneys (LPAs) and those appointed by the court as deputies.

Maintaining a register of powers of attorney and deputyship appointments

The Public Guardian maintains a register of registered EPAs and LPAs and a search of this would be useful starting point in discovering who has been appointed, under what kind of power and, if there is more than one attorney appointed, whether that appointment is joint or joint and several or a deputy appointed.

Search of the register

An application can be made on form OPG100. There is no fee for this search. There are two different types of searches: first tier and second tier.

First tier searches

Information you receive after a first tier search includes:

- the allocated case number;
- known other names of the donor/person the order is about;
- date of birth of the donor/person the order is about;
- name(s) of any deputy/deputies;
- name(s) of any attorney(s);
- whether the LPA, EPA or deputyship order relates to 'property and affairs' or 'personal welfare';
- the date the LPA, EPA or deputyship order was made;
- the date the LPA, EPA or deputyship order was registered;
- the date the LPA or EPA was revoked (if applicable);
- the date the deputyship order expires (if applicable);
- the date the deputyship order was cancelled (if applicable);
- name(s) of any replacement deputy/deputies/attorney(s);
- whether any replacement deputy/deputies/attorney(s) are active;
- whether deputies/attorneys are appointed jointly (ie they must all agree before any action is taken);
- whether deputies/attorneys are appointed jointly and severally (ie they can act independently of each other or act together); and
- whether there are conditions or restrictions on the LPA, EPA or deputyship order (but not details about the conditions or restrictions).

Such a search will not reveal:

- details about LPAs or EPAs that have not yet been registered;
- Court of Protection ('court') order applications that are pending (ie in progress), including applications for deputyship orders; or
- details of any other court orders. You will need to apply to the court for those details, and disclosure is governed by the court rules.

The Data Protection Act normally applies to information held by the OPG; however, it does not apply to the information you can access in a first tier search of the registers.

Second tier searches

A second tier search will reveal additional information to that given after a first tier search. Only information relating to the donor/client can be obtained through a second tier search. The OPG will carefully consider the application before deciding whether additional information can be released. It will depend on factors including your relationship to the case, the information you request and why you wish to access it.

To make a second tier search request, write to the OPG and include the following information:

- the name of the donor (for LPAs) or the name of the client (for deputyship orders);
- the specific information you require;
- the reason you require the information; and
- why you have been unable to obtain the information from the person themselves or from another source.

Any information provided to you will be at the discretion of the OPG and will vary according to the individual circumstances of the case.

The results of the search will enable you to decide what further action is appropriate. If you suspect that financial abuse is taking place and a power of attorney is registered then you should contact the OPG and report those suspicions.

In the year 2015/16 there were 30,323 requests to search the register. The average time for register searches was reported as five days.

Supervision of deputies

Where a deputy has been appointed by the Court of Protection, the OPG has supervisory functions over them. The OPG is authorised to contact the deputy or pay them a visit to ensure they are complying with their duties under the Act. They can also give advice and support. When you are appointed as a deputy you will be assessed by OPG to decide how much supervision and support you need. Most deputies get a 'general' level of supervision. If so, a lower fee is payable and you may not have to write a report each year.

Supervision visits

A deputy may be visited by a Court of Protection visitor to check that they:

- understand their duties;
- have the right level of support from OPG;
- are carrying out those duties properly; or
- if they are being investigated because of a complaint.

Classification of supervision of deputies

In September 2015, the OPG made changes to classifications for supervision of deputies following a review of how supervision is carried out. They have now introduced deputy-specific teams and a new more sophisticated risk assessment tool to try and identify at an early stage abuse cases.

Previously, the levels were classified as types 1, 2A, 2 and 3. The new classification moves away from a tiered approach and deputies will simply be given either a general or minimum level of supervision.

From September 2015, all new deputies were to be allocated to a general level of supervision in the first year of their deputyship. Existing deputies at that date, who manage the affairs of someone with assets below £21,000, were to be placed into minimal supervision, unless there were any concerns about the case.

If there are concerns, the case will receive a general level of supervision. When deputies manage the affairs of someone with assets above £21,000, these cases will also receive a general level of supervision.

Deputy annual reports

On 1 March 2016, the OPG introduced new report forms. Changes were made to increase safeguarding measures. As the Public Guardian, Alan Eccles, said:

'We have a duty of care to our deputies and their clients, and the redesign of the form addresses the needs of both groups. Deputies now have tailored report forms to suit their needs with a new look and feel, which makes for a more straightforward process. With additional questions and the introduction of the new safeguarding section, we can better support the deputies who need it the most, while protecting vulnerable members of society.'

There are different deputy annual reports required depending on the property and financial decisions required:

- OPG102 – for a general level of supervision;
- OPG103 – for a minimum level of supervision;
- OPG103 – for a general level of supervision if you are in your first year of being a deputy and the client's assets are under £21,000.

For professional deputies and public authority deputies there are other forms that need to be completed in respect of the fees to be paid for you acting as a deputy – see OPG105 and OPG106 respectively.

Previously there was one report form which covered both financial decisions and health and care decisions made by a deputy. Now there are two separate forms. In section 4 of *Property and Financial Decisions Form* (OPG102), deputies are now asked to detail the level of contact they have with their client, how the client's care is funded and whether the client is receiving all benefits to which they are entitled. The OPG had identified these key areas as early indicators that a client may be at risk of neglect or a red flag that the client is not receiving adequate support.

By way of example, form OPG102 provides for the following information for property and financial decisions:

- Section 1: Deputy and client information

- Section 2: Decisions made over the reporting period: the deputy must report whether the client's mental capacity has changed over the reporting period and also detail significant decisions taken and the examples provided included buying and selling property, making gifts and paying for care. They must also detail who was involved in the decisions and whether the client was involved.

- Section 3: People you consulted: such as an accountant, solicitor or member's of the client's family. You have to explain why they were consulted. Similarly, if you did not consult anyone you also need to explain that.

- Section 4: Safeguarding: This section details how the client is cared for and what contact they have with the deputy and checks how their needs are being met. You must answer whether the client is getting the care that they have paid for and how this is funded. It asks if there is a care plan and when was it last reviewed.

Client's accounts and assets

- Section 5: bank account details and funds

- Section 6: Client's assets and debts

- Section 7: Decisions in the next reporting period: Here the deputy has to explain whether there will be any significant financial decisions to be taken in the next reporting period and whether the deputy has any concerns about their deputyship for example if funds are running low or wanting to make gifts.

- Section 8 provides a declaration in the following terms:

    'I confirm that the information I have given in this report is true and correct to the best of my knowledge information and belief. I understand I have obligations to the Court of Protection and the OPG and that if I knowingly provide false or misleading information there may be legal consequences.

'I am signing this report on behalf of myself and each of the deputies named in the court order (unless I have stated otherwise and provided reasons).

'I confirm that I have had regard to the Mental Capacity Act 2005, its Code of Practice and the court order in this case. I understand the duties and obligations placed on me.'

Online completion of report for lay deputies

A deputy must send a report to the OPG each year explaining the decisions they have made. For lay deputies it is now possible for the annual report to be completed online.

Assurance visit for professional and local authority deputies

These are designed to assist in the review of cases and to ensure the proper management and administration of the deputyship work. They also have the objective of ensuring that the deputy standards are being met. In particular, the visits cover the following:

Stage 1 – cases

Invoices, contact, correspondence and decisions and future plans

Stage 2 – managing the caseload

Deputyship management, MCA principles and Code of Practice, Safeguarding, fees, how you deal with the client's property and conflicts of interest, accounting & banking, IT security and information assurance, consulting and contracting with third parties and Court of Protection orders.

After the visit the visitor will send a report to the OPG.

They are also designed to ensure that these deputies are meeting the relevant standards. These have been categorised by the OPG as follows:

- Standard 1: securing the client's finances and assets both when you receive the deputyship order and on an ongoing basis.

- Standard 2: Gain insight into the client to make decisions in their best interests.

- Standard 3: Maintain effective internal office processes and organisation.

- Standard 4: Have the skills and knowledge to carry out the duties of a deputy.

- Standard 5: Health and Welfare standards.

Standards 1 to 4 cover deputies appointed for property and financial decisions. Standards 2 to 5 cover health and care deputies.

The OPG's annual report for 2015/16 confirmed that the number of deputyship orders the OPG supervises had increased by 8% to just over 53,000 in April 2015 to over 57,243 at the end of the 2015/16. This follows a 6% increase in 2014/15.

Visitors and panel deputies: Court of Protection visitors completed 9,829 visits during the year 2015/16. Cases involving suspected abuse were prioritised and the majority allocated to a visitor within 24 hours (in the year 2014/15 Court of Protection visitors completed 10,650 visits).

In 2015/16, the Court of Protection made 366 panel deputy referrals and OPG made 186 panel deputy referrals. 29 assurance visits were made to panel deputies, along with 117 visits to their clients. (In 2014/15, 532 panel deputy referrals were made, and 17 assurance visits were made to panel deputies.)

Investigations unit

The OPG's responsibilities are to

- take action where there are concerns about an attorney or deputy;
- registering lasting and enduring powers of attorney;
- maintaining the public register of deputies and people who have been given lasting and enduring powers of attorney;
- supervising deputies appointed by the Court of Protection, and ensuring they abide by the terms of the MCA 2005;
- looking into reports of abuse against registered attorneys or deputies.

Safeguarding referrals to the OPG

If a referral is made to the OPG then an investigation will be undertaken by the OPG compliance unit and an investigating officer appointed to the case. In the case of a complaint against an attorney under a registered power the offending attorney or attorneys will be sent an initial letter by the officer confirming that concerns have been raised with the OPG, but will not confirm who has raised those concerns. As we saw above, the Lasting Power of Attorney, Enduring Power of Attorney and Public Guardian Regulations 2007 regs 47 and 48 empower the OPG to request information and documents within a specified time. In practice, it is often a matter of responding with the information required within a period of three weeks.

It is sensible to be as cooperative as possible. For example, if you feel that the time period given is insufficient, telephone the officer and explain. What is clear from the cases that reach the Court of Protection is that poor communication, delay and generally obstructing the OPG may lead to the court imposing an adverse costs order against the attorney or deputy personally. See, for example, the case of *The Public Guardian v CT* [2014] EWCOP 51 where Senior Judge Lush said:

'I consider that a departure from the general rule is justified and I shall order EY (the sole attorney under an LPA for property and financial affairs) to pay her own costs because her conduct, before and during the proceedings, has been aggressive and disingenuous and has resulted in both sides' costs being far greater than they would otherwise have been.'

The OPG will request that the attorney completes two forms and returns them to the investigating officer within the time period:

(1) Information provision form

    (a) Case specific information

    (b) Questions to be answered will include some of the following:

        (i) Tell us how you make sure the donor has enough money for her living expenses

        (ii) Provide receipts and invoices to support expenditure

        (iii) Have social services or anyone else carried out any mental capacity assessments or financial assessments for the donor? If so attach copies

        (iv) Tell us how you make decisions for the donor. How do you work together with the other attorney. If the appointment is a joint one rather than joint and several how do you undertake all decisions together

        (v) Tell us about any significant decisions you and your co-attorney have taken

        (vi) Do you consult the donor about decisions?

        (vii) When did you start acting in your role as attorney? What prompted you to start acting?

        (viii) Provide evidence of out of pocket expenses

        (ix) Specific allegations: here the officer will put the allegation directly to the attorney so that they can address it in their answers

(2) Financial account form

    (a) This is similar to providing a deputy's annual report insofar as the attorney will need to supply bank statements, investments statements, rental accounts, copy of the donor's will, receipts for expense and other spending

    (b) This will cover the reporting period only – that is – from the date of registration of the power of attorney to the date of the start of the investigation

    (c) Specific details need to be completed in the form including about the donor's assets, income, how you manage the bank accounts, investment sales and purchases, property, debts, general and specific spending, gifts, your allowances and expenses.

The OPG will then investigate the allegations in the light of the detail supplied. There may simply have been a misunderstanding or poor communication between family members or co-attorneys that has resulted in someone in the family or a close friend reporting the attorney to the OPG.

The OPG will require a Court of Protection visitor to see the donor if they still have capacity and find out what their views were. Investigations were concluded on average within 69 days in the year 2015/16.

Next steps?

When the investigation has been concluded the options available to the OPG are as follows:

- No further action – where it is shown you have been acting in the donor's best interests.

- Further action or monitoring is required – the OPG will recommend further action required – for example full accounts to be prepared and supplied, bank accounts to be managed better.

- Referral to another agency – if there are sufficient concerns but the OPG does not have the necessary authority to act.

- Referral to Police – if there is clear evidence of a criminal offence.

- Apply to the Court of Protection – for example to freeze donor's bank account, place a restriction on the HM Land Registry register, remove the attorney(s) and appoint a deputy in their place.

An interesting comment on the differences between an OPG and a police investigation arose in the case of *DP (Revocation of Lasting Power of Attorney)* [2014] EWHC B4 (COP). Senior Judge Lush explained that:

'There are significant differences between a police investigation and an investigation conducted by the OPG. When the police investigate an alleged crime, they need to consider whether there is sufficient evidence to present to the Crown Prosecution Service ("CPS") to guarantee a realistic prospect of conviction, which in this case would have been on a charge of theft or fraud by abuse of position. The CPS would have had to prove that JM was aware that he was acting dishonestly and they would have had to prove this "beyond reasonable doubt", the standard of proof in criminal proceedings. The decision not to prosecute him simply means that the CPS was not totally confident that it would be able to prove JM's guilt so as to ensure a conviction. It does not imply that his behaviour has been impeccable.

'By contrast, an investigation by the OPG is concerned primarily with establishing whether an attorney or deputy has contravened his authority under the Mental Capacity Act 2005, or has acted in breach of his fiduciary duties under the common law of agency, or has behaved in a way that is not in the best interests of the person who lacks capacity. The standard of proof, 'on the balance of probabilities', is lower than the criminal standard.

'Like the police and the CPS, the OPG carries out a comprehensive sifting process, and the Public Guardian will only make an application to the Court of Protection in cases where he has good reason to believe that an attorney or deputy has acted inappropriately and that it is in the best interests of the person who lacks capacity for the attorney or deputy to be discharged.'

Instances of court action

- *Re RG* [2015] EWCOP 2: Here EPA attorneys were appointed to act jointly and severally. One of the attorneys was managing the donor's money but excluded the other attorney from acting. He left care fees unpaid, commingled the donor's funds with his own money, and used his credit card. When the donor went into a care home the attorney failed to make his mortgage payments. The court found that the donor's finances had not been managed in his best interests. The attorney also failed to produce an account of dealings, and as a result he was deemed unsuitable to be an attorney. The court revoked appointment and continued with other attorney, and limited registration to that other attorney.

- *The Public Guardian v SR* [2015] EWCOP 32: A brother and sister were appointed LPA attorneys jointly and severally. The sister spent £451,000 of her mother's money and put her house on the market. The other attorney entered restriction at HM Land Registry to prevent the sale. There were also unpaid care fees. Three different firms of solicitors were involved in the donor's affairs which meant that no one had a complete understanding of her property and financial arrangements. The court revoked only the first-named attorney's appointment.

- *In Re ARL* [2015] EWCOP 55: The court found that there was a debt of £39,000 in respect of unpaid care fees, which the attorney was unwilling to pay because he believed that his mother should be receiving NHS Continuing Health Care. He also purchased a property in his own name, using £174,950 of his mother's funds, retaining the rental income from the property for the last two years. There was other unauthorised expenditure amounting to £36,524.17. Finally, he could not account for the remainder of the £90,500. The judge remarked that he had instructed six different firms of solicitors and this was a smokescreen to cover up extent of his deceit.

Contact is received from a number of sources, including relatives, local authorities, care homes and financial institutions. If cases are not suitable for investigation, advice is offered to the parties concerned. Alternatively, they might be referred on to the appropriate agency such as the local authority or police.

In the year 2014/15 the OPG introduced a pilot fast track procedure called 'aspect investigations' aimed to progress investigations of suspected abuse more quickly in non-complex cases. Out of 50 cases in the pilot, 25 were concluded in an average of 42 working days, well within the target of 75 days for full investigations. Seven of the 25 concluded cases needed further enquiries beyond the original scope. Resolving cases quickly reduces the impact upon attorneys and deputies and reduces stress on the person who may lack capacity. This new approach has now been incorporated into normal business.

Safeguarding referral numbers

Year	Number	Cases referred to full investigation
2014/15	1970	743
2015/16	2681	876

Typical examples of cases the OPG looked at in 2015/16 included undervalued house sales, the client's home being sold to the attorney, large financial sums transferred from the client's bank account to another bank account and creating fraudulent LPAs.

Information-sharing with other agencies

In July 2015, a memorandum of understanding with the Department for Work and Pensions was put in place to share information to jointly protect adults at risk. In December 2015, an information sharing protocol with the National Police Chiefs' Council was agreed. This was to ensure that best practice was put in place for referrals made to the police where any criminal activity is suspected.

Mediation

The OPG is trying to adopt a new approach to resolving issues with deputies and attorneys through in-house mediation. This is with the objective of avoiding costly court proceedings. A pilot scheme ran between December 2013 and March 2015. The OPG reported that 56 cases were identified where mediation would benefit parties. Mediation was eventually successful in nine of these cases, and in each of these a satisfactory formal agreement was reached.

MCA 2005, s 49 Mental Capacity Act 2005 power to call for reports

The court may require a report to be made to it by the Public Guardian or by a Court of Protection Visitor. The court may also require a local authority, or an NHS body, to arrange for a report to be made. The report must deal with such matters relating to the patient (P) as the court may direct.

The Public Guardian or a Court of Protection Visitor may examine and take copies of any health record, any record of, or held by, a local authority and compiled in connection with a social services function, and any record held by a person registered under the Care Standards Act 2000, Pt 2, so far as the record relates to P.

If the Public Guardian or a Court of Protection Visitor is making a visit in the course of complying with a requirement, he may interview P in private.

If a Court of Protection Visitor who is a Special Visitor is making a visit in the course of complying with a requirement, he may, if the court so directs, carry out in private a medical, psychiatric or psychological examination of P's capacity and condition.

The usefulness of a s 49 report to the court is that it is organised by the Public Guardian through the OPG. It is usually prepared by a general or special visitor of the Court of Protection. The court can, however, request that a local authority or NHS body can be ordered to prepare such a report. The funding of such a report was brought into question by the case of *RS v LCC* [215] EWCOP 56.

GN v Newland [2015] EWCOP 43 in this case Senior Judge Lush ordered such a report to made by a Court of Protection visitor to ascertain the donor's answers to the following questions:

> 'In her application papers Julia Newland (the intending deputy) stated that CN (the patient) has four children "whom she does not wish to assist her nor did she wish them to be appointed as deputy". The court is particularly interested in the following issues or questions and these should be addressed in the report:
>
> (1) Did CN hold this view?
>
> (2) Does CN still hold this view?
>
> (3) If so, why does she not wish any of her children to assist her or to be appointed as deputy?
>
> (4) In particular, why does she not wish GN to assist her or to be appointed as her deputy?
>
> (5) Is CN satisfied with her existing deputy, Julia Newland?
>
> (6) Any other matters that may assist the court in dealing with this matter.'

Such a report is helpful to the court in resolving difficulties and also ascertaining the wishes of a patient or donor.

Reporting concerns

The OPG website provides the following contact details where there is a registered LPA or registered EPA in place or a deputy has been appointed by the Court of Protection.

The Office of the Public Guardian and Supervisory and Investigatory Powers

Office of the Public Guardian

PO Box 16185

Birmingham

B2 2WH

opg.safeguardingunit@publicguardian.gsi.gov.uk

Telephone: 0300 456 0300

Textphone: 0115 934 2778

Monday to Friday, 9am to 5pm

Wednesday, 10am to 5pm

Safeguarding Powers

The Care Act 2014 (CA 2014), amongst other provisions, defines the current roles and responsibilities of local authorities to safeguard adults who are at risk of abuse or neglect. Sections 42–47 set out the law relating to enquiries by local authorities, Safeguarding Adults Boards, Reviews, duties to supply information and protection of property of adults who are being cared for away from home. The Act was specifically designed to ensure that local authorities took the lead in co-ordinating future safeguarding roles.

The Act came out of the Law Commission's Report No 326, 'Adult Social Care', in 2011. This acknowledged the disparate number of laws governing adult social care and the obvious need to rationalise legislation. The law up to that point was found in the Mental Health Act 1983, the MCA 2005, the Safeguarding Vulnerable Groups Act 2006 and the inherent jurisdiction of the High Court and other civil and criminal legislation.

CA 2014 brings together the powers and duties of safeguarding into one Act. There is, however, one notable exception concerning rights of entry which will be considered below. The Act is accompanied by the Care and Support Statutory Guidance issued by the Department of Health in October 2014. This guidance is legally binding and introduces the concept of promoting wellbeing as its core purpose. Adult safeguarding guidance appears in Chapter 14.

The Guidance confirms that it replaces 'No secrets – Guidance on developing and implementing multi-agency policies and procedures to protect vulnerable adults from abuse', which was issued jointly by the Department of Health and the Home Office in March 2000.

The duties apply only to particular adults as follows:

'An adult who has needs for care and support (whether or not the local authority is meeting any of those needs, and; is experiencing, or is at risk of, abuse or neglect; and as a result of those care and support needs is unable to protect themselves from either the risk of, or the experience of abuse or neglect. Accordingly, the duties apply whether or not the adult has mental capacity and regardless of the setting.'

The guidance sets out its aims to include:

'Stopping abuse or neglect wherever possible, preventing harm and reduce the risk of abuse or neglect to adults with care and support needs, safeguarding adults in a way that concentrates on improving life for the adults concerned and addressing what has caused the abuse or neglect.'

What is meant by financial abuse in the Act?

The Act provides that abuse includes financial abuse and further defines 'financial abuse' to include having money or other property stolen, being defrauded, being put under pressure in relation to money or other property, and having money or other property misused. It elaborates on this by defining financial or material abuse to include theft, fraud, internet scamming, coercion in relation to an adult's financial affairs or arrangements, including in connection with wills, property, inheritance or financial transactions, or the misuse or misappropriation or property, possessions or benefits.

It is also clear from case law and research that one type of abuse does not preclude the adult suffering another kind. For example, when financial abuse escalates it may well be accompanied by acts of domestic violence or psychological abuse. The latter being defined in the Guidance as including emotional abuse, threats of harm or abandonment, deprivation of contact, humiliation, blaming, controlling, intimidation, coercion, harassment, verbal abuse, cyber bullying, isolation or unreasonable and unjustified withdrawal of services or supportive networks.

Examples of indicators of financial abuse recorded in the Guidance are as follows:

- change in living conditions;
- lack of heating, clothing or food;
- inability to pay bills/unexplained shortage of money;
- unexplained withdrawals from an account;
- unexplained loss/misplacement of financial documents;
- the recent addition of authorised signers on a client or donor's signature card; or
- sudden or unexpected changes in a will or other financial documents.

Which adults are considered at risk by the Act and the Guidance?

In the pre-Act consultation, there was considerable debate about the meaning of those at risk and what constituted 'harm'. There was also a drive to follow the definition of 'adult at risk' in the Adult Support and Protection (Scotland) Act 2007, s 3. It was also suggested that the definition should extend to adult abuse in its entirety.

There was also debate about the definition of those at risk and a demand to move away from the term 'vulnerable adults', which was defined in the 'No Secrets and In Safe Hands' statutory guidance. Many felt that that term was inappropriate as it linked the cause of the abuse to the victim rather than placing it firmly with the actions or omissions of others.

Which adults fall within the category of those who are experiencing, or who are at risk of, abuse or neglect? These are defined as:

- Where the local authority has reasonable cause to suspect.

- An adult in its area.

- Who has needs for care and support and whether or not the local authority is already providing for those needs.

- Who is as a result of those needs unable to protect himself or herself against the abuse or neglect or the risk of it.

Enquiry by local authority

The local authority must make (or cause to be made) whatever enquiries it thinks necessary to enable it to decide whether any action should be taken in the adult's case (whether under this Part or otherwise) and, if so, what and by whom.

The consultation raised issues about whether a community care assessment or a safeguarding investigation should take place. There needed to be some clarification here. This would ensure that, for example, that an investigation takes place only if all attempts to provide services had failed or if service provision was inappropriate. The consultation raised issues about the investigation process and it was recognised that there needed to be less a focus on a need for services than on establishing the facts and the validity of allegations.

Safeguarding Adults Boards

The intention here is that each local authority has responsibility at a local level for setting up a board (SAB) for its area to help and protect adults in its area. 'An SAB may do anything which appears to it to be necessary or desirable for the purpose of achieving its objective': Care Act 2014, s 43(4).

Before the Act came in there was no express statutory duty on local authorities to investigate cases where adults using care services were at risk of harm. The Act provides that they must take the lead in co-ordinating responsibilities and ensure multi-agency arrangements between not just social services but also the NHS, the police, DWP, etc. The Guidance states that the SAB must include representatives of the local authority, the Clinical Care Commissioning Group in the area, and the chief officer of police in the area. It may also contain representatives of other organisations including DWP and Trading Standards. The SAB must prepare strategic plans and for each financial year produce an annual report containing details of the work carried out and the objectives delivered.

Safeguarding adult review

The SAB must also carry out a safeguarding adult review (SAR) where an adult in its area experiences abuse or neglect or dies as a result of abuse or neglect, whether known or suspected, and there is concern that partner agencies could have worked together more effectively to protect the adult. A SAR should be undertaken locally according to the specific circumstances of individual circumstances. The SAR should communicate with the adult, their family and in some cases with the person who caused the abuse. Such an SAR should be completed within a reasonable period and in any event within six months of initiating it, Unless there is good reason for a longer period being required, for example because of court proceedings.

SAR findings

These should provide an analysis of what happened, why, and what action is needed to prevent a reoccurrence.

Information-sharing

Records must be kept and each agency is required to identify procedures for recording all action taken when a complaint or allegation is received. SABs must be able to access the information held and therefore procedures must be put in place to ensure this can happen. The Guidance refers back to instances where the withholding of information from one agency to another has in the past prevented lessons being learnt and action taken.

Information will be shared on a need-to-know basis. It also stresses that confidentiality must not be confused with secrecy. Informed consent should be obtained wherever possible. Information for the public should enable them to know how to express concern and how to make a complaint.

Independent advocate

Adults who have no appropriate person to support them must be informed of their right to an independent advocate.

Designated adult safeguarding manager

Each member of the SAB should have a designated adult safeguarding manager (DASM) responsible for the management and oversight of individual complex cases. They should provide advice and guidance within their organisation and liaise with other agencies. They should monitor progress of cases for speed of resolution, consistency and a fair process. They must ensure appropriate record-keeping processes.

The guidance also provides information about the recruitment processes and background checks that should be in place when providing appropriate staff in this area.

A typical example that may arise:

Mrs Jones lives alone in her own home. She is very frail and mobility is restricted and her eyesight is poor. She has signs of dementia. She pays privately for home care services through a private care agency. A carer comes in three times a day to help her.

Her son believes that the carer is stealing from her as cash and small possessions are missing. He has spoken to the agency. He does not know whether Mrs Jones is making gifts of her property.

Enquiry required

The care agency should alert adult services department of the local authority and the Care Quality Commission. Note that not all agencies are registered with them. The local authority should now hold an enquiry or find out whether the agency has done so in a satisfactory manner. The agency's rules should prohibit receipt of gifts from their clients and therefore a breach of rules may have taken place.

Police involvement

The police may be involved if the family want to pursue this. If other clients of the agency are also victims then the carer should be suspended to remove further risk.

In the above example consider whether Mrs Jones is actually giving the property away and if so, does she have sufficient capacity to do so? A capacity assessment may be required and in the light of this either obtain her consent to the 'gift' or carry out a best-interests decision taken on her behalf.

6C

Right of Entry Powers

One of the more surprising debates on the Care Act 2014 (CA 2104) was the refusal of the Government to provide a statutory right of entry where abuse or neglect was suspected. Furthermore, s 46 of the Act abolished the local authority's power to remove persons in need of care. This was the National Assistance Act 1948, s 47 power. The Government issued a separate consultation on this power. It reported in 2009 that out of 212 respondents 60% agreed that there should be a power to enter premises where is it suspected that a vulnerable was being abused (27% did not support such a measure).

The Government's response may have been influenced by the Law Commission's view that consideration of new compulsory powers was outside its remit. It concluded that if the Government identified a need for new compulsory or emergency powers then they could be included. The Commission felt that the duty of co-operation between different agencies and other measures would mean that further powers would not be required. It felt that an additional duty to make enquiries on local authority social services departments would reinforce their obligations to take action where appropriate.

The repeal of the National Assistance Act 1948, s 47 was necessary because it was incompatible with the European Convention on Human Rights. This section had given local authorities powers to remove to suitable premises a person who is suffering from a grave chronic disease, is aged, infirm or physically incapacitated, is living in insanitary conditions and unable to devote themselves (sic), and is not receiving from other persons proper care and attention.

The consultation found that this power had been little used especially since the advent of the MCA 2005. However, it was pointed out that s 47, whilst used, rarely could be a useful safeguarding tool where the adult at risk has sufficient mental capacity but needs to be removed from their home and no other legal option is available. It was also noted that, with the new duty to provide safeguarding by local authorities, the need to use powers like those in s 47 would only increase.

The existing powers under current law were reviewed and considered to be sufficient for most cases.

Powers of entry: statutory and High Court

Statutory powers

The Police and Criminal Evidence Act 1984, s 17(1)(e) allows the police to enter and search premises without a warrant in order to save life or limb or to prevent serious damage to property. This power may only be used in an emergency and not simply for a general welfare concern. This means that if the abuse is not related to serious bodily injury the power will be of no use.

The power can also be used to effect an arrest without a warrant for an indictable offence (s 17(1)(b). The police would then have the power to enter premises. Such offences would include here ill-treatment or wilful neglect (MCA 2005, s 4 and Mental Health Act 1983 (MHA 1983), s 127), theft (Theft Act 1968, s 1) and fraud (Fraud Act 2006).

Under the Police and Criminal Evidence Act 1984, s 24 there is power to arrest a person without a warrant who is committing, or is about to commit, or has committed, an offence. The police need reasonable grounds for believing an arrest is necessary for one of the reasons set out in the section. For example:

- to protect a vulnerable person likely to be harmed, or at risk of being harmed, if the person in question is not arrested and other arrangements for the prevention of harm cannot be made;

- to prevent a person from causing physical injury to another person.

As we have seen, MCA 2005 provides a statutory framework for decision-making for those who have lost their mental capacity. The Court of Protection can make orders appointing deputies to act for such a person in respect of care and welfare and financial decisions. At the outset a determination of mental incapacity must be obtained. See, for example, the case of *London Borough of Redbridge v G* [2014] EWHC 485 (COP), where there was initial uncertainty as to whether to apply under the MCA 2005 or under the inherent jurisdiction of the court. Once the court had a capacity assessment the case was referred to the Court of Protection.

The court can make interim orders and directions under MCA 2005, s 48 if the matter is a type covered by the powers of the court and it is in that person's best interests to make an order or give directions without delay.

Whenever the court is considering the use of such a power they will be mindful of applying the principles set out in MCA 2005, s 1:

- assuming that a person has mental capacity unless it can be shown otherwise;

- not mistaking unwise decisions for decisions taken without capacity;

- acting in the person's best interests;

- considering less restrictive ways of achieving those best interests.

Right of Entry Powers

For example, such orders could be made if there are immediate safeguarding concerns relating to the person's personal welfare. The order can include directions to permit a person to gain entry to premises and access to that person. Obstruction would be contempt of court. A penal notice could be attached. The order or direction will only be made against a third party and if necessary. That third party may give an undertaking to co-operate, which would avoid the need for the order or direction.

Fraud Act 2006

The Police and Criminal Evidence Act 1984, s 1 (powers to stop and search) is extended to the Fraud Act 2006. A person is guilty of fraud if he is in breach of the following sections of the Act:

- section 2 fraud by false representation;

- section 3 fraud by failing to disclose information; and

- section 4 fraud by abuse of position.

Mental Health Act 1983

MHA 1983, ss 135–136 provide a power for a magistrate to issue a warrant authorising a police officer to enter premises and to use force if necessary and, if it is thought fit, to remove individuals who have a mental disorder to a place of safety for a mental health assessment. However, s 135 will not be available in all circumstances and limitations in the MCA 2005 mean it may not be sufficient where someone is resisting being removed from their property. This only leaves an application to the Court of Protection assuming the person lacks capacity, which is an expensive procedure and may leave local authorities unwilling to take action. In practice, this section is limited to adults who need to be detained in hospital and this is limited only to a 72-hour period.

MHA 1983, s 115 provides powers of entry and inspection to a mental health professional if the professional has reasonable cause to believe that the mentally disordered person is not receiving proper care. This does not permit forced entry, but obstruction without reasonable cause by a third party could constitute an offence under the Act.

Inherent jurisdiction of the High Court

The High Court has wide powers here, including both declaratory relief and the use of injunctions. In the past the court used its powers to intervene where an adult lacked capacity, but recent case law suggests that it is more inclined to intervene now where an adult may have capacity but is vulnerable. See, for example, *Re SA (Vulnerable Adult with Capacity: Marriage)* [2005] EWHC 2942 (Fam), *G (An Adult) (Mental Capacity: Court's Jurisdiction)* [2004] EWHC 2222 and *Sunderland City*

Council v PS [2007] EWHC 623 (Fam). Mr Justice Munby (as he then was) defined a vulnerable adult for these purposes as one who is not necessarily lacking mental capacity but is reasonably believed to be:

- under constraint;

- subject to coercion or undue influence; or

- for some other reason deprived of the capacity to make the relevant decision, or disabled from making a free choice, or incapacitated or disabled from giving or expressing a real or genuine consent.

New legislation would have to be compatible with the European Convention on Human Rights. In particular, Articles 2 (the right to life) and Article 3 (prohibition of inhuman and degrading treatment) both impose positive obligations on the Government to take measures to protect its citizens. Articles 5 (the right to liberty) and 8 (right to respect for private and family life) are also relevant. Interestingly, Article 16 requires states to take legislative and other measures 'to protect persons with disabilities, both within and outside the home from all forms of exploitation, violence and abuse'.

It is noteworthy that the Law Commission's paper 'Mental Incapacity' No 231 (1995) had recommended the introduction of new compulsory intervention powers aimed specifically at adults at risk of abuse or neglect.

The case of *A Local Authority v A* [2010] EWHC 978 (Fam) illustrated the problem of where local authorities can act in too heavy-handed a fashion and may appear too eager to intervene without sufficient legal authority.

There was concern that certain groups would be left unprotected by the abolition of the s 47 power; in particular, people with capacity, and people whose capacity is uncertain and whose lifestyle creates a significant risk of harm to themselves or others. It was pointed out that existing laws do not assist with these groups of adults. In particular:

- use of MHA 1083, s 135(1) only applies to those who need to be detained in hospital;

- removal to a place of safety under that section is only permitted up to 72 hours. This may be inadequate to put in place robust safeguarding arrangements;

- the amount of force required to remove someone is uncertain under MCA 2005, s 5 in regard to a 'best interests' decision;

- applications to the High Court under its inherent jurisdiction are subject to delay and expense.

The case of Mayan Coomeraswamy who died in 2009 illustrated in the words of the coroner 'a piecemeal legal framework' riddled with contradictions and inadequacies.

The Scottish Government's approach

The Adult Support and Protection (Scotland) Act 2007 provides in s 14 a power of removal. This permits a council to apply to a sheriff for a removal order which, if granted, allows the council to remove the adult at risk to a specified place. The purpose is to assess the adult's situation and to support and protect them. It lasts for a maximum of seven days. The order can only be granted if the sheriff is satisfied that the adult may be seriously harmed if not moved to another place. The council also has a duty to protect their property whilst they are subject to this order.

There is a 72-hour period in which to execute the order. The order should only be considered once all other options have been explored and considered. The adult's wishes and needs must always be considered. Consideration must be given to whether the adult will consent or not. The council must consider whether the adult has mental capacity or not.

The Act also provides banning and temporary banning orders in s 21. Such an order will be granted if the adult at risk is in danger of being seriously harmed, and where banning the subject of the order from a specified place is likely to safeguard the adult's well-being and property more effectively than would the removal of the adult at risk. This can last up to six months. The order may attach conditions as follows:

- ban the subject from being in a specified area in the vicinity of a specified place;

- authorise the summary ejection of the subject from the specified place and the specified area;

- prohibit the subject from moving any specified thing from the specified place;

- direct any specified person to take specified measures to preserve any moveable property owned or controlled by the subject which remains in the specified place while the order has effect.

The Welsh experience

It is hoped that the new Social Services and Well-being (Wales) Act 2014 will introduce a new interventionist approach through new adult protection supervision orders. This will give agencies the power to enter an environment where abuse is taking place to allow social care practitioners to make an assessment of the situation. The professional will need to have a reasonable belief that the individual is suffering harm.

6D

Police Action

Involving the police in cases of financial abuse is a significant step but one that should be taken if the evidence of abuse is clear and it is the only means to stop the financial abuse continuing. Only by bringing the matter to the attention of the police can one stop the current abuse, prevent the perpetrator repeating the offence and ensure that a suitable compensation order is obtained and a suitable penalty imposed on the perpetrator. It is by no means an easy step to take and it is understandable that close relatives will not want to report a relative. This is why it is even more important for concerned third parties to alert the police and that the police take reports seriously and investigate.

The offences that may require police action include the following:

- theft;
- fraud by abuse of position;
- forgery;
- handling stolen goods; and
- false accounting.

There are various offences that a perpetrator of financial abuse may have committed and so it is important to consider their definitions. The criminal standard of proof is *beyond all reasonable doubt* (as compared to the *balance of probabilities* in a civil claim).

Theft

The Theft Act 1968, s 1(1) provides a straightforward definition:

'A person is guilty of theft if he dishonestly appropriates property belonging to another with the intention of permanently depriving the other of it.'

If a son takes money from his mother's bank account and transfers it to his own bank account without his mother's knowledge or consent and with no intention of using it for his mother's benefit then this is theft. It does not matter whether the mother has her mental capacity or not. It is common for no police action to be taken even where the Office of the Public Guardian (OPG) has investigated and there is clear evidence of misappropriation. The Court of Protection becomes involved in order to remove the attorney or deputy, and the new appointee is left to take civil action to recover assets. There should be an obligation on the part of the authorities or professionals to report this to the police. There should then be a firm obligation on the part of the police to investigate and prosecute. As the charity Action on Elder Abuse says: 'Theft is theft'.

Prior to the passage of the Theft Act 1968 it was necessary to prove that the property alleged to have been stolen was taken 'without the consent of the owner' (Larceny Act 1916, s 1(1)).

Hinks v R [2000] UKHL 53 illustrates one of the problems of dealing with offences against a vulnerable person, whether elderly or not. In 1996 the appellant was 38 years old and the mother of a young son. She was friendly with a 53-year-old man, John Dolphin, who displayed limited intelligence. The appellant described herself as the main carer for John Dolphin. It is not in dispute that in the period April to November 1996 Mr Dolphin withdrew sums totalling around £60,000 from his building society account and that these sums were deposited in the appellant's account. During the summer of that year Mr Dolphin made withdrawals of the maximum permissible sum of £300 almost every day. Towards the end of this period Mr Dolphin had lost most of his savings and moneys inherited from his father. In 1997 the appellant was charged with six counts of theft, five counts covering moneys withdrawn and one count of a television set being transferred by Mr Dolphin to the appellant.

The appellant said that Mr Dolphin had handed over the moneys, as well as the colour television set, as gifts to her or her young son, or as part of a loan. Two police officers testified that after cautioning the appellant she denied 'having any money' from Mr Dolphin except for a single cheque which she said represented a loan. She denied this. The prosecution case was that the appellant had taken Mr Dolphin for as much as she could get. She asserted that she had acted honestly throughout. On appeal her conviction for theft was quashed.

Lord Hobhouse summed up the court's judgement by concluding that:

> 'The definition of theft therefore embraces cases where the property has come to the defendant by the mistake of the person to whom it belongs and there would be an obligation to restore it – s 5(4) – or property in which the other still has an equitable proprietary interest – s 5(1). This would also embrace property obtained by undue influence or other cases coming within the classes of invalid transfer recognised in *In re Beaney*.

> 'In cases of alleged gift, the criteria to be applied are the same. But additional care may need to be taken to see that the transaction is properly explained to the jury. It is unlikely that a charge of theft will be brought where there is not clear evidence of at least some conduct of the defendant which includes an element of fraud or overt dishonesty or some undue influence or knowledge of the deficient capacity of the alleged donor … and it will not suffice simply

to invite the jury to convict on the basis of their disapprobation of the defendant's conduct and their attribution to him of the knowledge that he must have known that they and other ordinary and decent persons would think it dishonest. Theft is a crime of dishonesty but dishonesty is not the only element in the commission of the crime.'

Lord Hutton summarised his conclusions as follows:

(1) It was necessary for the judge to make clear to the jury that if there was a valid gift the defendant could not be found to be dishonest no matter how much they thought her conduct morally reprehensible.

(2) If the Crown were making the case that the gifts were invalid because Mr Dolphin was mentally incapable of making a gift, it was necessary for the judge to give the jury a specific direction as to what degree of mental weakness would, in the light of the value of the gifts and the other circumstances of the case, make the donor incapable of making a valid gift.

(3) The jury should have been directed that if they were satisfied that Mr Dolphin was mentally incapable of making a gift, they should not convict unless they were satisfied that what the defendant did was dishonest by the standards of ordinary decent people and that the defendant must have realised this.

(4) If the Crown were making the case that the gift was invalid because of undue influence or coercion exercised by the defendant, it was necessary for the judge to give the jury a specific direction as to what would constitute undue influence or coercion.

(5) The jury should have been directed that if they were satisfied that the gifts were invalid by reason of undue influence or coercion, they should not convict unless they were satisfied that what the defendant did was dishonest by the standards of ordinary decent people and that the defendant must have realised this.

Accordingly, in cases where an abuser is charged with theft a vitiating factor like mental incapacity, coercion or undue influence need to be shown in order to prove the offence under the Act.

Fraud by abuse of position

This offence was introduced by the Fraud Act 2006, s 4. The section provides:

(1) A person is in breach of this section if he:

    (a) occupies a position in which he is expected to safeguard, or not to act against, the financial interests of another person,

    (b) dishonestly abuses that position, and

    (c) intends, by means of the abuse of that position:

        (i) to make a gain for himself or another, or

      (ii) to cause loss to another or to expose another to a risk of loss.

(2) A person may be regarded as having abused his position even though his conduct consisted of an omission rather than an act.

Section 5: Gain and loss

The provisions of this section are as follows:

(1) The references to gain and loss in sections 2 to 4 are to be read in accordance with this section.

(2) 'Gain' and 'loss'—

    (a) extend only to gain or loss in money or other property;

    (b) include any such gain or loss whether temporary or permanent;

    and 'property' means any property whether real or personal (including things in action and other intangible property).

(3) 'Gain' includes a gain by keeping what one has, as well as a gain by getting what one does not have.

(4) 'Loss' includes a loss by not getting what one might get, as well as a loss by parting with what one has.

The CPS guidance for prosecutors provides that in order to prove the offence they must show that the defendant:

- occupied a position in which he was expected to safeguard, or not to act against, the financial interests of another person;
- abused that position;
- behaved dishonestly;
- intended by that abuse to make a gain/cause a loss.

The abuse may consist of an omission rather than an act.

The offence is entirely offender-focused. The offence is complete once the defendant carries out the act that is the abuse of his position. It is immaterial whether or not he is successful in his enterprise and whether or not any gain or loss is actually made. The consequences of the offending will determine the type of sentence, compensation and confiscation. In many instances it is the fact of the gain or loss that will prove the defendant's dishonesty beyond reasonable doubt.

The Law Commission report on Fraud (No 276) explained the reasoning behind the new offence. This was that the Theft Act 1968 had introduced a requirement for 'deception' for an offence to take place. It was accepted that there were many instances where the victim was completely unaware of a deception taking place. A vulnerable person may very well be unaware until a much later date or not at all of being deceived by a person in a positon of trust in relation to them.

The Court of Appeal in *R v Ghosh* [1982] EWCA Crim 2, laid down a two-stage test as follows:

(1) The first question is whether the defendant's behaviour was dishonest by the ordinary standards of reasonable and honest people. If the answer is no, that is the end of the matter and the prosecution fails.

(2) If the answer is yes, then the second question is whether the defendant was aware that his conduct would be regarded as dishonest by reasonable, honest people.

Non-disclosure of information

It is in the nature of the situation that the person who trusts the defendant to disclose the information in question will act, or omit to act, in reliance on the defendant's failure to do so.

Fraudulent behaviour

Some kinds of conduct can properly be described as fraudulent on the ground that they amount to an abuse of an existing position of trust, even if there is no question of the victim having been induced to act or omit to act. The difference between this case and that of non-disclosure is that the defendant does not need to enlist the victim's co-operation in order to secure the desired result. An example would be the employee who, without the knowledge of his employer, misuses his position to make a personal profit at the employer's expense.

The relationship/privileged position

The victim has voluntarily put the defendant in a privileged position, by virtue of which the defendant is expected to safeguard the victim's financial interests or given power to damage those interests. Such an expectation to safeguard or power to damage may arise, for example, because the defendant is given authority to exercise a discretion on the victim's behalf, or is given access to the victim's assets, premises, equipment or customers. In these cases the defendant does not need to enlist the victim's further co-operation in order to secure the desired result, because the necessary co-operation has been given in advance.

Example of such relationships include:

- trustee and beneficiary;
- director and company;
- professional and client;
- agent and principal;
- employee and employer;

- between partners;
- within a family;
- in the context of voluntary work;
- any context where the parties are not at arm's length.

Fiduciary duties

Civil law will recognise this as importing fiduciary duties, and any relationship that is so recognised will suffice. We see no reason, however, why the existence of such duties should be essential. This does not of course mean that it would be entirely a matter for the fact-finders whether the necessary relationship exists.

The abuse of position may be an omission as well as a positive act – for example, where an employee omits to take up a chance of a crucial contract, intending to enable an associate to pick up the contract instead.

Forgery

The Forgery and Counterfeiting Act 1981, s 1 provides:

> 'A person is guilty of forgery if he makes a false instrument, with the intention that he or another shall use it to induce somebody to accept it as genuine, and by reason of so accepting it to do or not to do some act to his own or any other person's prejudice.'

The carer forging the elderly client's signature on a cheque or building society withdrawal form will be guilty of this offence.

Handling stolen goods

The Theft Act 1968, s 22 provides that a person handles stolen goods if (otherwise than in the course of the stealing), knowing or believing them to be stolen goods, he dishonestly receives the goods, or dishonestly undertakes or assists in their retention, removal, disposal or realisation by or for the benefit of another person, or if he arranges to do so.

A person who destroys, defaces, conceals or falsifies accounts, records or documents with a view to gain or to cause loss to somebody else may be charged with false accounting under the Theft Act 1968, s 17 and can extend to making use of these, when the person knows they may be misleading, false or deceptive.

Other possible offences include the following:

- blackmail under the Theft Act 1968, s 21;
- forgery under the Identity Cards Act 2006, s 25;
- forgery under the Forgery and Counterfeiting Act 1981;
- fraud by false representation under the Fraud Act 2007, s 2;
- fraud by failure to disclose information under the Fraud Act 2007, s 3.

Police refusal to investigate

If the police refuse to investigate they should be reported to a senior officer. Under guidelines drawn up by the Independent Police Complaints Commission, if the police refuse to record a crime that you have reported then you can complain about the officers involved. There are suspicions that many situations in which there was direct evidence of theft from an elderly person were not followed up after being reported to the police. At the very least, if a perpetrator is prepared to steal from an elderly person it is likely that will do so again. Very often we have presented sufficient evidence to the police that not much further investigation is required. In such a case it is important to press the police to do more to ensure that perpetrators are not able to commit further offences.

Very often the perpetrators will defend their actions by saying that the money transferred was a gift by the victim. Unless there is written proof of this it should not be accepted. There should be no unexplained debits or transfers from a bank account. The recipients should always be asked for full details of how they received the funds and the reason for this.

The Metropolitan Police have a Victim Code of Practice which includes a commitment that vulnerable and intimidated victims will receive an enhanced service under the Code.

These are defined as follows:

> 'all victims under 17 years old or whose quality of evidence is likely to be reduced because they have a mental disorder or learning disability or a physical disability or disorder. Intimidated victims are victims whose quality of evidence is likely to be reduced because they are in fear or distress about giving evidence. If you have been a victim of domestic violence or sexual assault or have lost a family member through murder or manslaughter, you will also be defined as a vulnerable victim. You will be told if you are identified as vulnerable or intimidated as this depends on your personal circumstances and the details of your case.'

Their service commitments include:

- if a victim is vulnerable or a repeat victim police will provide an enhanced response, including the offer of a follow-up visit;

- if a victim reports a crime face-to-face or at a front counter, police will give them a Victim Care Card containing basic information regarding their crime, what will happen next and outlining the minimum standards they can expect;

- police will be polite, courteous and treat victims with respect;

- police will inform victims of their crime number within 36 hours of the initial investigation;

- victims will be informed in writing whether police will further investigate their crime within five days of it being reported;

- if a crime is passed to a secondary investigator, that officer will contact the victim within 24 hours of being assigned the crime and adhere to the Victim Code of Practice.

In September 2016 the Ministry of Justice announced a new policy called 'Supporting vulnerable victims and witnesses':

'Making sure that the voices of victims and witnesses are heard is crucial for a just criminal justice system, and supporting them however we can is a central part of our reform programme. Already, vulnerable victims and witnesses can give evidence from behind a screen, or over video link, but we want to do more to give the court more choice and so give witnesses greater protection. We have increased the number of locations from where victims and witnesses can give their evidence. In many cases this means that they do not even have to be in a court building, saving them time and allowing them to give evidence in an environment that feels comfortable. Following the roll out of digital case management across all Crown Court centres, statements, including victims' personal statements, are now available to judges earlier in the proceedings, allowing more time for them to be considered.'

But there is still more that could be done. Having piloted pre-trial cross-examination, allowing vulnerable witnesses to pre-record their evidence ahead of the trial taking place, the police will be rolling this out nationally from 2017. This is to be welcomed and should allow more vulnerable elderly witnesses to obtain the justice they need. But it does assume that the police take the necessary action at the outset to investigate the crimes.

Chapter 7

Delegating Decision-making Powers to Others

As individuals get older, more forgetful and less mobile they begin to rely on others to help them do all those routine day-to-day tasks that previously they had accomplished easily. Putting in place formal arrangements which will be helpful at a later date, when your faculties are less acute, is sensible planning. However, we do not all think ahead. We tend to postpone, think it will not be necessary or that we trust those closest to us to take over the reins without any formality being required. As we shall see, timely planning can give us peace of mind and protect us from the unscrupulous and those who are only motivated by financial gain. Whilst the best laid plans cannot prevent abuse they certainly reduce unchecked abuse.

There are various ways to delegate decisions to others. Some are fairly informal and others involve careful thought, advice and formality. The more formal they are, the greater the degree of protection and oversight by, for example the Office of the Public Guardian, or ultimately the Court of Protection, when mental capacity has been lost. We shall consider the dangers that can arise if more formal paperwork is not put in place. Having no one appointed to look after a client's affairs can make a client more vulnerable to abuse, involve extra expense and ultimately delay protection. As we shall see, putting in place a more formal appointment of an attorney under an lasting power of attorney (LPA) does take time, not only for the client to consider carefully the choices involved, but also the registration process itself can take some weeks to achieve.

We shall also see that where a client has not appointed an attorney then, if they have lost their mental capacity, a deputy must be appointed to look after their affairs. This generally is a longer and more expensive process than the client deciding in their own time to appoint their own choice of attorney. However, as we shall also see, the deputyship route does provide additional protection for the client that most LPAs do not. Simply by the fact that the deputy must provide annual accounts and be supported by the purchase of a surety bond means that the client is protected from the outset from financial abuse. This is not to say that it will not occur, but generally the Court of Protection sees far more cases involving abuse by attorneys than by deputies.

7A

Informal Arrangements

If an individual makes ad hoc informal arrangements with another person to, for example, to manage funds or assets for them, then they run the risk to losing those funds. Not only could the transferee die, get divorced or go into bankruptcy, but they could simply argue that the money was a gift from the transferor which did not need to be held for transferor's benefit or use. Unless the arrangement is with someone well trusted, the arrangement is short-term and documented, then it is advisable to avoid this.

A good example of what can go wrong with informal arrangements is the case of *JS v KB (Property And Affairs Deputy for DB)* [2014] EWCOP 483. Here Mr Justice Cobb stated:

'This cautionary tale illustrates vividly the dangers of informal family arrangements for an elderly relative who lacks mental capacity, made without proper regard for:

(i) the financial and emotional vulnerability of the person who lacks capacity; and

(ii) the requirements for formal, and legal, authorisation for the family's actions, specifically in relation to property and financial affairs.

'An application was made by the patient's daughter JS when she sought appointment by the Court of Protection as her mother's deputy. She thereby sought to have the authority to continue to make decisions on behalf of her mother (which she had been making for some time) given that she was unable to make such decisions for herself, in relation to her property and financial affairs.

'However, the informal, and as I find improper, means by which DB's finances were utilised by JS to fund the current care arrangement led to the sale of the home in which she had lived for over fifty years effectively "over her head", and the proceeds of sale being placed out of her immediate reach, rendering her financially highly exposed; state benefits and retirement pension payable to DB have subsequently been diverted into an account in JS's name. All of this was done without legal authority. Only with the intervention of the court appointed deputy was the situation regularised.'

It was accepted at this hearing that in 2009 (and at the latest by the start of 2010), DB did not have capacity to manage her property or financial affairs. Specifically, on the facts of this case, at the material time, she did not have the capacity to:

- enter into a legal contract to sell her house;

- appoint an Attorney to act on her behalf;

- make an informed decision about whether to loan or gift the proceeds of sale of her home to JS, or to purchase another house in the name of JS, and/ or use the surplus funds to renovate the property to a high standard, without preserving a beneficial interest for herself.

It illustrates the ease with which an elderly parent can find themselves trusting an adult child with power over their estate with no legal protection and leaving them exposed to serious financial loss. As we shall see later, it is often when care home fees are left unpaid that indicates financial abuse is taking place. Abuse can mean that the care of the elderly parent is at risk either unintentionally or more often as a result of deliberate action. As local authorities come under financial pressures themselves, a more rigourous scrutiny of client's financial arrangements may be required to ensure that long-term care can be provided and sustained.

There are various degrees of formality involved in appointing another person to act on behalf of an individual. These range from appointeeship and powers of attorney governed by the Powers of Attorney Act 1971 (POAA 1971) through to LPA attorneys under MCA 2005. Beyond that there is the court appointment of deputies where a donor no longer has mental capacity to appoint their own attorney.

Appointeeship

Become an appointee for someone claiming benefits

You can apply for the right to deal with the benefits of someone who cannot manage their own affairs because they have lost their capacity or are severely disabled.

Only one appointee can act on behalf of someone who is entitled to benefits (the claimant) from the Department for Work and Pensions (DWP).

An appointee can be an individual, eg a friend or relative, an organisation or representative of an organisation, eg a solicitor or local council.

Appointee's responsibilities

The DWP sets out the appointee's responsibilities as follows:
- '• sign the benefit claim form;

- tell the benefit office about any changes which affect how much the claimant gets;

- spend the benefit (which is paid directly to [*the appointee*]) in the claimant's best interests;

- tell the benefit office if you stop being the appointee, eg the claimant can now manage their own affairs.'

If the benefit is overpaid, depending on the circumstances, the appointee could be held responsible.

Once the application has been made, the DWP arranges to visit the claimant to assess if an appointee is needed, then interviews the proposed appointee to approve their suitability, filling out Form B56 (appointee application form). Confirmation as appointee is communicated on Form BF57; appointee duties commence upon receipt of this form.

Once the appointee is authorised, the DWP will monitor the situation to make sure it remains suitable for both appointee and claimant.

Stop being an appointee

Contact DWP immediately if you want to stop being an appointee. Phone the benefit office that deals with the claim – the number will be on any letters they've sent you.

Your appointment can be stopped if:

- you don't act properly under the terms of the appointment;

- the claimant is clearly able to manage their own benefits;

- you become incapable yourself – let DWP know immediately.

Formal arrangements

Powers of Attorney

Ordinary Powers of Attorney

POAA 1971 provides that a donor can grant a general or specific power to another (the donee). The form is as set out in the Act as follows:

This General Power of Attorney is made this day of 19 by AB of

I appoint CD of

[or CD of and

EF of jointly or

jointly and severally] to be my attorney[s] in accordance with section 10 of the Powers of Attorney Act 1971.

In Witness etc,

An instrument creating a power of attorney shall be executed as a deed (since the Law of Property (Miscellaneous Provisions Act 1989) by the donor of the power.

Another important provision of this Act is the regulation governing proof by certified copies. These state that the contents of an instrument creating a power of attorney may be proved by means of a copy which is a reproduction of the original made with a photographic or other device for reproducing documents in facsimile; and contains the following certificate or certificates signed by the donor, a solicitor, or an authorised person (since 2007 this has included a notary public or a stockbroker).

The certificate provides as follows:

'a certificate at the end to the effect that the copy is a true and complete copy of the original; and if the original consists of two or more pages, a certificate at the end of each page of the copy to the effect that it is a true and complete copy of the corresponding page of the original.'

Revocation of an ordinary power of attorney

POAA 1971, s 5 states:

(1)   A donee of a power of attorney who acts in pursuance of the power at a time when it has been revoked shall not, by reason of the revocation, incur any liability (either to the donor or to any other person) if at that time he did not know that the power had been revoked.

(2)   Where a power of attorney has been revoked and a person, without knowledge of the revocation, deals with the donee of the power, the transaction between them shall, in favour of that person, be as valid as if the power had then been in existence.

(3)   Where the power is expressed in the instrument creating it to be irrevocable and to be given by way of security then, unless the person dealing with the donee knows that it was not in fact given by way of security, he shall be entitled to assume that the power is incapable of revocation except by the donor acting with the consent of the donee and shall accordingly be treated for the purposes of subsection (2) of this section as having knowledge of the revocation only if he knows that it has been revoked in that manner.

(4)   Where the interest of a purchaser depends on whether a transaction between the donee of a power of attorney and another person was valid by virtue of subsection (2) of this section, it shall be conclusively presumed in favour of the purchaser that that person did not at the material time know of the revocation of the power if the transaction between that person and the donee was completed within twelve months of the date on which the power came into operation; or that person makes a statutory declaration, before or within three months after the completion of the purchase, that he did not at the material time know of the revocation of the power.

(5)   Without prejudice to subsection (3) of this section, for the purposes of this section knowledge of the revocation of a power of attorney includes knowledge of the occurrence of any event (such as the death of the donor) which has the effect of revoking the power.

Additional protection for transferees under stock exchange transactions

POAA 1971, s 6 states:

(1)   Without prejudice to section 5 of this Act, where—

(a) the donee of a power of attorney executes, as transferor, an instrument transferring registered securities; and

(b) the instrument is executed for the purposes of a stock exchange transaction,

it shall be conclusively presumed in favour of the transferee that the power had not been revoked at the date of the instrument if a statutory declaration to that effect is made by the donee of the power on or within three months after that date.

Execution of instruments by donee of power of attorney

The execution provisions for such powers of attorney is set out in POAA 1971, s 7:

(1)   If the donee of a power of attorney is an individual, he may, if he thinks fit—

(a) execute any instrument with his own signature, and

(b) do any other thing in his own name,

by the authority of the donor of the power; and any instrument executed or thing done in that manner shall, subject to subsection (1A) of this section, be as effective as if executed by the donee in any manner which would constitute due execution of that instrument by the donor or, as the case may be, as if done by the donee in the name of the donor.

(1A) here an instrument is executed by the donee as a deed, it shall be as effective as if executed by the donee in a manner which would constitute due execution of it as a deed by the donor only if it is executed in accordance with section 1(3)(a) of the Law of Property (Miscellaneous Provisions) Act 1989.

POAA 1971, s 10 provides that 'a general power of attorney in the form set out in Schedule 1 to the Act, or in a form to the like effect but expressed to be made under this Act, shall operate to confer on the donee of the power; or if there is more than one donee, on the donees acting jointly or acting jointly or severally, as the case may be, authority to do on behalf of the donor anything which he can lawfully do by an attorney.'

Enduring Powers of Attorney

Enduring Powers of Attorneys (EPAs) could be created up until 1 October 2007. The Enduring Powers of Attorney Act 1985 (EPAA 1985) provided donors with the power to appoint someone as an attorney and that appointment could endure even if the donor subsequently lost their mental capacity. Any such powers are still valid today provided they were executed before 1 October 2007 and were validly executed. EPAA 1985 was repealed by the Mental Capacity Act 2005 (MCA 2005) and this Act now applies to EPAs (see in particular Schedule 4).

An EPA only applies to a donor's property and affairs and not any health, welfare or care issues. A duly executed EPA can take effect immediately like an ordinary power of attorney.

It is impossible to say how many EPAs there are in existence. Apart from the numbers that are sent for registration when mental incapacity supervenes, EPAs are generally held for safekeeping and not always used. There was a spike in applicants to execute EPAs just before the deadline on 30 September 2007. The Office of the Public Guardian (OPG) stated that the registration of EPAs peaked at 25,000 in 2007 and since that date the number has been gradually falling. In the year 2014/15 there were 15,000 registration applications.

Once incapacity supervenes the attorney is under an obligation to register the EPA with the OPG. MCA 2005, Sch 4, para 1 provides that the donee of the power may not do anything (if capacity has been lost) with a few notable exceptions, under the authority of the power unless or until the instrument creating the power is registered.

The attorney may at this point only take action under the power to maintain the donor or prevent loss to his estate, or to maintain himself or other persons in so far as Sch 4, para 3(2) permits him to do so.

Where the attorney purports to act as provided in para 3(2) then, in favour of a person who deals with him without knowledge that the attorney is acting otherwise than in accordance with sub-para (2)(a) or (b), the transaction between them is as valid as if the attorney were acting in accordance with sub-para (2)(a) or (b). Those sub-paragraphs provide that:

(a) he may so act in relation to himself or in relation to any other person if the donor might be expected to provide for his or that person's needs respectively, and

(b) he may do whatever the donor might be expected to do to meet those needs.

Characteristics of an EPA

A power of attorney is an EPA provided it is in the prescribed form and was executed in the prescribed manner by the donor and the attorney, and incorporated the prescribed explanatory information. There have been four different forms under the different regulations in 1986, 1987, 1990 and in 2000.

Attorneys under EPA

An attorney must be an individual who has reached 18 and is not bankrupt or a trust corporation. An EPA will be revoked by the bankruptcy of the donor or attorney. But where the donor or attorney is bankrupt merely because an interim bankruptcy restrictions order has effect in respect of him or where the donor or attorney is subject to an interim debt relief restrictions order, the power is suspended for so long as the order has effect.

A power of attorney which gives the attorney a right to appoint a substitute or successor cannot be an enduring power. This contrasts with lasting power of attorneys, where replacement attorneys can be appointed on the prescribed forms.

Revocation

A court can revoke the enduring power under MCA 2005, ss 16–20 in relation to the donor. Note also that a EPA can be validly disclaimed by deed or otherwise, only when the attorney gives notice of it to the donor or, in particular circumstances to the Public Guardian.

Scope of an EPA

MCA 2005, s 3 sets out the scope of authority under an EPA. If the instrument which creates an EPA is expressed to confer general authority on the attorney, the instrument operates to confer, subject to the restriction imposed by sub-s (3), and any conditions or restrictions contained in the instrument, authority to do on behalf of the donor anything which the donor could lawfully do by an attorney at the time when the donor executed the instrument.

Subject to any conditions or restrictions contained in the instrument, an attorney under an EPA, whether general or limited, may (without obtaining any consent) act under the power so as to benefit himself or other persons than the donor to the following extent but no further. He may so act in relation to himself or in relation to any other person if the donor might be expected to provide for his or that person's needs respectively, and he may do whatever the donor might be expected to do to meet those needs. Note that this is in contrast to LPAs.

Making gifts for a donor of an EPA

Subject to any conditions or restrictions contained in the instrument, an attorney under an EPA, whether general or limited, may (without obtaining any consent) dispose of the property of the donor by way of gift of a seasonal nature, or on an anniversary, a birth, a marriage or the formation of a civil partnership, to persons (including himself) who are related to or connected with the donor, and he may make gifts to any charity to whom the donor made or might be expected to make gifts, provided that the value of each such gift is not unreasonable having regard to all the circumstances and in particular the size of the donor's estate.

Duties of attorney in event of actual or impending incapacity of donor

If the attorney under an EPA has reason to believe that the donor is or is becoming mentally incapable they must, as soon as practicable, make an application to the Public Guardian for the registration of the instrument creating the power. The attorney must complete form EP2PG.

Before making an application for registration the attorney must comply with the provisions as to notice set out in MCA 2005, Sch 4, Part 3.

An application for registration must be made in the prescribed form, and must contain such statements as may be prescribed. The attorney may, before making an application for the registration of the instrument, refer to the court for its determination any question as to the validity of the power, and must comply with any direction given to him by the court on that determination.

No disclaimer of the power is valid unless and until the attorney gives notice of it to the Public Guardian; and the Public Guardian must notify the donor if he receives a notice under the Part 3 notice provisions.

A person who, in an application for registration, makes a statement which he knows to be false in a material particular is guilty of an offence and is liable on summary conviction, to imprisonment for a term not exceeding 12 months or a fine not exceeding the statutory maximum or both; on conviction on indictment, to imprisonment for a term not exceeding two years or a fine or both.

What is interesting is that there is no detailed declaration required when making the application for registration. All that the attorney(s) must confirm is:

'I (We) certify that the above information is correct and that to the best of my (our) knowledge and belief I (We) have complied with the provisions of the Mental Capacity Act 2005'.

At this point it would be good opportunity to remind attorneys of their obligations not least in respect of acting in the best interests of the donor, limitations on gifts and the requirements to keep accounts. As we shall see when looking at the reported cases, many attorneys seem quite cavalier in the way they handle their donor's property and finances. Some means by which the attorney's obligations are brought to their attention at this point would be sensible. It is unreasonable to think that lay attorneys will know their way around the MCA 2005. This is one area which could be tightened up. The booklet EPA101 provides greater detail, but a reminder on the registration form would bring the attorney's duties and obligations into focus.

The EPA form itself contains prescribed information on the first page including the following:

- number of attorneys to be chosen and whether jointly or jointly or severally appointed;

- general or specific powers;

- restrictions;

- out-of-pocket expenses;

- obligation to register at the onset of the donor's mental incapacity;

- notification rules.

In Part C of the EPA form the attorney must confirm as follows:

'I understand that I have a duty to apply to the Court for the registration of this form under the Enduring Powers of Attorney Act 1985 when the donor is becoming or has become mentally incapable. I also understand my limited power to use the donor's property to benefit persons other than the donor.'

By way of contrast, when signing an LPA form, as we shall see below, an attorney has to confirm that he understands all of the following:

'He or she is aged 18 or over, has read the lasting power of attorney including the section entitled "Your legal rights and responsibilities", or I have had it read to them, that they have a duty to act based on the principles of the Mental Capacity Act 2005 and to have regard to the Mental Capacity Act Code of Practice, that they must make decisions and act in the best interests of the donor, that they must take into account any instructions or preferences set out in the LPA and that they confirm that they can make decisions and act only when the LPA has been registered and at the time indicated in section 5 of that LPA.'

Notification prior to registration

The attorney or attorneys are under a duty to give notice to relatives.

Before making an application for registration the attorney must give notice of his intention to do so to all those persons (if any) who are entitled to receive notice. The usual rule is that no more than three persons are entitled to receive notice (subject to exceptions in MCA 2005).

The persons entitled to be notified include the following relatives:

- the donor's spouse or civil partner;

- the donor's children;

- the donor's parents;

- the donor's brothers and sisters, whether of the whole or half blood;

- the widow, widower or surviving civil partner of a child of the donor;

- the donor's grandchildren;

- the children of the donor's brothers and sisters of the whole blood;

- the children of the donor's brothers and sisters of the half blood;

- the donor's uncles and aunts of the whole blood;

- the children of the donor's uncles and aunts of the whole blood.

If a person's name or address is not known to the attorney and cannot be reasonably ascertained by him, or the attorney has reason to believe that he has not reached 18 or is mentally incapable then they are not entitled to be served with such notice.

There are separate rules for notifying the donor and any joint attorneys in MCA 2005, ss 10–11.

The notices themselves are currently set out in form EP1PG. This contains prescribed information including informing that relative of his right to object to the registration under MCA 2005, Schedule 4, Part 4, paragraph 13(4). The form specifies the grounds on which an objection to registration may be made, (see paragraph 13(9)). The grounds are:

- that the power purported to have been created by the instrument was not valid as an enduring power of attorney;

- that the power created by the instrument no longer subsists;

- that the application is premature because the donor is not yet becoming mentally incapable;

- that fraud or undue pressure was used to induce the donor to create the power;

- that, having regard to all the circumstances and in particular the attorney's relationship to or connection with the donor, the attorney is unsuitable to be the donor's attorney.

The donor is informed that while the instrument remains registered, any revocation of the power by him will be ineffective unless and until the revocation is confirmed by the court.

Registration of instrument creating power will proceed at the OPG unless there is a valid objection.

If any of those grounds is established to the satisfaction of the court it must direct the Public Guardian not to register the instrument, but if not so satisfied it must direct its registration.

If the court directs the Public Guardian not to register an instrument because it is satisfied that the ground in MCA 2005, Sch 4, Pt 5, para (9)(d) (fraud or undue pressure) or (e) (attorney is unsuitable to be the donor's attorney), is established, it must by order revoke the power created by the instrument.

If the court directs the Public Guardian not to register an instrument because it is satisfied that any ground in para (9) except that in sub-para (c) is established, the instrument must be delivered up to be cancelled unless the court otherwise directs.

Legal position after registration

Effect and proof of registration

The effect of the registration of an instrument under para 13 is that:

- no revocation of the power by the donor is valid unless and until the court confirms the revocation;

- no disclaimer of the power is valid unless and until the attorney gives notice of it to the Public Guardian;

- the donor may not extend or restrict the scope of the authority conferred by the instrument and no instruction or consent given by him after registration, in the case of a consent, confers any right and, in the case of an instruction, imposes or confers any obligation or right on or creates any liability of the attorney or other persons.

Functions of court with regard to registered power

Where an instrument has been registered under para 13, the court has the following functions with respect to the power and the donor of and the attorney appointed to act under the power.

The court may—

(a) determine any question as to the meaning or effect of the instrument;

(b) give directions with respect to—

    (i) the management or disposal by the attorney of the property and affairs of the donor;

    (ii) the rendering of accounts by the attorney and the production of the records kept by him for the purpose;

    (iii) the remuneration or expenses of the attorney whether or not in default of or in accordance with any provision made by the instrument, including directions for the repayment of excessive or the payment of additional remuneration;

(c) require the attorney to supply information or produce documents or things in his possession as attorney;

(d) give any consent or authorisation to act which the attorney would have to obtain from a mentally capable donor;

(e) authorise the attorney to act so as to benefit himself or other persons than the donor otherwise than in accordance with paragraph 3(2) and (3) (but subject to any conditions or restrictions contained in the instrument);

(f) relieve the attorney wholly or partly from any liability which he has or may have incurred on account of a breach of his duties as attorney.

[Para 16(2).]

Revocation

On application made for the purpose by or on behalf of the donor, the court must confirm the revocation of the power if satisfied that the donor has done whatever is necessary in law to effect an express revocation of the power, and was mentally capable of revoking a power of attorney when he did so (whether or not he is so when the court considers the application).

The court must direct the Public Guardian to cancel the registration of an instrument registered under MCA 2005, Sch 4, para 13 in any of the following circumstances (para 16):

(2)

    (a) on confirming the revocation of the power under sub-paragraph (3);

    (b) on directing under paragraph 2(9)(b) that the power is to be revoked;

    (c) on being satisfied that the donor is and is likely to remain mentally capable;

    (d) on being satisfied that the power has expired or has been revoked by the mental incapacity of the attorney;

(e) on being satisfied that the power was not a valid and subsisting enduring power when registration was effected;

(f) on being satisfied that fraud or undue pressure was used to induce the donor to create the power;

(g) on being satisfied that, having regard to all the circumstances and in particular the attorney's relationship to or connection with the donor, the attorney is unsuitable to be the donor's attorney.

(3) If the court directs the Public Guardian to cancel the registration of an instrument on being satisfied of the matters specified in sub-paragraph (4)(f) or (g) it must by order revoke the power created by the instrument.

(4) If the court directs the cancellation of the registration of an instrument under sub-paragraph (4) except paragraph (c) the instrument must be delivered up to the Public Guardian to be cancelled, unless the court otherwise directs.

Cancellation of registration by Public Guardian

Paragraph 17:

The Public Guardian must cancel the registration of an instrument creating an enduring power of attorney:

(a) on receipt of a disclaimer signed by the attorney;

(b) if satisfied that the power has been revoked by the death or bankruptcy of the donor or attorney or the making of a debt relief order (under Part 7A of the Insolvency Act 1986) in respect of the donor or attorney or, if the attorney is a body corporate, by its winding up or dissolution;

(c) on receipt of notification from the court that the court has revoked the power;

(d) on confirmation from the court that the donor has revoked the power.

Joint and joint and several attorneys

An instrument which appoints more than one person to be an attorney cannot create an EPA unless the attorneys are appointed to act jointly, or jointly and severally.

A failure by any one attorney to comply with the requirements for the creation of EPAs prevents the instrument from creating such a power in his case, but does not affect its efficacy for that purpose as respects the other or others, or its efficacy in his case for the purpose of creating a power of attorney which is not an enduring power.

If one or more, but not both or all, the attorneys makes or joins in making an application for registration of the instrument, an attorney who is not an applicant, as well as one who is, may act pending the registration of the instrument as provided in para 1(2), notice of the application must also be given under Sch 4, Part 3 to the other attorney or attorneys, and objection may validly be taken to the registration on a ground relating to an attorney or to the power of an attorney who is not an applicant as well as to one or the power of one who is an applicant.

The Public Guardian is not precluded from registering an instrument and the court must not direct him not to do so if an enduring power subsists as respects some attorney who is not affected by the ground or grounds of the objection in question; and where the Public Guardian registers an instrument in that case, he must make against the registration an entry in the prescribed form.

This does not preclude the court from revoking a power in so far as it confers a power on any other attorney in respect of whom the ground above is established; and where any ground affecting any other attorney is established the court must direct the Public Guardian to make against the registration an entry in the prescribed form.

Joint attorneys

The reference to the time when the attorney executes the instrument is to be read as a reference to the time when the second or last attorney executes the instrument.

References to the attorney are to be read as including references to any attorney under the power.

Joint and several attorneys

The reference above (in para 17) to the bankruptcy of the attorney is to be read as a reference to the bankruptcy of the last remaining attorney under the power; and the bankruptcy of any other attorney under the power causes that person to cease to be an attorney under the power.

Financial abuse by attorneys acting under an EPA

Senior Judge Lush of the Court of Protection has reported that in respect of EPAs in the cases that came before him in 2013, 22 were safeguarding applications to the Public Guardian. In the following year this rose to 40. There were comparable increased cases recorded in respect of LPAs and deputyships, as we shall see below.

Application by the Public Guardian to revoke an EPA

In *Re AB* [2014] EWCOP 12 the Public Guardian applied to revoke the EPA on the ground that in all the circumstances the attorneys (the donor's nephews) were unsuitable to be the donor's attorneys. Concerns were raised when it transpired that the donor's residential care home fees were not being paid. The attorneys had given £15,000 of the donor's money to their mother to buy a car, had made loans of £10,000 and £40,000 to their brother, and furthermore could not explain withdrawals of over £60,000 from the donor's funds.

The judge reminded the court of the provisions of The Mental Capacity Act 2005 Code of Practice; paragraph 7.60 refers to the fiduciary duties of an attorney and provides that:

'A fiduciary duty means attorneys must not take advantage of their position. Nor should they put themselves in a position where their personal interests conflict with their duties. They must also not allow any other influences to affect the way in which they act as an attorney. Decisions should always benefit the donor, and not the attorney. Attorneys must not profit or get any personal benefit from their position, apart from receiving gifts where the Act allows it, whether or not it is at the donor's expense.'

The judge held they were unsuitable to be the attorneys and a local authority deputy was ordered to be appointed in their place.

In *Re DT* [2015] EWCOP 10 an application was made to revoke an EPA as the attorneys had failed to discharge outstanding care fees of nearly £20,000. This rose to £68,000 a year later. However, following a visit by the court's special visitor it was found that the donor did have capacity and although his wishes appeared to be irrational they were hard to ignore. Despite the attorneys' failure to produce accounts their conduct was not such as to lead to a detrimental effect on the donor's finances. There was no animosity between the three attorneys and the donor wanted the attorneys to continue to act for him. The court found that revoking the EPA would not be in the donor's best interests.

In *Re SF* [2015] EWCOP 68 the donor's son has been appointed as her attorney under an EPA. An application to revoke the EPA and its registration was made by the Public Guardian. An investigation showed that there were unpaid care fees totalling £29,000. Her property had been sold for £189,000, her son (Martin) wasn't providing a personal allowance to pay for her toiletries, hairdressing and chiropody, he rarely visited her and had paid himself over £117,000 in out-of-pocket expenses, which the OPG regarded as excessive. There was an ongoing dispute as to whether her fees should be publicly funded. The local authority had already reimbursed her with continuing care payments totalling £82,000. In response to the application the attorney replied: 'I see no need to replace myself. I am the sole heir and because of my mother's dementia and current poor health, there is no need to protect the estate's financial interests, which are effectively mine …On the face of it, the OPG's desire for me to repay money from my mother's estate makes little sense. I am the sole beneficiary of the estate and any restitution I made would come straight back to me on my mother's death, which considering her present state of health, is likely to be sooner rather than later.'

The decision is illustrative of cases such as these where attorneys are simply not fit to manage someone else's money and this is set out in full below:

'One would be hard pressed to find a more callous and calculating attorney, who has so flagrantly abused his position of trust. Martin hasn't paid his mother a personal allowance since June 2014 because toiletries were free in her previous residential care home and he resents having to pay for them now in the nursing home in which she has been living since February 2013. He even begrudges her having her hair tinted.

'The assertion that he hasn't taken "any gifts from the estate" adds nothing to his credibility. If anything, it highlights his lack of it. He was referring to the £3,000 annual exemption for inheritance tax ("IHT") purposes, but Sheila's estate is well below the threshold at which IHT becomes chargeable and no one is entitled, as of right, to receive a gift of £3,000 each year.

'As regards the non-payment of Sheila's care fees, I agree with the Public Guardian's stance that:

"whilst Martin attempts to resolve the dispute (with Powys Local Health Board), it would be in Sheila's best interests that he continues to pay her care fees."

'There is no evidence to support Martin's suggestion that "if my mother's care fees are paid from now onwards, Powys LHB will seek to avoid refunding monies owed." The letter from Powys Local Health Board to the OPG, dated 12 March 2015, to which I referred in paragraph 21 above, shows that the Health Board has acted in good faith and reimbursed any fees that were overpaid in the past. Martin, on the other hand, has persistently acted in bad faith.

'As for his claim for reimbursement of out-of-pocket expenses for acting as his mother's attorney, paragraph 6 of Part A of the prescribed form of Enduring Power of Attorney, which he and his mother signed on 23 October 2004, stated that:

"Your attorney(s) can recover the out-of-pocket expenses of acting as your attorney(s). If your attorney(s) are professional people, for example solicitors or accountants, they may be able to charge for their professional services as well. You may wish to provide expressly for remuneration of your attorney(s)."

'Sheila did not expressly provide for Martin to be remunerated and if he intended to charge a daily rate of £400 for acting as her attorney, he should have applied to the court for authorisation pursuant to paragraph 16(2)(b)

(iii) of Schedule 4 to the Mental Capacity Act 2005. By not doing so, he behaved in a way that contravened his authority and was not in the donor's best interests.

'The Public Guardian believes the amount of £117,289.45 is an excessive amount to claim for out of pocket expenses. I would put it more strongly than that. I believe that charging one's elderly mother a daily rate of £400 for visiting and acting as her attorney is repugnant.

'Martin suggested that the appointment of a panel deputy would be a waste of time and money because his mother's estate is effectively already his. I disagree. The panel deputy will, for the first time in eleven years, place Sheila at the centre of the decision-making process, rather than view the preservation and enhancement of Martin's inheritance as the paramount consideration.

'Having regard to all the circumstances, therefore, I am satisfied that Martin is unsuitable to be Sheila's attorney, and I shall revoke the EPA and direct the Public Guardian to cancel its registration. I shall also direct an officer of the court to invite a panel deputy to apply to be appointed as Sheila's deputy for property and affairs.'

In *Re HS* [2015] EWCOP 33 an application was made to revoke the EPA where the donor's partner as her attorney had failed to keep accounts and £40,000 appeared to be unaccounted for. The county council wanted a panel deputy to be appointed, but the court decided that the least restrictive option would be to appoint the donor's son to take over from his father.

Revocation of an EPA

In *Re ED* [2015] EWCOP 26 there was significant rivalry and hostility between the two daughters who had been appointed as their mother's attorneys under an EPA, their appointment being joint rather than joint and several. One of the attorneys changed the appointment in page 2 of the EPA to a joint and several appointment as she thought this was in her mother's best interests. However, the amendment was not made with the donor's involvement, was made after the time when EPAs could no longer be executed, and the amendment was not witnessed. The EPA was subsequently sent for registration. However, the law is quite clear that a person who, in an application for registration, makes a statement which he knows to be false in a material particular is guilty of an offence (MCA 2005, Sch 4, para 4(7)). The EPA was revoked and the Public Guardian was directed to cancel the registration. A panel deputy was appointed in the attorneys' place.

In *Re P* [2015] EWCOP 37 an application was made by the Public Guardian for an order to revoke an EPA on the grounds that the donor was unsuitable to be his wife's attorney. The Public Guardian's application was on the grounds that he had concerns that the attorney's decisions were unwise and not in the donor's best interests. The donor's properties were badly managed and provided no income for her and the attorney had made undocumented loans to himself from her funds.

The Public Guardian's application was for an order under Sch 4, paras 16(4)(g) and 16(5). Paragraph 16(4) states that:

> 'The court must direct the Public Guardian to cancel the registration of an instrument registered under paragraph 13 in any of the following circumstances—
>
> [...]
>
> (g) on being satisfied that, having regard to all the circumstances and in particular the attorney's relationship to or connection with the donor, the attorney is unsuitable to be the donor's attorney.'

Paragraph 16(5) provides that:

> 'If the court directs the Public Guardian to cancel the registration of an instrument on being satisfied of the matters specified in sub-paragraph (4)(f) or (g) it must by order revoke the power created by the instrument.'

In the circumstances the court ordered the revocation of the EPA and ordered the appointment of deputies.

Application to revoke an EPA

In *Re RG* [2015] EWCOP 66 an application had been made by a county council for the court to order the revocation of an EPA and the appointment of a professional deputy. The donor had appointed her son to be her sole attorney. The council investigated after being alerted by an anonymous tip-off that the attorney and his brother were selling off her personal effects and planning to let her property out. The council identified numerous debts in the donor's name and arrears of care home fees. Before the donor went into the care home she was not provided with basic care and support. It was also believed that the attorney had delegated his authority to his brother, which is not permitted unless they are seeking professional or expert advice. The court accordingly revoked the EPA and directed the Public Guardian to cancel its registration.

Unsuitability of individuals to be attorneys

See, for example, *Re AB* [2014] EWCOP 12: in all the circumstances the attorneys (the donor's nephews) were unsuitable to be the donor's attorneys.

The Law Commission briefly discussed the meaning of the expression 'unsuitable to be the donor's attorney' in its 1993 report, 'The Incapacitated Principal', which led to the enactment of the Enduring Powers of Attorney Act in 1985. It said:

'This needs some explanation. It would amount in effect to a criticism of the donor's choice of attorney. But we would not wish this ground to be sustained merely because the attorney was not the sort of person that a particular relative would have chosen. It is our wish that the donor's choice of attorney should carry considerable weight. Thus, for example, a mother might be content to appoint her son as her EPA attorney despite being aware of a conviction for theft. We would not want her choice of attorney to be upset simply because a particular relative would not want the son to be his attorney. The question should be whether the particular attorney is suitable to act as attorney for the particular donor. In short, the court should examine carefully all the circumstances, particularly the relationship between the donor and the attorney.'

There was a string of reported decisions on the 'unsuitability' of attorneys some ten to 15 years ago:

- *Re W (Enduring Power of Attorney)* [2000] 3 WLR 45, where the decision of the first instance judge was subsequently upheld by the Court of Appeal in *Re W (Enduring Power of Attorney)* [2001] 2 WLR 957.
- *Re E (Enduring Powers of Attorney)* [2000] 3 WLR 1974.
- *Re F* [2004] 3 All ER 277.

Differences between revoking an EPA and an LPA

Senior Judge Lush in *Re P* [2015] EWCOP 37 explained that the criteria whereby the court may revoke an EPA are different from those for revoking an LPA:

'Rather than applying a general or abstract criterion of "unsuitability", and instead of requiring the court to have regard to 'all the circumstances', section 22 of the Mental Capacity Act 2005 is narrower and more focused. It provides that the court may revoke an LPA only if:

(a) the donor lacks the capacity to revoke it, and

(b) the attorney has behaved, or is behaving, or proposes to behave in a way that contravenes his authority or is not in the donor's best interests.

'One further difference between EPAs and LPAs is that attorneys acting under an EPA must comply with the fiduciary duties described in paragraphs 7.58 to 7.68 of the Mental Capacity Act 2005 Code of Practice (Code, paragraph 7.79), whereas an attorney acting under an LPA must not only comply with these fiduciary duties, but also must:

(a) act in accordance with the provisions of the Mental Capacity Act and in particular sections 1 (the principles) and 4 (best interests) (MCA 2005, section 9(4)(a)); and

(b) have regard to the Mental Capacity Act Code of Practice in a wider sense (MCA 2005, section 42(4)(a)).

'Notwithstanding the absence of an express requirement in either the MCA 2005 or the Code of Practice for an attorney acting under an EPA to act in the donor's best interests, in my judgment, any attorney acting under an EPA who has contravened his authority or has behaved, or is proposing to behave, in a way that is not in the donor's best interests is potentially "unsuitable", although the court needs to have regard to all the circumstances, and to consider "the bigger picture", before it can finally determine whether the attorney is unsuitable to be the donor's attorney.'

Issues with EPAs

When EPAs were withdrawn in 2007 there was considerable debate about how they had become open to abuse due to the registration procedure and lack of oversight. The statistics now seem to suggest that it is not the forms that were the problem, but the way some attorneys feel able to use their donor's funds in either a chaotic or abusive way. It would be possible to bring in registration for all EPAs immediately if they were to be used. This would ensure that they were listed on a searchable register, subject to immediate oversight and that the attorneys would be under the aegis of the OPG.

The registers should be used as a database to keep attorneys up to date with good practice. One of the significant problems of managing powers of attorney is that attorneys are not necessarily competent to manage their own money, let alone someone else's. It is surprising that accountants have not stepped in to provide simple accounting for attorneys. Alternatively, simple software packages designed to provide attorney accounts could be marketed. It seems strange that the MCA 2005 draftsmen did not insist on the same regulation of EPAs as for LPAs.

Key differences between EPAs and LPAs are as follows:

- forms;
- registration;
- notice provisions;
- replacement attorneys;
- revocation;
- finances and property only for EPAs;
- EPA attorneys have no express requirement to act in donor's best interests unlike LPA attorneys.

7C

Lasting Powers of Attorney

Lasting powers of attorney (LPAs) were introduced by the Mental Capacity Act 2005 (MCA 2005). Sections 9 to 14 deal with the definition of an LPA, the types, appointment of donees, restrictions, gifts and protection of donees and others. Schedule 1 provides for the formalities for creation of an LPA, the registration process, cancellation, severance and alteration provisions.

The provisions of the Act are reinforced by the Code of Practice to the Act which gives practical illustrations of what LPAs are and how they should be used. It also shows how they differ from enduring powers of attorney (EPAs), the types of decisions attorneys can make, situations where an LPA can or cannot be used, the duties and responsibilities of attorneys, the standards applicable to attorneys, and what measures can be taken if attorneys do not meet those standards.

There have been various revisions to the MCA 2005, not least the amendments brought in in 2015 by the Lasting Powers of Attorney, Enduring Powers of Attorney and Public Guardian (Amendment) Regulations 2015, SI 2015/899.

What is an LPA?

MCA 2005, s 9 provides that an LPA is a power of attorney under which a donor confers on a donee or donees (the attorneys) authority to make decisions about the personal welfare and property and affairs of the donor, and includes authority to make such decisions when that donor no longer has capacity.

There are certain requirements as to who can be a donor and an attorney. A donor must be 18 years of age and have capacity to execute the LPA. An attorney must also be 18 or be a trust corporation in respect of a property and affairs LPA. A trust corporation cannot act as an attorney for health and welfare matters.

Bankruptcy of the donor

The donor's bankruptcy or the making of a debt relief order against the donor has the effect of revoking the power so far as it relates to their property and affairs. But where the donor is bankrupt merely because an interim bankruptcy restrictions order has effect in respect of him, or where the donor is subject to an interim debt relief restrictions order, the power is suspended, for so long as the order has effect.

Bankruptcy of an attorney

An attorney appointed under a property and affairs LPA must not be bankrupt or someone for whom a debt relief order has been made. This does not apply in respect of a health and welfare LPA attorney. If there is more than one attorney appointed joint and severally these rules apply only to the attorney who is bankruptcy or subject to the debt relief order and not the other attorney(s) appointed under the LPA. Where the attorneys have been appointed to act jointly neither attorney can act in this situation and the Act provides that this will prevent the LPA from being created.

Joint or joint and several appointments

Where there is more than one attorney appointed they can be appointed to act jointly so that all decisions must be taken together. Alternatively, they could be appointed jointly and severally so that one can act alone. They can also be appointed to act jointly in respect of some matters and jointly and severally in respect of others. If the LPA does not specify how they are to act they it is to be assumed that they act jointly.

Note if the appointment is a joint one and one of those attorneys is found to be not acting in the donor's best interests then the court will be bound to revoke the whole power. This contrasts with the appointment of joint and several attorneys.

See, for example, the case of *The Public Guardian v SR [2015] EWCOP 32* where the other joint and several attorney could remain in place when the appointment of the co-attorney, under the joint and several LPA, was revoked and registration cancelled.

Contrast that with *ID (Revocation of LPA)* [2015] EWCOP 19 where the jointly appointed attorneys had their power revoked because of the actions of one of them.

Replacement attorneys

An attorney cannot appoint a successor to act for them. However, the donor can appoint a person to replace an attorney(s). The appointment of the replacement will take effect if one of the following events (as set out in MCA 2005, s 13) takes place:

* disclaimer by an attorney;

- death of an attorney;

- bankruptcy of an attorney or the making of a debt relief order in respect of the attorney (or, if the attorney is a trust corporation, its winding-up or dissolution);

- dissolution or annulment of a marriage or civil partnership between the donor and an attorney;

- attorney no longer has capacity.

How is an LPA created?

MCA 2005, Sch 1 provides that an LPA must be in the form prescribed by the Act, containing statements by the donor, the attorney(s) and a certificate provider.

The prescribed form LP1F for financial decisions contains the following information:

Section 1: The donor

Full names, date of birth (they must be over 18 years old) and contact details.

Section 2: The attorneys

Full names, date of birth (they must be over 18 years old) and contact details. They must not be bankrupt or subject to a debt relief order. They can also be a trust corporation, for which continuation sheet 4 must also be signed. If more than four attorneys are appointed, continuation sheet 1 needs to be completed with the attorneys' details.

Section 3: How should attorneys make decisions?

In this section the donor must decide whether the attorneys (if more than one) are to be appointed to act jointly, jointly and severally, or jointly for some decisions and jointly and severally for other decisions. All decisions taken where attorneys are appointed jointly must be taken unanimously. There is no equivalent majority decision-making power as there could be for trustees. A joint and several appointment allows more flexibility for one attorney to act on their own or together as they choose.

Sometimes clients express a wish that they would like more important or higher value financial transactions to be taken jointly by their attorneys. So, for example, you could have an instruction requesting that all property sale and purchase decisions must be unanimous decisions. Also, you could limit their power so that transactions involving assets worth over a certain value, for example, all investment sales and purchases in excess of £10,000 should be taken jointly.

Section 4: Replacement attorneys

As the form explains, 'Replacement attorneys are a back-up in case one of your original attorneys can't make decisions for you any more'. It is sensible to provide for this. If one of your original attorneys dies or they become mental incapable themselves then a replacement is helpful. However, surviving attorneys do not have the power to appoint others to act with them and the donor cannot appoint further attorneys if they no longer have capacity. If there is more than one replacement attorney then they will all step in and act at once. If they replace the original attorneys they will usually act jointly.

The Public Guardian v Miles [2014] EWCOP 40 showed that complications can arise; in this case, the Public Guardian's application to the court to determine whether the donor of an LPA can appoint more than one attorney to act jointly with survivorship by expressly reappointing the continuing attorney or attorneys.

Senior Judge Lush stated:

> '**27.** In order to create the effect of appointing more than one attorney to act jointly with survivorship, the donor could appoint A, B and C jointly to be the attorneys and appoint them subsequently to act jointly and severally. When one of the events mentioned in section 13(6) of the Mental Capacity Act 2005 occurred, which terminated the joint appointment, the joint and several appointment would come into operation and enable the surviving attorneys to continue to act.

> '**28.** However, because of the design of section 4 of the prescribed form, I do not think it would be possible to achieve this by appointing A, B and C to act jointly and severally as replacement attorneys in the same instrument. Having already ticked the box to appoint the original attorneys to act jointly, there is no facility for the donor to state that the replacement attorneys shall act jointly and severally.

> '**29.** In my view, the safest way of achieving the effect of joint attorneyship with survivorship would be for the donor to execute two LPAs: the first appointing the attorneys to act jointly, and the second appointing them to act jointly and severally with a condition that the second LPA will come into operation when the first LPA fails for any reason. The second LPA could also provide for the appointment of one or more replacement attorneys, if that is what the donor wishes.'

The court held that the donor of an LPA cannot appoint more than one attorney to act jointly with survivorship by expressly reappointing the continuing attorney or attorneys.

Section 5: When can your attorneys make decisions?

In the case of health and welfare LPAs the attorneys can only act when the LPA has been registered and the donor has lost their mental capacity. However, in respect of a financial decisions LPA, an attorney can act as soon as the LPA has been registered and before the donor has lost their mental capacity. The donor can decide this in this section.

Section 6: People to notify when the LPA is registered

This section is now optional. Originally the MCA 2005 introduced mandatory notice provision to replicate that required for registering an EPA. If a client did not want to provide notice to any other person then a second certificate provider was required. It seems that as a result of a desire by the OPG to make the forms as easy to complete as possible the second certificate provider requirement was dropped and necessarily the notice provisions are no longer a mandatory requirement. They do, however, remain a sensible protection for a client. The notice gives a third party (chosen by the donor) notice in form LP3 that the LPA is being registered either by the donor themselves or by an attorney. It gives details of who the attorneys are and how they have been appointed. It does not give details of any instructions or preferences the donor may have included in the LPA.

Objections to registration

The important aspect for protection purposes is that it gives the person notified a three-week period within which to object to the LPA being registered. Page 4 of the notice sets out the following factual and prescribed grounds on which to object:

'Factual objections:
- the donor or an attorney has died
- the donor and an attorney were married or had a civil partnership but have divorced or ended the civil partnership
- an attorney doesn't' have the mental capacity to be an attorney
- an attorney has chosen to stop acting (has disclaimed the appointment)
- the donor or an attorney is bankrupt, interim bankrupt or subject to a debt relief order
- the attorney is a trust corporation and is wound up or dissolved

A factual objection must be set out in form LPA007 and sent to the OPG

Prescribed objections:
- the LPA is not legally valid – for example if you do not believe that the donor had the mental capacity to make the LPA
- the donor cancelled their LPA when they had mental capacity to do so
- there was fraud or the donor was pressured to make the LPA

- an attorney is acting above their authority or against the donor's best interests.'

A prescribed objection can be made on Court of Protection form COP7 and must be sent to the court. Alternatively, it can be made on form LPA008 and sent to the OPG.

As practitioners will be aware, now that the rules have changed and a donor no longer needs to notify any one, an important safeguard has been removed. Interestingly, in the OPG's online guidance for making an LPA under the section 'Safeguards', the OPG explains that the OPG must be sure that the LPA is legally correct, has no errors and that people have had the opportunity to object if they have concerns. It is difficult to see how anyone can now object to an LPA being registered as they will be given no notice of its registration. Those who were fortunate enough to sign EPAs before October 2007 will still have that protection as the EPA rules provide that at least three members of their closest family must be informed when registration is about to take place. It seems a backward step at a time when safeguards should not only be kept in place but reinforced.

Section 7: Preference and instructions

This section is described on the form as optional. However, it is sensible for the client to consider specific instructions to their attorneys to assist and guide them in carrying out their responsibilities. The more detail the attorneys have, the better their decision-making should be. What are the differences between these?

Preferences

These are expressions of your wishes, guidance, values and choices. They are not legally binding on the attorneys but they should bear them in mind when taking decisions for the donor.

Examples of such preferences would include the following as suggested by the OPG:

- I would like to maintain a minimum balance of £1,000 in my current account.
- I prefer to invest in ethical funds.
- I would like my attorneys to consult my doctor if they believe I may not have the mental capacity to make decisions about my home.
- I would like to donate £100 each year to Age UK.

Other examples could include:

- I want to continue to give £250 each year to each of my children either at Christmas or on the occasion of their birthdays.

- I want my attorneys to pay for a taxi at least once a week for my friends and/ or members of my family to visit me either at home or in any care home to which I was then residing up to the limit of £20 per week.

- I want my attorneys to continue my annual subscription to ... magazine even if I have lost my mental capacity.

Instructions

These are matters that the attorneys must or must not do when making decisions for the donor.

The OPG provides the following examples:

- My attorneys must continue to make donations to charities that I have previously supported or for which I have set up standing order payments.

- My attorneys must not make gifts.

- My attorneys must not sell my home unless in my doctor's opinion I can no longer live independently.

- My attorneys must send annual accounts to my brother and sister.

- My attorneys must instruct a tax accountant to prepare my annual tax return.

- My attorneys must use AB Investment Management Limited who manage my investments.

- My attorneys must review my estate and tax on an annual basis.

It should be noted here that attorneys have very limited gift-making powers. As explained in Chapter 5A, the donor cannot authorise an attorney to go beyond such limits.

The following gifts cannot be authorised:

- gifts intended to reduce inheritance tax liability;

- trust funds for grandchildren;

- payment of school fees for grandchildren;

- interest-free loans to family;

- maintenance for any family member other than your wife, husband, civil partner or child under 18.

Section 8: Your legal rights and responsibilities

This sets out the rules by which the LPA is governed, that is, MCA 2005 and the MCA Code of Practice. This section also reminds the attorneys that they must follow the five principles of the Act and sets those out in detail. They are also reminded to act in the donor's best interests and that the LPA must be registered before it can be used.

Section 9: Donor

The donor must sign the LPA before anyone else signs it. Their witness must be independent of them and be present at the same time as the donor signs. The witness must complete the details of their full name and address.

Section 10: Certificate provider

Unlike EPAs, an LPA requires an independent person to certify various matters in connection with the donor of the LPA. This is the certificate provider (CP). The role is perhaps the most important one in this process and should be taken seriously by the parties. Their responsibilities are:

- to discuss the LPA with the donor;
- to ensure that the donor understands what they are doing;
- to ensure that nobody is forcing them to sign the LPA.

MCA 2005, Sch 1, para 2(e) provides for a certificate by a person of a prescribed description that, in his opinion, at the time when the donor executes the instrument:

- the donor understands the purpose of the instrument and the scope of the authority conferred under it;
- no fraud or undue pressure is being used to induce the donor to create a lasting power of attorney; and
- there is nothing else which would prevent a lasting power of attorney from being created by the instrument.

Who can be a CP?

Either:

- someone who has known the donor personally for at least two years (a friend, neighbour, colleague or former colleague); or
- someone with relevant professional skills such as the donor's GP, a healthcare professional or a solicitor.

There are certain categories of people who are barred from being the CP, including the attorney or replacement attorney, any member of the donor's or attorneys' families, or the owner, manager or employee of a care home in which the donor resides.

The boyfriend of an attorney could not act as a CP in a LPA because he was disqualified as a member of her family and lacked independence, the Court of Protection has found (*Phillips v The Public Guardian* [2012] MHLO 60).

Problems with capacity in which the CP is certifying are as follows:

(a) As the case of *Phillips* above indicates, the problem of who is independent of the donor or not and therefore can act as a CP. This may not now be detected by the OPG. It is no longer a requirement on the form introduced from 1 July 2015 to state in what capacity the CP is acting. The CP in that case had described himself as follows: 'I am the partner of [attorney] and have known [Mrs Phillips] for three years'.

(b) As the CP no longer has to state in what capacity they are acting it is almost impossible for the OPG to verify whether they are truly independent of the donor. It does seem short-sighted to remove the box in which the capacity was stated in the previous forms

Some statistics collated by Senior Judge Lush illustrated that even where professionals are involved in acting as the CP abuse can still occur. He reported that in a random sample of 100 cases that went to court, 18 CPs were friends of the donor and in 47 cases they were solicitors. Interestingly, GPs acted as CPs in only eight of those cases.

Section 11: Attorney or replacement

How do the clients know which choices to make and what provides the best level of protection? Experience suggests that greater protection is afforded where the client:

* appoints more than one attorney;

* sets out clear limits to decision-making;

* sets out wishes and preferences;

* provides for independent oversight of annual accounts;

* appoints a professional to act as one of the attorneys;

* ensures that there are limits to joint and several decisions (as mentioned above).

Clearly having a good understanding of your client's family situation is paramount in order to advise them regarding who would be suitable to act as financial attorneys. As we have seen above, there are some initial requirements that need to be clarified:

* Is the attorney over 18?

* Is the attorney bankrupt or subject to a debt order?

- Do the attorneys understand financial decision-making and in particular your finances?

What if the donor has signed an instrument that deviates from the prescribed form?

Even if the LPA is not in the prescribed form, MCA 2005, s 3 provides that where there are immaterial differences the form can still take effect as an LPA and, perhaps more importantly, it also states that 'the court may declare that an instrument which is not in the prescribed form is to be treated as if it were, if it is satisfied that the persons executing the instrument intended it to create a lasting power of attorney'.

An interesting example of this was *Re XZ* [2015] EWCOP 35. XZ was a wealthy individual with estate in several countries but who lived mainly in London. He executed an LPA for property and financial affairs and appointed attorneys to act jointly in respect of some decisions and jointly and severally in respect of others. He imposed restrictions and conditions running to seven continuation sheets and it was these that were the subject of the Court of Protection proceedings. The Public Guardian refused to register the LPA on the grounds that the conditions imposed an unreasonable fetter on the attorneys' power to act and were therefore ineffective as part of an LPA. The LPA contained, for example, a precondition that no attorney could act under the LPA unless:

- the attorneys reasonably believe at the time of the decision that XZ lacks capacity to make that decision himself; and

- there is a genuine financial need for the action which is under consideration.

The LPA went on to provide that if the above is satisfied then two additional hurdles had to be satisfied, including obtaining a psychiatrist's opinion and a time delay.

There was no doubt that the provisions were unusual, but it was purely designed to ensure that the attorneys did not act until XZ's incapacity had been properly confirmed. The court held that the LPA had been correctly completed on the prescribed form.

For the vast majority of individuals the standard form of LPA will be the form adopted. Where affairs are complex or multi-jurisdictional, involving various advisors and substantial wealth, the forms will need extending. This will mean that Section 7, which sets out instructions and preferences, could extend to several pages of binding instructions and non-binding wishes as in *XZ* above.

It is clear that an attorney should take seriously the statement on the LPA confirming that he has read the prescribed information on the form, and that they understand the duties imposed on them under MCA 2005, ss 1 and 4. In particular, that they have a duty to act based on the principles of the Act and to have regard to the MCA Code of Practice. They must also confirm that they will act in the best interests of the donor. As we shall see, this is a big undertaking for any attorney. The Code of Practice itself is nearly 300 pages long. It is most unlikely that any attorneys will have read the Code, which surely they would need to do in order to meet this obligation.

Professional advisers would be well advised to stress test their client's choice of attorneys. Some simple but effective questions would be a start. For example:

(1) Family appointees:

    (a) bankruptcy search;

    (b) financial acumen;

    (c) how they manage their own finances;

    (d) timely bill payments;

    (e) savings rates checking;

    (f) investment management;

    (g) bank account;

    (h) property management;

    (i) pension decisions;

    (j) document – wills, pension, life assurance paperwork – and whether they have an LPA themselves.

(2) Friend appointees

    All as above, but also:

    (a) How well do you really know them?

(3) Professional appointees:

    (a) Has the client considered what charges the professional can make for acting?

    (b) Will there be annual accounting of all financial decisions?

    (c) Who will keep records of important decisions?

What can be done if the client wants to revoke the LPA?

How this is done depends on what stage has been reached. See below as to how the rules operate.

(1) *If the client has capacity and the LPA has not been registered:* the donor can execute a deed of revocation. They should inform the attorneys and recover any copies. The LPA can be revoked as a whole or partially; for example, the donor could revoke the appointment of an attorney.

(2) *If the client has capacity and the LPA has been registered:* As the LPA has been registered, an application to the OPG must be made in form the donor can execute a deed of revocation. They should inform the attorneys and recover any copies. The LPA can be revoked as a whole or partially; for example, the donor could revoke the appointment of an attorney. In this case the deed of revocation must be sent to the OPG so that the LPA's registration can also be cancelled.

The wording suggested by the OPG is as follows:

'I granted a lasting power of attorney for Property and Financial Affairs/Health and Welfare (delete as appropriate) on [date you signed the lasting power of attorney] appointing [name of first attorney] of [address of first attorney] and [name of second attorney] of [address of second attorney] to act as my attorney(s).

'I revoke the lasting power of attorney and the authority granted by it.

'Signed and delivered as a deed [your signature] Date signed [date] Witnessed by [signature of witness] Full name of witness [name of witness] Address of witness [address of witness]'

(3) *If the client does not have capacity and the LPA has not been registered:* It is therefore impossible for the client to revoke the LPA. The donor must have mental capacity to execute a deed of revocation. The LPA will remain in place and should be registered. If the donor objects to the use of the LPA by the attorneys then an application to the Court of Protection will be required to resolve the problem.

(4) *If the client does not have capacity and the LPA has been registered:* As in (3) above, the LPA cannot be revoked by the donor once they have lost their capacity.

MCA 2005, s 13 provides the rules whereby an LPA can be revoked automatically on the occurrence of particular events. As we have seen above, the bankruptcy of the donor will also have the effect of automatically revoking the LPA.

The other events are:

- the disclaimer of the appointment by the attorney;

- the death of the attorney;

- bankruptcy of the attorney;

- the making of a debt relief order in respect of the attorney or, if the attorney is a trust corporation, its winding-up or dissolution;

- the dissolution or annulment of a marriage or civil partnership between the donor and the attorney;

- the attorney losing capacity.

The LPA will also come to an end if the sole attorney is removed by the Court of Protection under the Court's revocation power in MCA 2005, s 22(4)(b):

The court may, if the patient lacks capacity to do so, revoke the instrument or the lasting power of attorney.

The factual tests to be met are set out in s 22(3):

(3) Subsection (4) applies if the court is satisfied—

(a) that fraud or undue pressure was used to induce P—

(i) to execute an instrument for the purpose of creating a lasting power of attorney, or

(ii) to create a lasting power of attorney, or

(b) that the donee (or, if more than one, any of them) of a lasting power of attorney—

(i) has behaved, or is behaving, in a way that contravenes his authority or is not in P's best interests, or

(ii) proposes to behave in a way that would contravene his authority or would not be in P's best interests.

The discretion has to be exercised in accordance with ss 1(5)–(6):

(5) An act done, or decision made, under this Act for or on behalf of a person who lacks capacity must be done, or made, in his best interests and

(6) Before the act is done, or the decision is made, regard must be had to whether the purpose for which it is needed can be as effectively achieved in a way that is less restrictive of the person's rights and freedom of action.

What kind of decisions can an attorney appointed for property and affairs take?

The MCA Code of Practice lists the following activities:

7.36

- buying or selling property;

- opening, closing or operating any bank, building society or other account;

- giving access to the donor's financial information;

- claiming, receiving and using (on the donor's behalf) all benefits, pensions, allowances and rebates (unless the Department for Work and Pensions has already appointed someone and everyone is happy for this to continue);

- receiving any income, inheritance or other entitlement on behalf of the donor;

- dealing with the donor's tax affairs;

- paying the donor's mortgage, rent and household expenses;

- insuring, maintaining and repairing the donor's property;

- investing the donor's savings;

- making limited gifts on the donor's behalf;

- paying for private medical care and residential care or nursing home fees;

- applying for any entitlement to funding for NHS care, social care or adaptations;

- using the donor's money to buy a vehicle or any equipment or other help they need;

- repaying interest and capital on any loan taken out by the donor.

Delegation by the attorney

An attorney may not delegate their authority to another person without being expressly authorised by the donor in the LPA. Each decision they take must be taken personally.

See *The Public Guardian v Marvin* [2014] EWCOP 47, where the 25-year-old sole attorney under an LPA effectively delegated his decision-making to his mother, who was not an attorney.

A common example that arises here is where investments are managed by an investment manager. The LPA must state that the attorney can continue to use that investment manager. A suitable clause to deal with this in the LPA would be as follows:

'My attorneys may transfer my investments into a discretionary management scheme. Or, if I already had investments in a discretionary management scheme before I lost capacity to make financial decisions, I want the scheme to continue. I understand in both cases that managers of the scheme will make investment decisions and my investments will be held in their names or the names of their nominees.'

Cases of abuse by attorneys under an LPA

In *DP (Revocation of Lasting Power of Attorney), Re* [2014] EWCOP B4, the attorney (DP) had failed to keep proper accounts and financial records and was in breach of his fiduciary duties as an attorney. DP had, amongst other things, made a gift to himself of £38,000.

In *Public Guardian v DH* [2014] EWCOP 15 the attorney arranged a loan to renovate attorney's partner's property. This drew the following comment:

'The Public Guardian's position is that, if VH had the necessary capacity and was aware of her financial affairs and the low level of her accessible capital, she would have been unlikely to enter into a mortgage which incurred fees to be paid from her account on a monthly instalment basis, which would add an additional burden to an account which already had a low balance and she had little or no other reserve to call upon. Therefore it is the Public Guardian's view that DH has breached his fiduciary duty by making an unapproved and excessive gift which has substantially depleted VH's capital.'

In *OL, Re* [2015] EWCOP 41 a costs order departed from the usual rule because of the attorney's conduct. OL's maisonette in Stockwell was sold for £730,000 on 23 May 2014. The property in which she subsequently with her daughter, DA (one of the attorneys under an LPA), was bought for £430,000 entirely with OL's funds.

OL and the two attorneys had subsequently executed a declaration of trust stating that OL had only a 20% share in the property (worth £86,000), whereas the attorneys, neither of whom had contributed anything towards the purchase price, had a 40% share each. This represented an outright gift of £172,000 to each of the attorneys. £127,885 of OL's money was used to pay off DA's mortgage on her former home in South Norwood, which she still owns. It was divided into two flats, one of which was let at a rent of £850 a month. A further £80,000 of OL's money was spent on building work and a loft conversion at DA's property in South Norwood.

In a period of six months OL had gone from having a property worth £730,000 to having only £7,000 in her bank account plus, of course, a 20% share of the house in Croydon. The attorneys were not acting in the donor's best interests and had contravened their authority. The power was revoked and a panel deputy appointed.

In *DWA, Re* [2015] EWCOP 72, one of the three LPA attorneys breached her fiduciary duty as an attorney by taking advantage of her position and obtaining a personal benefit from her position. She also continued to receive a carer's allowance after her mother was admitted into residential care. She also failed to account satisfactorily for all the transactions she had carried out on her mother's behalf as an attorney. In particular, there were several inconsistencies in her evidence as to amounts expended for which she had retained no receipts or other records; and contravened the duty to keep her money separate from the donor's. The court revoked her appointment as an attorney.

Statistics

The OPG annual report for 2015/16 reported significant volumes of powers of attorneys being registered:

Applications for registration	2014/15	2015/16	Increase
EPAs	14,970	13,792	−7.87%
LPAs	394,079	533,229	+35.31%
Total	**409,049**	**547,021**	**+33.73%**

At the end of the year they reported a total of 1,870,393 powers of attorney registered with the OPG.

These statistics show the phenomenal take up of LPAs. It also shows what a considerable job the OPG will have in the future. The take-up is good news for those donors who have taken the trouble to consider carefully who they are appointing to manage their property and financial affairs when capacity has gone. It also demonstrates potential supervision problems and, as we will see in the final chapters of this book, strengthening the OPG's powers to supervise those attorneys should be at the forefront of future developments.

Deputyship

If a person has neither an enduring power of attorney (EPA) nor a lasting power of attorney (LPA) for property and financial decisions, an application will need to be made for the appointment of a deputy to manage their affairs. If, however, the patient's estate comprises only income from social security benefits and they have no property or savings then a deputyship appointment is not required. A DWP appointee can manage their benefits on their behalf.

In all other cases where a patients' assets are over a specified amount, where a sale of their property is required in the future, or where their income or capital is such that management is required, then a deputyship application should be made.

By virtue of MCA 2005, s 16(2) the Court of Protection may:

- by making an order, make the decision or decisions on P's behalf in relation to the matter or matters; or

- appoint a person (a 'deputy') to make decisions on P's behalf in relation to the matter or matters.

Sub-section 4 provides that when deciding whether it is in P's best interests to appoint a deputy, the court must have regard to the principles that:

- a decision by the court is to be preferred to the appointment of a deputy to make a decision; and

- the powers conferred on a deputy should be as limited in scope and duration as is reasonably practicable in the circumstances.

In practice, this means that the court will prefer to take one-off decisions rather than appointing a full-time deputy to act. However, the reality is that if a client did not sign an EPA or LPA before they lost their mental capacity then a deputy does need to be appointed where their estate needs careful management.

It is by no means clear as to who is the most appropriate person to undertake this role. Very often it is the person who puts themselves forward who has the best chance of being appointed – that is, provided that they meet the court's suitability requirements.

Different types of deputies

- Lay deputies – these are usually close relatives or friends of the patient.

- Professional deputies – these are appointed usually from specialist solicitors who maintain a Court of Protection practice. They will step to assist a client who has not appointed an attorney and has no close relatives or friends able or willing to undertake the task.

- Panel deputies – those on the appointed panel of deputies who will be called on by the Court to step in where a deputy is required for example where a power of attorney has been revoked by the court and the attorney is no longer permitted to act.

- Local authority deputies – these will act in most cases where the estate is not large but there are assets that need managing and usually the patient is in the care home whose fees need to be paid.

'The Fundamental Review of the Supervision of Court Appointed Deputies' (2014)

In December 2014 the OPG reported to Parliament in their report, 'The Fundamental Review of the Supervision of Court Appointed Deputies'. This commented that the OPG's supervision caseload had more than doubled since the commencement of the MCA 2005 and this growth was predicted to continue. The number of new deputy orders received by OPG is approximately 12,000 a year, with about 10,000 cases concluding each year. The average time that an order is active is 3.5 years. The current number of orders being supervised is over 51,000. This was expected to grow with the ageing population.

The OPG then introduced a new model providing proportionate oversight, building engagement around the needs of the deputy and OPG's judgement of risk in the case at any given time. Where issues are raised, they will be investigated and managed swiftly. The OPG reported at para 53 of the Review that the design of the new model will include:

- Better information to the general public about the need to create an LPA.

- Better guidance to people who apply to the Court of Protection.

- Early OPG contact shortly after the deputyship order – for lay deputies and new professional deputies.

- A digital communication channel option, designed to ease the deputy's burden and improve the two-way contact.

- Targeted visits to those deputies who need face-to-face support.

- Standards for professional and local authority deputies which set out good practice.

- An emphasis on assurance visits to professional and local authority deputies.

- Staff who specialise in their deputy type, who take an end-to-end issue resolution approach to their allocated cases, who build relationships with their deputies, and who are trained, qualified and accountable, sustained by the entire resources available to the OPG to support and supervise their deputies.

- Evidence-based risk assessments conducted throughout the lifetime of the case, resulting in risk ratings (Red, Amber, Green) which will be transparent and will determine the extent of OPG's engagement.

- Compliance and investigations resources, which will be more closely engaged with case managers in order to maintain the circle of knowledge, action, lessons learned.

- Improved legal resources and support.

- Continuous improvement culture.

- Better control of professional deputy charges through annual plans; asset inventories; estimates of charges; fuller annual reporting; and the better understanding of the professional deputy caseload resulting from the specialist teams building their knowledge and relationships.

- New back-office technology supporting the case managers effectively and efficiently.

This new model now provides specialist end-to-end deputyship support and supervision teams for the four following separate categories:

(1) lay deputies;

(2) local authority deputies;

(3) professional and panel deputies;

(4) health and welfare cases.

Who will the court appoint as a lay deputy?

A deputy must be over the age of 18; they must consent to the appointment; and must not be someone who is being paid for caring for the patient. They must have the necessary skills, knowledge and commitment to carry out the tasks and duties of a deputy.

Duties of a deputy

They must:

- abide by the MCA 2005's statutory principles as set out in s 1;

- make decisions in the patient's best interests;

- have regard to the guidance in the MCA code of practice;
- only make decisions that the court has authorised them to make.

The duties

The deputy's duties are as follows:

- duty of care;
- fiduciary duty;
- duty not to delegate;
- duty of good faith;
- duty of confidentiality;
- duty to comply with the directions of the Court of Protection;
- duty to keep accounts; and
- duty to keep the patient's money and property separate.

The application

An applicant applying to become a deputy must complete and or provide the following forms:

- COP1: Application form: this details what the application relates to, the applicant and patient's details and to whom notice of the application should be given.

- COP1A: Annex A Supporting information for property and affairs applications: this sets out full details of the patient's income and assets, and damages or compensation awards, investments, property and expenditure.

- COP3: Assessment of Capacity: this must be partially completed by the applicant and then handed to the assessor – usually a medical practitioner for completion.

- COP4: Deputy's declaration: this provides details about the applicant including their financial circumstances. In particular, it asks about any judgement debts and bankruptcy orders and in addition whether it is likely that their own financial interests might conflict with those of the patient. There are a total of 17 separate undertakings that the applicant must complete. These include undertakings not to delegate their powers to another person unless expressly authorised by the Court, to visit the patient regularly, and keep accounts of dealings and transactions.

The Court of Protection will review the application and make a decision 14 days after the applicant has told the other people involved that the application has been made – provided the application was complete and no one objected.

The court will tell them if:

- the application has been approved or rejected;
- you have to provide more information to support your application, for example a report from social services;
- it is going to hold a hearing to get more information.

You then must give notice to the patient and other close relatives (if any).

You'll be sent a 'court order' telling you what you can and can't do as a deputy. You can start acting on behalf of the person:

- as soon as you're appointed if you're a personal welfare deputy;
- when you pay a 'security bond' – a type of insurance to protect the person's money – if you're a property and affairs deputy.

Problems that arise

The cases that come to the attention of the Court of Protection are the cases that cannot be resolved by any other means. Where it is a straightforward case of the deputy using the patient's money to fund their own expenditure, house repairs or mortgages then this is pure financial abuse and the court removes the deputy from acting.

In extreme cases such as *Re GM, MJ and JM v The Public Guardian* [2013] COPLR 290, the deputies clearly pillaged the patient's funds to pay for their extravagant lifestyles.

In *London Borough of Haringey v CM* [2014] EWCOP B23 the court found that the applicant applying to be a deputy was someone who had been taking advantage of an elderly relative – in this case there were suggestions of undue influence in getting him to sign a will in her favour and spending up to £28,000 on unaccounted for expenditure. The court concluded that such an applicant was clearly not suited to being appointed as his deputy. The court found that: (a) the weight of evidence showed that CM was unable to put his interests first; and (b) CM had also been unable to recognise when her actions had not been in his best interests.

In *Re HC* [2015] EWCOP 29 the deputy spent money on renovating his mother's property which exceeded the scope of the deputyship order and expenses of £1,300 per month. There accounting was also vague, which led to concerns being raised about the deputyship reports. The court approved the payments retrospectively as the deputy could show the benefit to his mother of being cared for at his home and that the payments made to the deputy were not unreasonable in the circumstances.

PAW, Re (appointment of a deputy) [2015] EWCOP 57 sets out considerations for appointing deputies.

Disputes as to who is to be a deputy

See, for example, the following cases.

Re FT [2015] EWCOP 49 confirmed the appointment of the deputies. Here the factor of magnetic importance was that the patient had appointed the deputies also as the executors. It should also be noted that the behaviour of the deputies had a direct impact on the resulting costs order made by the court. In this case the applicants did not file responses or turn up for the hearing. The costs order departed from the usual rule, but the court agreed an interest-free loan (for the costs) from the estate to be paid on the patient's death.

Re AW [2015] EWCOP 16 involved competing applications for deputy appointments.

David and Barry v Peter [2014] EWCOP 31 was a dispute about who should be a deputy. Peter disagreed with decisions being made and was described as a serial complainer by the judge. Furthermore, he lived too far away from the patient. The court confirmed that the other applicants should be appointed. The tone here was important. It was also a matter of attitude and approach.

In conclusion, there does appear to be some evidence to show that the appointment of a deputy provides much more security for a patient and their finances than appointing someone as an attorney. This may seem controversial, but the cases show that where there is annual supervision in place coupled with annual reports and accounts to be submitted then the deputy's actions are subject to annual scrutiny. An attorney, on the other hand, will be under no obligation to submit accounts to the OPG (although they are under a duty to keep accounts), they do not need to take out a security bond, nor do they have to have visits from the OPG to see how they manage the donor's affairs. It is only when the OPG is informed that there may be problems with an attorney that the OPG will start investigating an attorney's management of finances.

When Attorneys Fall Out, What can the Courts Do?

We should all take considerable care to ensure that our clients understand the powers of attorney they want to sign. Do we, however, spend enough time with them considering the suitability of their choice of attorneys? Frequently clients will want to appoint their children to be their attorneys and sometimes sibling rivalry can get the better of them. When this happens it is worth reminding ourselves as to the differences in law as the treatment of enduring powers of attorney (EPA) and lasting powers of attorney (LPA).

If an EPA has been registered due to the onset of the donor's mental capacity then the Court of Protection that must take steps to revoke the power. The court then directs the Office of the Public Guardian (OPG) to cancel its registration (see Mental Capacity Act 2005 (MCA 2005), Sch 4, para 16(4)(g)). The court must direct the Public Guardian to cancel the registration of an instrument registered under Sch 4, para 13 'where it is satisfied that having regard to all the circumstances and in particular the attorney's relationship to or connection with the donor, the attorney is unsuitable to be the donor's attorney'.

Revoking a registered EPA

An EPA may be revoked by the court where it is satisfied that:

- fraud or undue pressure was used to induce the donor to create the EPA;

- the attorney is unsuitable to be the donor's attorney, having regard to all the circumstances, and in particular the attorney's relationship to or connection with the donor.

A number of cases considered the concept of unsuitability in the context of disputes between attorneys or their siblings, culminating in *Re F* [2004] 3 All ER 277, in which Patten J said that removing an attorney because of hostility from a sibling or other relative must, in the absence of effective challenge to that attorney's competence or integrity, be on the basis of clear evidence that the continuing hostility will impede the proper administration of the donor's affairs or cause significant distress to the donor.

Revoking a registered LPA

There are some differences in the way that LPAs can be revoked. Under MCA 2005, s 22(3) and (4) an LPA can be revoked if:

- the attorney (or if more than one, any of them) has behaved, or proposes to behave in a way that contravenes his authority or is not in the donor's best interests; and
- the donor lacks capacity to revoke the LPA.

Clearly the Law Commission felt that linking the revocation of an LPA to a best-interests decision was preferable to deciding it on the grounds of the suitability or otherwise of an attorney or attorneys.

In both cases the donor will have lost their capacity and it is noted that entirely separate problems arises when someone has mental capacity but refuses to revoke their power of attorney due to other vulnerabilities.

The Law Commission's report number 231, 'Mental Capacity', published in 1995, concluded: 'We therefore think it necessary to stress, by way of an explicit provision, that a donor should always retain the power to revoke his or her [LPA]'. However, this does present problems where a donor is subject to pressure or undue influence but still has capacity.

There could be instances where an attorney could be deemed unsuitable to act as an EPA attorney but would be suitable as an LPA attorney.

An LPA can be revoked by any one of the following methods:

- deed of revocation;
- express notice to the attorney.

Revocation by the donor

It is best practice to revoke an LPA by deed. This provides clear evidence of the revocation to all interested parties.

The donor must notify the attorneys and the OPG that the LPA is revoked (Lasting Powers of Attorney, Enduring Powers of Attorney and Public Guardian Regulations 2007, SI 2007/1253, Reg 21).

Revocation by the Court

If the donor does not have capacity to revoke the LPA, the Court of Protection can revoke it on his behalf (MCA 2005, s 22(4)(b)). The court may only revoke an LPA on the donor's behalf if:

- fraud or undue pressure was applied to the donor to make him create the LPA;

- the attorney has behaved, or is proposing to behave, in a way that is not in the donor's best interests.

In the Law Commission's report, 'The Incapacitated Principal' (Law Com No 122) published in 1983, which explains the policy behind the 1985 Act. Paragraph 4.49, so far as material, states as follows:

'This needs some explanation. It would amount in effect to a criticism of the donor's choice of attorney. But we would not wish this ground to be sustained merely because the attorney was not the sort of person that a particular relative would have chosen. It is our wish that the donor's choice of attorney should carry considerable weight. Thus, for example, a mother might be content to appoint her son as her EPA attorney despite being aware of a conviction for theft. We would not want her choice of attorney to be upset simply because a particular relative would not want the son to be his attorney. The question should be whether the particular attorney is suitable to act as attorney for the particular donor. In short, the Court should examine carefully all the circumstances – particularly the relationship between donor and attorney.'

See also the judgment of Mr Jules Sher QC (sitting as a Deputy Judge of this Division) in the case of *Re W (Enduring Power of Attorney)* [2000] Ch 343. This was a case in which there was hostility between the donor's children. He considered the unsuitability of the attorneys in the context of hostility between various members of the donor's family. In this case the donor, Mrs W, appointed her daughter to be her attorney under her EPA. Her other two children objected to the registration of the EPA on the grounds that their mother lacked the capacity to execute the EPA and secondly that the attorney daughter was an unsuitable choice in the light of the dispute between the siblings.

'The second ground of unsuitability is the hostility between the three children. The Master concluded that that fact alone rendered any one of them unsuitable to be Mrs. W's attorney. In my judgment such hostility may well have such consequences but it all depends upon the circumstances. For example, had the estate of Mrs W been complex and had it required strategic decisions in relation to its administration, one would expect the attorney to have had to consult and work with her siblings in relation to the administration. In such circumstances the evident hostility between them would impact adversely on the stewardship of the attorney, no matter who was at fault in creating the hostility in the first place.

'But in this case the estate is simple … In other words there is nothing of any significance left to be done. The assets are under proper control. The income simply needs to be fed through to the nursing home. The evidence is that this has been done by Mrs X very efficiently. She has indicated more than once that she has never intended to charge for her services under the power of attorney and she does not intend to do so. Against this, if the Public

Trustee were to come in, there would be an appointment fee and an annual fee of between £2,350 and £3,600 per annum. If a solicitor were appointed the total cost would be likely to be somewhat less than that.

'It seems to me that it is not right to say that (irrespective of the background) hostility of the kind we have seen in this case between the children renders any one of them unsuitable to be Mrs W's attorney. In this case the hostility will not impact adversely on the administration. It would, in my judgment, be quite wrong to frustrate Mrs W's choice of attorney in this way. Whether it is or is not a good idea for a parent in Mrs W's position, when such hostility exists, to appoint one child alone as attorney is another question. But Mrs W did so and, on the evidence, did so knowing of the hostility. That is her prerogative and in my judgment, when the hostility does not interfere with the smooth running of the administration, the court should not interfere of the ground of unsuitability.'

That decision was subsequently upheld by the Court of Appeal, in *Re W (Enduring Power of Attorney)* [2001] 2 WLR 957, and was applied by Mr Justice Patten, in *Re F* [2004] 3 All ER 277. Here he said:

'It seems to me that to remove a chosen attorney because of hostility from a sibling or other relative, in the absence of any effective challenge to his competence or integrity, should require clear evidence either that the continuing hostility will impede the proper administration of the estate or will cause significant distress to the donor which would be avoided by the appointment of a receiver.'

There have been various other cases before the Court of Protection illustrating this problem.

Re RG [2015] EWCOP 2

RG appointed his second wife and his two step-children, PB and JW, to be his attorneys. He had four children from his first marriage. He lost his capacity and PB registered the EPA at the OPG. The relationship between the two attorneys was extremely poor and PB consistently excluded JW from acting as an attorney. JW objected to the OPG about PB's handling of the attorneyship including outstanding care home fees.

The Public Guardian challenged PB's competence as an attorney.

Judge Denzil Lush stated:

'I am satisfied that PB has contravened his authority and failed to act in RG's best interests and that, having regard to all the circumstances, he is unsuitable to be RG's attorney. He may be an affectionate and attentive stepson, but that's not the point. He has been a hopeless attorney, and has broken almost every rule in the book, and I sense that he has done so wilfully.'

He also referred to the rights, will and preference of the donor in accordance with Article 12.4 of the United Nations Convention on the Rights of Persons with Disabilities. Nevertheless, RG did not revoke JW's appointment as one of his attorneys, which, of course, he could have done, while he still retained capacity. The judge identified that there were strategic decisions (as in *Re W*) that would need to be made about the donor's property and for each of those decisions JW would have to consult and work closely with her brother, PB.

The judge decided that despite misgivings, 'I uphold my original decision to limit the registration of the EPA to JW acting as the sole attorney because':

(a) it was a less restrictive alternative to the appointment of a deputy;

(b) it complies with resolution 1859 (the Assembly of the Council of Europe) on protecting human rights and dignity by respecting the previously expressed wishes of patients;

(c) there was 'no evidence to suggest that JW would act other than in RG's best interests';

(d) JW will be acting gratuitously and therefore cheaper than those of an independent deputy;

(e) if the hostility between the siblings does interfere with the smooth running of the administration of RG's affairs, the court can then consider the appointment of a deputy of last resort; and

(f) it was in RG's best interests.

Re ED [2015] EWCOP 26

ED appointed her two daughters, JD and GB, to be her attorneys jointly under an EPA. They detested each other. Furthermore, the only communication between them was by email, and usually this was 'rancorous in tone'.

JD applied to register the EPA and she completed a form EP2PG, in which she stated that the attorneys had been appointed to act jointly and severally. She knew that this statement was false.

The judge said:

'In my judgment, any attorney who dishonestly attempts to undermine the registration procedure by making a statement she knows to be false is unsuitable to be the donor's attorney. JD is no exception and, notwithstanding the natural love and affection between them and the undoubted support she has provided to her mother in recent years, I find her unsuitable to be the donor's attorney.'

'In addition, I consider that JD and GB are both unsuitable to be their mother's attorneys, and also unsuitable to be her deputies for property and affairs, because of the intense acrimony between them.'

There were strategic decisions to be made, such as the sale of the house in Marlow, and the obvious hostility between the two sisters would almost certainly have a negative impact on the administration of ED's estate. Each would wilfully try to frustrate any action or decision initiated by the other and nothing would ever be achieved.

The judge said that the appointment of an independent person was not merely desirable but essential and, having regard to all the circumstances, including ED's advanced age, her anticipated life expectancy and the extent of her assets, it was unlikely that the additional costs incurred would be disproportionate. He therefore revoked the EPA and appointed a panel deputy to act in place of the attorneys.

Re KJP [2016] EWCOP 6

K signed an EPA appointing his son N and daughter J as his attorneys jointly and severally in respect of his property and affairs. He then remarried. His attorneys applied to register his EPA to which the OPG received no objections. Some months later his attorneys decided to restrict his access to his income and to his capital. The relationship with his attorneys deteriorated and he then executed a deed of revocation of the EPA.

The case demonstrated that where a donor has mental capacity to revoke his EPA he should be allowed to do so. His attorneys provided no evidence to suggest he had lost that capacity and therefore the court was bound to respect his wishes and cancel the registration by virtue of MCA 2005, Sch 4, para 16(3). The court also acknowledged that his children were no longer suitable to act as his attorneys because the relationship between the donor and the attorneys had broken down irreparably and their continued involvement in the management of his affairs was causing him embarrassment and distress.

Re EL (revoking a Lasting Power of Attorney) [2015] EWCOP 30

EL signed an LPA for property and financial affairs, appointing her daughter and son as her attorneys jointly. However, the attorneys did not trust each other and had differing views as to their mother's finances and care provision. Each made complaints against the other to the OPG.

The judge said:

'Because they cannot be trusted to act in the manner and for the purposes for which the LPA was intended, I am satisfied that the attorneys have behaved in a way that is not in the donor's best interests.

'I am also satisfied that they have contravened their authority by making gifts to themselves from their mother's funds, which are far in excess of the limited authority conferred upon attorneys generally by section 12 of the Mental Capacity Act.

'The outcome is the same as it would have been if EL had executed an EPA, instead of an LPA, and I had found that, having regard to all the circumstances, the attorneys are unsuitable to be her attorneys, but the methodology is different. In addition, I have to be satisfied that EL lacks the capacity to revoke the power of attorney herself, whereas this is not a requirement under the EPA legislation. The Court revoked the LPA and requested that a panel deputy should take over the attorney's roles.'

In conclusion, clients should be challenged on their choices of attorneys. Your discussion with them needs to be thought-provoking and focus on the specific people they intend to appoint. The clients will assume that their children are beyond reproach and the only sensible appointees. You need to open up the discussion by asking them: is there any existing sibling rivalry? Do they have any financial difficulties? Is there anyone who may put pressure on them concerning the management of their property and finances? Is there, rather, someone more independent with a proven financial track record who may be better choice?

Chapter 8

Other Issues

8A

Care Allowances

The subject of care allowances frequently features in the cases heard in the Court of Protection. It is easy to see why. Where a deputy or attorney has been appointed to act on behalf of another in managing their financial affairs they must act in the best interests of the patient or donor. If the appointee is paying themselves an 'allowance' from their funds then they are making a gift to themselves. Gifts are strictly controlled by the rules of the Court. In addition, the deputy or attorney is acting in the role of a fiduciary and as such owes a duty to the patient or donor not to profit from their position, take advantage of them, or put themselves in a position where their personal interests come into conflict with those of the person they should be protecting.

Problems from case law

In *Re HC* [2015] EWCOP 29 the deputy had failed to submit report forms for three years. The OPG investigation team discovered that he had provided himself with £1,300 per month out of the patient's funds for the care he provided. In addition, there were property renovation costs and deputyship expenses. The OPG found that he could not account for the expenditure and requested that he produce full accounts of his spending. However, he impressed the court with his explanation of the spending and was given retrospective approval of payments to date and the sum of £1,500 per month for future payments.

In *Re AGR* [2015] EWCOP 73 Lush SJ decided to revoke the appointment of two deputies where their combined expenses claim for £5,400 in the 2014/15 report for '"travelling expenses to and from care home approx 20 miles round trip by taxi two-three times weekly", when the care home manager states that, according to her records, the deputies have only visited their father three times in the last twelve months'.

Reasonable expenses

If the order appointing the deputy does not contain a clause providing for the deputy to receive payments from the patient's estate then the deputy is only permitted his reasonable expenses as set out in MCA 2005, s 19(7). This provides that a deputy is entitled to be reimbursed out of P's property for his reasonable expenses in discharging his functions, and if the court so directs when appointing him, to remuneration out of P's property for discharging them.

The MCA Code of Practice provides at para 7.60 that:

> 'A fiduciary duty means attorneys must not take advantage of their position. Nor should they put themselves in a position where their personal interests conflict with their duties. They also must not allow any other influences to affect the way in which they act as an attorney. Decisions should always benefit the donor, and not the attorney. Attorneys must not profit or get any personal benefit from their position, apart from receiving gifts where the Act allows it, whether or not it is at the donor's expense.'

What are care allowances or family care payments?

These are usually a combination of the following:

Remuneration for care support work – In *Re WVP (Deceased) and EP* [2015] EWCOP 84 (see below) the court allowed the payment for this. The attorneys' care and support allowed both parents to live at home for as long as possible and in the case of the father until his death.

Travel expenses – In *Re WVP* the mileage rates claimed were heavily discounted to reflect the fact that they were not on business and, where dealing with an elderly incapacitated relative, common decency would expect to ensure that the attorney does not profit from their position.

Remuneration for acting as an attorney – In *Re WVP* such a payment was disallowed. The court decided that there was nothing exceptional about the work carried out as an attorney as compared with care support work.

Hourly rates – In *Re HNL* [2015] EWCOP 77 the expert there quoted an hourly rate for care but noted that this would normally be discounted by 20% to acknowledge that neither national insurance not income tax is payable on amounts paid to carers.

Amount – In *Re WVP* the court agreed the sum of £150 per month that the attorneys were claiming. These were shown to be in their mother's best interests because:

- the services they provided were reasonably required to meet their parents' care needs, as were the services they continued to provide for their mother;
- the payments were currently affordable and sustainable;
- they represented a considerable saving on the commercial cost of providing these services; and

- in the absence of any express provision made by the donors in their EPAs for the attorneys to be remunerated for acting as attorneys and to be rewarded for providing care support services, these payments strike a reasonable balance between ensuring that Theresa and Stephen were neither financially disadvantaged by acting as their parents' attorneys, nor actually making a profit from their position.

In *HC, Re* [2015] EWCOP 29, the senior judge of the Court of Protection approached payments for care in the same way as a court would do when hearing a personal injury claim – by allowing a commercial rate, discounted by 20% because the payment is not taxable. He also provided for annual increases in line with the Annual Survey of Hours and Earnings (ASHE) 6145 – carers and home carers.

In *A, Re* [2015] EWCOP 46, the senior judge took into account the views of a professional deputy and found that the deputy had carefully gone through the checklist of matters to be taken into account when making a best interests decision.

In April 2016 the OPG issued a Practice Note that sets out the legal framework and the Public Guardian's view of how deputies should approach family care payments, including factors for them to consider when deciding on the level of such payments.

Note that the guidance only applies to financial affairs deputies and not health and welfare deputies. Similarly, the Practice Note does not apply to attorneys under a LPA or EPA as their powers will be dependent on the terms of the power of attorney which appointed them. However, there is no doubt that the OPG take similar factors into account when considering the actions of attorneys as they would for a deputy. For this reason, it is sensible to consider the guidance for both deputies and attorneys when taking best interests decisions for their donors in respect of care payments.

OPG Practice Note

Factors to consider

In deciding if family care payments are in the client's best interests, deputies should take the following factors into account:

- The care must be reasonably required to meet the client's needs and be of a good standard. If in doubt, the deputy may need to seek a care assessment from social services. If there has been any litigation claim for damages, the deputy should consider the level of care recommended by experts in the course of the litigation claim.

- The payments must be affordable, taking into account the client's resources, age and life expectancy. If the payments cannot be met out of the client's income, deputies must consider the effect on capital, having in mind the client's future care needs.

- Payments must properly reflect the input by the family/carer. There should be some evidence of how the care payment has been calculated in relation to the degree of care being provided. If the client is a very young child, deputies should consider whether care is over and above what a parent would normally give.

- The care must be actually provided. Temporary interruptions in provision of care, for example if the client is in hospital, do not mean the payments need to stop, but long-term changes in the client's living arrangements that affect the amount of care being provided must be considered – for example, a permanent move to a care home or supported living arrangement.

- Deputies should consider payments alongside the level of professional care in place, ie they should be necessary to supplement professional care.

- Payments should represent a saving on the cost of professional care.

- Payments should take into account any other contributions the client makes towards the running of the household or paying bills. Payments may need to be adjusted down if the carer is living in the client's property rent-free or is receiving other income.

- Payments should take into account the overall family situation; for example, whether anyone is in gainful employment. If two parents are providing care, what is their respective contribution? If the client needs two people at any time to manage their needs, payments may need to increase to reflect this.

- Payments should be agreed in consultation with the carer and other family members, where possible. It is good practice to consult others with an interest in the client's affairs to avoid situations of conflict.

How much to pay?

As we saw above in the case of *Re WVP (Deceased) and EP* [2015] EWCOP 84, the court will analyse closely the payments, the reason they are being carried out and the overall benefit to the elderly person.

The Practice Note sets out three alternative approaches to calculating the payment:

(1) Where the client's estate is sufficient and the family provide most care, the deputy may ask what allowance would be needed. If the amount is affordable, sustainable and reasonable in relation to the amount of care provided, then payment can be made.

(2) Where the client's estate is sufficient and a significant amount of professional care is being provided, then the deputy may wish to calculate the allowance with reference to the approach Senior Judge Lush recommended in the case of *Re HC* [2015] EWCOP 29. That involves calculating family care by taking the commercial cost of care in the client's home area and reducing it by 20%. This in turn follows the approach taken by the Queen's Bench Division of the High Court in quantifying heads of damages in personal injury litigation.

(3) Where the client's estate is limited, then the payment should reflect only what the client can reasonably afford. When considering affordability, if there is an annual periodic payment the client gets as part of a litigation claim, then such a payment is normally for care and case management. It can also be useful to refer to counsel's advice on settlement of a damages claim. This helps in accessing an overall budget for family care when any professional care costs and case management costs are eliminated from the equation. In some situations, the carer may have given up a well-paid job to care for the client. It is the Public Guardian's view that, in all but the most exceptional circumstances, family care payments are not intended to replace salaries and should not be calculated at the level of the carer's previous earnings. Deputies need to bear in mind that, when applying the different factors in this guidance, and particularly taking into account affordability, payments can vary widely. It is possible, for example, that two carers providing the same amount of care may get different family care payments. While on the face of it this appears unfair, it reflects the fact that carers' situations must be considered in the round rather than applying a simple formulaic approach.

8B

Lifetime Gifts

Introduction

Financial abuse of the elderly is most obviously evidenced by unauthorised gifts of one type or another. The unauthorised aspect comes from either a third party having the means to control the other person's finances or by the elderly person having another person exercising sufficient influence and/or pressure on them to part with money or assets. Where the third party has been appointed formally by the court in the case of a deputy appointment or by the elderly person themselves by executing a power of attorney, there are rules applicable and set out in the Mental Capacity Act 2005 (MCA 2005). Where the donor (the maker of gift) has the mental capacity to make a specific gift, the MCA 2005 rules do not apply. In such cases that person may still be an elderly vulnerable person but is treated as having sufficient capacity to make the gift. This is an area where that vulnerable person needs to be safeguarded from those who may want to prey on them.

We shall explore the situations that can arise, the rules applicable and the safeguards that should be put in place to protect such vulnerable people.

What is a gift?

A gift is a transfer of assets of whatever kind to another person or to another entity so that the donor no longer has any legal right to that asset and their estate is reduced accordingly by title and value. The value of the other person's estate is accordingly increased by the same value. The asset thereafter belongs to the donee or donees.

The transfer is a gift because it is made for no consideration in money or money's worth. The gift must be completed and therefore cash must be handed over, or a cheque or bank transfer must clear. A gift of chattels should be evidenced in some way, usually by writing, but conduct might be sufficient. However, in order to avoid any dispute or disagreement at a later date a signed and dated letter by the donor detailing the gift would be helpful. A transfer of a car would be usually effected by a signed vehicle registration document.

A gift of real property would be completed on either the delivery of keys and the unregistered title deeds and execution of a conveyance. For registered land a registered transfer would be sufficient to complete the transfer.

Case law has shown that sometimes unauthorised gifts may be disguised as either expenses and or care allowances incurred whilst looking after the elderly person. If such expenses are unwarranted or excessive then they are more likely to be treated by the courts as gifts and could therefore be set aside.

Other examples from case law show that perpetrators may go to considerable lengths to try and justify the transfer of funds out of an elderly person's estate. For example:

- housewarming presents;
- graduation presents;
- gifts on the occasion of marriages or civil partnerships which took place many years after that event;
- living expenses extended to include the purchase of cars so that visits to the elderly person can be made;
- house improvements to enable other family members to share the elderly person's house;
- providing for the needs of other members of the family.

Transfers into joint names

There may be good practical reasons to transfer bank accounts, property or other assets into the joint names of the elderly person and another. However, careful consideration and advice should be given to any such transfer. The transfers will have legal, tax and control implications for both joint owners.

Transfers into joint bank and building society accounts will mean that both joint owners will have access to the funds, share any income arising and be taxed on that income. The joint owners will be treated as 'joint tenants' and not 'tenants in common'.

The death of one joint owner will usually mean that the surviving owner will inherit the balance in the account by virtue only of their joint ownership and not by reason of any will or the intestacy rules. They will not be bound to hand over any of the funds to the deceased joint owner's executors. The bank will transfer it into the survivor's name on production only of a death certificate will not have to await the issue of a grant of representation.

If one of the joint owners loses their mental capacity you will need to consider what the bank will require in order for the joint account to be operated by the capacitous joint owner. The practice of banks varies in this instance.

In respect of the legal title to a property it is usual that dealings with the property can only be effected if both parties have their capacity. If one joint owner has lost their capacity then that party should be removed from the title and another trustee appointed; for example, if a sale is required.

Does the client have sufficient mental capacity to make a gift or execute a will?

There are different tests of capacity involved.

The common law

The case of *Re Beaney (Deceased)* [1978] 1 WLR 770 sets out the test and states that capacity to make a gift varies according to the size, nature and circumstances of the gift. Martin Nourse QC (as he then was) set out the test in general terms as follows:

'the question in each case is whether the person concerned is capable of understanding what he does by executing the deed in question when its general purport has been fully explained to him.'

Thus the overall test is one of ability to understand, rather than actual understanding. If the maker of the gift does not in fact understand the transaction, in circumstances, where its general purport has not been fully explained, that does not establish lack of capacity. The test is whether he or she would have understood it, if the consequences had been fully explained.

As to the degree of understanding required, he approved the following statement from the Australian case of *Gibbons v Wright* that the principle is:

'In the circumstances, it seems to me that the law is this. The degree or extent of understanding required in respect of any instrument is relative to the particular transaction which it is to effect. In the case of a will the degree required is always high. In the case of a contract, a deed made for consideration or a gift inter vivos, whether by deed or otherwise, the degree required varies with the circumstances of the transaction. Thus, at one extreme, if the subject matter and value of a gift are trivial in relation to the donor's assets a low degree of understanding will suffice. But, at the other extreme, if its effect is to dispose of the donor's only asset of value and thus, for practical purposes, to pre-empt the devolution of his estate under his will or on his intestacy, then the degree of understanding required is as high as that required for a will, and the donor must understand the claims of all potential donees and the extent of the property to be disposed of.'

On the facts, in *Re Beaney*, there was expert evidence from a professor of clinical neurology and from a consultant psychiatrist. The deceased suffered from senile dementia in a very advanced stage and it was getting worse. It was not possible for her to have a lucid interval. The deceased was not capable of understanding that she was even making an absolute gift.

Capacity to make a valid will

The common law test for mental capacity to make a will (testamentary capacity) is to be found in *Banks v Goodfellow* (1870) LR 5 QB 549. The key passage is in the judgment of Cockburn CJ at 565:

> 'It is essential to the exercise of a power that a testator shall understand the nature of the act and its effects; shall understand the extent of the property of which he is disposing; shall be able to comprehend and appreciate the claims to which he ought to give effect; and, with a view to the latter object, that no disorder of the mind shall poison his affections, pervert his sense of right, or prevent the exercise of his natural facilities – that no insane delusion shall influence his will in disposing of his property and bring about a disposal of it which, if the mind had been sound, would not have been made.'

The statutory test in the MCA 2005

MCA 2005, ss 1–3 set out the relevant principles for ascertaining mental capacity. Section 1 sets out the following principles:

- A person must be assumed to have capacity unless it is established that he lacks capacity.

- A person is not to be treated as unable to make a decision unless all practicable steps to help him do so have been taken without success.

- A person is not to be treated as unable to make a decision merely because he makes an unwise decision.

Section 2 provides, so far as relevant, as follows:

> 'A person lacks capacity in relation to a matter if at the material time he is unable to make a decision for himself in relation to the matter because of an impairment of, or a disturbance in the functioning of, the mind or brain. This must be decided on the balance of probabilities.'

Section 3 expands upon the meaning of 'unable to make a decision' and provides, so far as relevant, as follows:

> '(1) For the purposes of section 2, a person is unable to make a decision for himself if he is unable:
>
> (a) to understand the information relevant to the decision,

(b) to retain that information,

(c) to use or weigh that information as part of the process of making the decision, or

(d) to communicate his decision (whether by talking, using sign language or any other means).

(2) A person is not to be regarded as unable to understand the information relevant to a decision if he is able to understand an explanation of it given to him in a way that is appropriate to his circumstances (using simple language, visual aids or any other means).

(3) The fact that a person is able to retain information relevant to a decision for a short period only does not prevent him from being regarded as able to make the decision.

(4) The information relevant to a decision includes information about the reasonably foreseeable consequences of:

(a) deciding one way or another, or

(b) failing to make the decision.'

Sections 1(3) and 3(2) reflect the decision in *Re Beaney* insofar as the question is one of ability to understand rather than actual understanding in fact. It is clear that the s 3(1) test of capacity is not a general test of capacity, but simply applies where the Court of Protection is deciding matters within its statutory jurisdiction.

What does the MCA Code of Practice add to the above?

The Code of Pratice reinforces the message that the definition and the test as above are to be used in situations covered by MCA 2005. The Act's new definition of capacity is in line with the existing common law tests, and the Act does not replace them. The Code states that when cases come before the court on other issues, judges can adopt the new definition if they think that it is appropriate. The Act will apply to all other cases relating to financial, healthcare and welfare decisions.

The case of *Kicks v Leigh* [2014] EWHC 3926 (Ch) shows the interplay between the common law test as set out above in *Re Beaney* for making substantial lifetime gifts and the *Banks v Goodfellow* test of capacity to make a will. This case showed that in circumstances where there is a gift of such value that it constitutes the greater part of the donor's estate then the test is that akin to the test in *Banks v Goodfellow*, whereby the donor should:

'… understand the nature of the act and its effects; shall understand the extent of the property of which he is disposing; shall be able to comprehend and appreciate the claims to which he ought to give effect; and, with a view to the latter object, that no disorder of the mind shall poison his affections, pervert his sent of right, or prevent the exercise of his natural facilities – that no insane delusion shall influence his will in disposing of his property and bring about a disposal of it which, if the mind had been sound, would not have been made.' (Cockburn CJ)

The court showed a willingness to follow *Re Beaney* rather than the strict application of the MCA test of capacity to make a gift. The claimants in this case succeeded on the grounds of undue influence, but failed to show that the testatrix lacked capacity to make a substantial gift of the proceeds of sale of her house. They had to show that there was a sufficient case to raise doubts about the donor's capacity to make the gift. It was clear that the house was the donor's principal asset and therefore *Re Beaney* applied. That case set a high threshold. There was considerable evidence to show that the donor knew what she was doing. The judge looked at the totality of the evidence (following *Gorjat v Gorjat* [2010] EWHC 1537(Ch)). This included the medical evidence, evidence of other witnesses, and the evidence surrounding the transaction itself – the sale of the property and the gift of the proceeds. Considering all of this evidence the Judge concluded that there was insufficient evidence to shift the evidential burden to the defendant.

Can a client be helped to make a decision?

The Public Guardian's Practice Note No 02/2012 of September 2015 emphasised that the principal duty of both deputies and attorneys is to provide for the needs of the patient or donor. There may be circumstances where it would be reasonable to consider gifts of part of the donor or patient's estate. For example, to maintain a spouse or dependent, to continue to make gifts that the donor or patient had made in the past and would want to continue to make, and to utilise tax exemptions and enable tax planning opportunities to be used.

It is not, however, an opportunity to benefit people that the donor would not have considered, such as new charities or individuals with no connection with the patient. It should not be used to loan funds or invest in businesses of the deputy, attorney or others. Similarly, it should not be used to fund home improvements that are of no benefit to the donor. The case of *Re GM* illustrates the dangers of the unfettered purchasing power of deputies. In this case the deputies bought Rolex watches, designer handbags, rings and perfume for themselves. This was clearly beyond the remit of the order appointing them as deputies.

The Code makes it clear that you should always involve the patient in the gift decision-making process. This would include consideration of the patient's present and past expressed wishes. It may be that their past behaviour indicated whether they would ever want to make gifts, what types of gifts and who they would expect to benefit. *Re Gladys Meek* is a case in point, where the deputies made gifts to charities that the patient would not have considered.

The Code also explains what steps you should take to assist the patient in taking such a decision:

(1) *Provide them with relevant information*

To help someone make a decision for themselves, check whether they have all the relevant information they need to make a particular decision. If they have a choice, have they been given information on all the alternatives?

(2) *Communicating in an appropriate way*

- Could information be explained or presented in a way that is easier for the person to understand (for example, by using simple language or visual aids)?

- Have different methods of communication been explored if required, including non-verbal communication?

- Could anyone else help with communication (for example, a family member, support worker, interpreter, speech and language therapist or advocate)?

(3) *Make them feel at ease*

- Are there particular times of day when the person's understanding is better?

- Are there particular locations where they may feel more at ease?

- Could the decision be put off to see whether the person can make the decision at a later time when circumstances are right for them?

(4) *Supporting the person*

- Can anyone else help or support the person to make choices or express a view?

What information should be provided to people and how should it be provided?

All practical and appropriate steps must be taken to help people to make a decision for themselves. Information must be tailored to an individual's needs and abilities. It must also be in the easiest and most appropriate form of communication for the person concerned. How should people be helped to make their own decisions?

- Take time to explain anything that might help the person make a decision. It is important that they have access to all the information they need to make an informed decision.

- Try not to give more detail than the person needs – this might confuse them. In some cases, a simple, broad explanation will be enough. But it must not miss out important information.

- What are the risks and benefits? Describe any foreseeable consequences of making the decision, and of not making any decision at all.

- Explain the effects the decision might have on the person and those close to them – including the people involved in their care.

- If they have a choice, give them the same information in a balanced way for all the options.

- For some types of decisions, it may be important to give access to advice from elsewhere. This may be independent or specialist advice (for example, from a medical practitioner or a financial or legal adviser). But it might simply be advice from trusted friends or relatives.

Gift-making powers and rules related to an incapacitated principal where the decision has been delegated to another

1 Where a deputy has been appointed

Firstly, check the terms of the Order appointing the deputy to see what powers they have been given. The Order usually gives very limited gift-making powers and the usual terms would be:

- Make gifts on customary occasions to relatives or persons connected to the patient provided that the value of the gift is not unreasonable having regard to all the circumstances and, in particular, the size of the estate.

- Make gifts to charities which the patient might have made, provided that the gift is not unreasonable having regard to all the circumstances and, in particular, the size of the estate.

It should be noted that the deputy is under no obligation to make gifts but if they do want to make gifts outside the terms of the order appointing them, then they must make a separate application to the court for authorisation.

2 Attorneys appointed under a LPA for financial decisions

MCA 2005, s 12 provides that:

The attorney may make gifts for the donor on the following occasions

(a) on customary occasions to persons (including himself) who are related to or connected with the donor, or

(b) to any charity to whom the donor made or might have been expected to make gifts, if the value of each such gift is not unreasonable having regard to all the circumstances and, in particular, the size of the donor's estate.

(3) 'Customary occasion' means—

(a) the occasion or anniversary of a birth, a marriage or the formation of a civil partnership, or

(b) any other occasion on which presents are customarily given within families or among friends or associates.

(4) Subsection (2) is subject to any conditions or restrictions in the instrument.

If an attorney wishes to make more extensive gifts than permitted by the above section then they must apply for an order under s 23(4), which provides that 'The court may authorise the making of gifts which are not within section 12(2) (permitted gifts)'.

What does this mean in practice? Firstly, customary occasions are initially limited by statute to birthdays and occasions of marriage and civil partnerships. This is quite clear. However, it also is extended to 'any other occasion on which presents are customarily given to members of the family or to the donor's connections'. So, for example, there may be gifts for religious purposes other than Christmas or Eid. There may be other occasions when gifts are given or exchanged. However, the courts have shown that there are limits to this. See, for example:

- *Public Guardian v AGR & SYN* [2015] EWCOP 73, where one of the deputies had paid for her own divorce fees;

- *Public Guardian and MF* [2015] EWCOP 68, where excessive 'out of pocket' expenses were claimed by an attorney under an EPA.

It is important not to stretch the definition of customary occasions. It does not, for example, extend to gifts for housewarming presents of £2,500, graduation presents of £2,500 or gifts on the occasion of marriages or civil partnerships which took place many years after that event. In *Re Joan Treadwell (Deceased); OPG v Colin Lutz* [2013] EWHC 2409 (COP), the deputy Colin Lutz also set up trust funds of £9,000 for each of his two children.

There may, however, be occasions when the court will approve the use of the elderly person's funds for:

- living expenses extended to include the purchase of cars so that visits to the elderly person can be made but not if this is an unreasonable purchase or if the primary benefit is for the donee;

- house improvements to enable other family members to share the elderly person's house;

- providing for the needs of other members of the family. So, for example, in the case of a younger patient the court has authorised the payment of a sibling's school fees where it was successfully argued that this would be of benefit indirectly for the patient.

The gifts must also be reasonable bearing in mind the donor's estate, so for example in *The Public Guardian v AM* [2015] EWCOP 86 a gift of £10,000 for a grandson's wedding was outside the scope of the attorney's authority where the net estate was £186,000.

3 Where an EPA is registered

MCA 2005, Sch 4, Part 1 provides that:

> (2) Subject to any conditions or restrictions contained in the instrument, an attorney under an enduring power, whether general or limited, may (without obtaining any consent) act under the power so as to benefit himself or other persons than the donor to the following extent but no further
>
> (a) he may so act in relation to himself or in relation to any other person if the donor might be expected to provide for his or that person's needs respectively, and
>
> (b) he may do whatever the donor might be expected to do to meet those needs.
>
> (3) Without prejudice to sub-paragraph (2) but subject to any conditions or restrictions contained in the instrument, an attorney under an enduring power, whether general or limited, may (without obtaining any consent) dispose of the property of the donor by way of gift to the following extent but no further
>
> (a) he may make gifts of a seasonal nature or at a time, or on an anniversary, of a birth, a marriage or the formation of a civil partnership, to persons (including himself) who are related to or connected with the donor, and
>
> (b) he may make gifts to any charity to whom the donor made or might be expected to make gifts, provided that the value of each such gift is not unreasonable having regard to all the circumstances and in particular the size of the donor's estate.

As seen above, there is a subtle difference from the provisions relating to lasting powers of attorney and that concerns provisions for the needs of others. The Act does not define what is meant by 'needs', but it is accepted that where a donor has in the past provided for the needs of family members or others and that they would continue to do so if they were able to, then the court would allow such provision to continue. However, prior approval should be obtained to confirm this in order to avoid any future dispute or challenge.

4 Where an EPA has not yet been registered

Where the donor has not lost his or her mental capacity then the attorney appointed under the unregistered EPA can use it to make gifts in accordance with the above provisions provided that also he has the consent of the donor. It is important that such gifts are evidenced in some way (for example, in writing or in the presence of a witness or witnesses) so that any dispute about the circumstances can be resolved at a later date. The best practice is for a contemporaneous letter or note signed by the donor and dated. This should show details of the gift, value and recipient's name. If there is any question about the donor's capacity to make the gift then a separate medical report at the time would be important.

In all the above it is important to consider the particular circumstances. The following checklist may assist before considering any gifts:

1   Is the amount or value of the gift appropriate in relation to the size of the patient's estate?

2   Are you favouring one member of the family over another or others?

3   Has the subject matter of the gift in the case of a chattel or property been mentioned in the patient's will as a specific gift?

4   What is the reason for the gift?

5   Is the gift to the deputy or attorney and what is the reason for this?

6   Are the patient's needs being taken care of and in particular are the patient's care fees being paid?

7   Do you have authority to make the gift?

8   Do you need the court's permission?

9   Would the patient have authorised the gift if they had the capacity to do so?

10   If it is a gift to a charity is it one which the patient would have benefited?

11   What form does the gift take? Is it outright, a loan or an investment?

12   Is the gift a transfer into joint names? Is there a declaration of trust governing the ownership, income and dealings with the assets?

13   Are there restrictions in the deputyship order or power of attorney restricting gifting powers?

Have any specific restrictions been imposed?

Deputyship order

As mentioned above, the order appointing the deputy should be checked. There will usually be limited gifts as provided by the rules imposed by statute. Where a specific order of the Court of Protection authorising a particular gift or series of gifts has been obtained, it is important to abide by the strict terms of that order.

Powers of attorney

Make sure that if there are to be gifts of any items that are left as specific legacies in the will that the attorneys have the power to see the donor's will; otherwise a court order will be required.

Consider imposing some restrictions in an LPA, which could include the following:

- setting a maximum amount of a cash gift;
- distribution of chattels on sale of house in accordance with terms of will;
- ensuring that the consent of a third party is required;
- ensuring that the Attorneys make a court application for approval of gifts;
- providing for the maintenance of spouse or dependants.

Finally consideration should be given to two other gift-making rules

(1) **Donatio mortis causa**

This is the rule whereby an individual makes a present gift which takes effect in the future and remains conditional until the donor dies (*Sen v Headley* 1991 Ch 425). It is an exception to the Wills Act formality requirements. It is important that the facts of each case distinguish between a genuine donatio and an attempt to make a testamentary gift outside the provisions of the Wills Act 1837.

In *Re Craven's Estate* [1937] Ch 423 the court set out the essential conditions required. They were:

- a clear intention to give but to give only if the donor dies;
- the gift must be made in contemplation of death and that is death within the near future;
- the donor must part with 'dominion' over the subject matter of the gift. (This must not just be more than just physical possession of the subject matter (*Sen v Headley* [1991] Ch 425).

The question of 'parting with dominion' has exercised many of the cases. For example:

- *Sen v Headley* [1991] Ch 425, where unregistered land was the subject of the donation and the donor handed over the keys to the deeds box to the done;
- *Birch v Treasury Solicitor* [1951] Ch 298, where the donor handed over the Post Office and bank deposit books.

The court must still be satisfied that the donor had the necessary capacity to make the donation.

(2) **Rule against double portions**

This provides that where a 'portion' is left to a child of the testator either by way of legacy or a part of the residue, and thereafter the same testator makes a substantial lifetime gift to the same child, the rule states that there is a presumption that the gift replaces the portion left in the will. That is, it is a payment on account of the legacy or share of residue left by will, not in addition to it. In this situation, it is important to establish the testator's intentions at the time of such a lifetime gift.

Finally, consider whether a change to the patient's will should be made to rebalance the lifetime gifts. A statutory will or codicil application may be required to ensure fairness amongst family members and or dependants.

8C

Conflicts of Interest

Taking instructions from an elderly or vulnerable person requires a great deal of understanding, patience and experience. It is not just that we must ensure that the client can hear and see what we are discussing, but also that they can give us clear, independent instructions without being under pressure or influence from a third party. It is often the case that the first contact about a client is when a 'concerned' member of the family or a friend telephones to request a meeting on behalf of the client. A few pointers at this stage will help you determine who the client is and what common warning signs you need to watch out for.

How does a conflict arise here?

The Solicitor's Regulation Authority code of conduct for solicitors provides that conflicts of interests can arise between two or more current clients. This is defined as a client conflict. A separate conflict known as 'own interest conflict' can arise between you and current clients. The code provides that you can never act where there is a conflict, or a significant risk of conflict, between you and your client.

It further provides that 'if there is a conflict, or a significant risk of a conflict, between two or more current clients, you must not act for all or both of them unless the matter falls within the scope of the limited exceptions set out at Outcomes 3.6 or 3.7. In deciding whether to act in these limited circumstances, the overriding consideration will be the best interests of each of the clients concerned and, in particular, whether the benefits to the clients of you acting for all or both of the clients outweigh the risks'.

Who is my client?

In taking instructions from any client, but in particular an elderly or vulnerable one, you should ensure that the instructions come from the client alone, not through a third party unless independently confirmed by the client, and that the client is not under undue pressure or influence from another person.

Common situations	Who is my client?	Steps required
LPA instructions	Donor	Take instructions from donor separately from attorney(s) to be appointed
Gift from parent to child	Parent	Ensure both are separately represented. See the Law Society's Practice Note on gifts
Equity release to provide funds for gift to child	Parent	Ensure that you are not advising both parent and ultimate beneficiary of funds
Property transfer to child	Parent	Ensure separate representation
Deputyship	Patient	Ensure no confusion over interests of the donor and those of the deputy
Statutory will applications	Applicant	Official Solicitor represents the patient
Spouses/civil partners	Spouses/civil partners	Advise both as to potential for conflict and obtain consent to act for both provided they have a common interest
Instructions received from third party for a client	Client	Take steps to confirm those instructions in person or if not possible then decline to act

Common warning signs

Transaction	Danger indicators	Steps to take
Parent moving in with adult child	Parent providing funds for annex but not having any charge on property nor share of the legal title	Advice to parent, amend will to reflect gift, obtain legal charge repayable on death or a share of the legal title
Gift of cash to child	Depleting parent's estate and insufficient left in estate to pay care fees	Advise parent to request return of funds, alter will to reflect gift, apply to have gift set aside due to undue influence

Transaction	Danger indicators	Steps to take
Equity release	Leaves insufficient for parent if needs to go into care home	Follow guidelines, ensure experienced solicitor advises and written advice and written evidence that client understands implications
Transfer of property	Parent not understand implications for their home, care fees provision and tax	Separate full advice required and full understanding of reasons for the transfer especially if it is family home
Bankruptcy of child	Financial insecurity and pressure on parent to make cash gifts	Implications if child is an attorney or deputy – can no longer act in respect of finances and property, secure the parent's finances and appoint independent attorney
Adult child living with vulnerable parent	Emotional and financial pressure on parent to provide for child	Social services should be aware and other members of the family should maintain contact and communication to ensure no isolation
Bank accounts in joint names of parent and child	Child depleting parent's money on an ongoing basis	Establish reasons for this and explain financial and tax implications
Care fees unpaid	Indicator that the attorney or deputy is spending money on themselves and not for the donor's benefit	Call Adult Safeguarding to alert them to potential financial abuse
Third party holding client's bank cash card	May be convenience, but should be returned to owner after use each time	Establish reasons for this and ensure proper systems in place to prevent abuse

Family dynamics

Parent and child

McDonnell v Loosemore [2007] EWCA 1531 shows that there is potential for a negligence claim if the solicitor does not make full enquiries as to whether significant influence has been brought to bear on one of the parties.

In *Re JW* [2015] EWCOP 82, the patient's son, a builder, applied to replace the county council as his mother's deputy. He stood to benefit from building works to be carried out on a property owned by his mother and the court placed conditions on him. The court set his proposed budget of £35,000 for the refurbishment works. Any anticipated expenditure in excess of that sum required approval in advance by the court. He was given authority to sell the property when the building works were completed. He was not given authority to sell his mother's other property in which his siblings Sheila and Desmond resided, without further order of the court. He was required to give security in the sum of £250,000. Finally, he was required to account annually to the Public Guardian and to ensure that his personal interests did not conflict with his duty to act in his mother's best interests.

Couples

In most cases where you are taking instructions from a couple their interests will be the same and the potential for any conflict will not exist. However, whether you are taking instructions for a will or LPA you need to consider the possibility of a conflict of interest. For example, where one party to the marriage has been married before and has children from that earlier marriage then they will, with good reason, want to provide for those children whether by will or in respect of appointing them as substitute attorneys. This may be at odds with what the second spouse would like the couple to do. You therefore need to establish whether they are comfortable with you advising both at the same meeting or holding separate meetings.

The case of *Gill v Woodall (Rev 1)* [2010] EWCA Cov 1430 illustrates the problem of a domineering husband who may well have unduly influenced his wife in signing a will with which she did not wholeheartedly agree. This shows that if it can be proved that the testator did not know and approve of the contents of a will then the courts will set this aside. It is an illustration of the importance of ensuring that both spouses or civil partners fully understand and approve of the contents of the will that they are signing and not simply rely on instructions from one party alone.

Where you take instructions for the preparation of a LPA make sure that where they each want to appoint the other as attorney that the certificate provider can meet them separately to ensure there is no undue pressure being placed on one party. On the original version of the LPA forms there used to be a requirement that the donor and attorneys were not present in the same room when advice was given about the LPA. This has been removed from the later versions of the forms which further reduces the safeguards for donors. There is a mention of this in the online notes 'making a lasting power of attorney' where it is stated 'if possible, they should discuss your LPA with you in private, without attorneys or other people present, before they sign to "certify" their part of the LPA'. This should be a mandatory safeguard.

Note the effect on an appointment if an attorney and donor divorce. The spouse or civil partner attorney can no longer act for the donor unless there is a restriction mentioned in the LPA saying that they can continue to act.

Transactions

Gifts

Unequal gifts between family members are a constant source of problems. The Law Society Practice Note on making gifts states at paragraph 3.2:

> 'You should clarify who you will be acting for and who you will be receiving instructions from. You must consider any possible conflict of interest where you receive instructions from a donee, especially if you already act for the donor. Chapter 3 of the SRA Code indicates when instructions must be refused.
>
> 'If you are asked to act for both parties, you must make them both aware of the possible conflict of interest, and should advise one of them to take independent advice. You should explain you may be unable to disclose all that you know to each of them. You may also be unable to give advice to one of them which conflicts with the interests of the other. Both parties must give their consent to the arrangement in writing. If you remain in any doubt, you should not act for both parties.'

It is essential that the client receives full independent legal advice here. This should be supported by detailed attendance notes and follow up meetings preferably at the client's home to try to establish the client's motives and whether there is real evidence of the influence of a third party.

Equity release

Many negligence claims have arisen as a result of solicitors viewing their role in the execution of third party charge documentation as little more than a formality. The important House of Lords decision in *Royal Bank of Scotland v Etridge* was delivered on 11 October 2001 and as a result all conveyancing lawyers should consider carefully their procedures when faced with a transaction where a third party provides security for another person's borrowing. The risk to solicitors' professional indemnity cover remains acute. *Etridge* involved a wife claiming that she had charged her interest in the matrimonial home as a result of the undue influence of her husband.

Lord Nicholls summarised at paragraph 65 of the judgment the core minimum requirements for advice, which typically will include:

- the nature of the documents and the risk that the client will lose the home if the borrower's business does not prosper, and even the possibility that the client could be made bankrupt;

- the seriousness of the risks involved by reference to the purpose, amount and terms of the new facility and whether the client understands the value of the property being charged and if there are any other assets out of which repayment could be made if the business fails;

- the fact that the lender may alter the terms of the loan including increasing the amount borrowed without reference to the client;

- asking whether the client is content for the solicitor to write to the bank confirming that the solicitor has explained the nature of the documents to the client and the practical implications they may have;

- discussing whether the client wishes the solicitor to negotiate with the bank on the terms of the transaction (eg limitation on the amount borrowed);

- providing the advice at a face to face meeting in the absence of the borrower and giving the advice using non-technical language;

- explaining that the client does have a choice on whether to sign the charge/ guarantee or to consent to mortgage with the decision being up to the client alone.

However, it must be appreciated that additional requirements may become appropriate depending on the specific facts of the case. It should be appreciated by the solicitor that 'the solicitor's task is an important one. It is not a formality' (Lord Nicholls, para 65). To comply properly with the House of Lord's judgment guidance is likely to take several chargeable hours.

Confirmation

The advice given should be recorded in a full attendance note and confirmed in detail in writing in a letter sent promptly after the meeting. A draft letter is available on the Law Society website.

Summary

All conveyancing solicitors should be certain that before advising on third party charges:

- they have the necessary expertise;

- there is no conflict;

- there is no suspicion of undue influence or impropriety;

- the bank provides full financial information;

- the advice covers, at the very least, the core minimum requirements;

- the advice is confirmed in writing.

The SRA Code of Conduct shows that there are exceptions where you may act, with appropriate safeguards, where there is a client conflict. So, for example, in Outcome 3.6 where the clients have a substantially common interest in relation to a matter or a particular aspect of it, you can only act if:

- you have explained the relevant issues and risks to the clients and you have a reasonable belief that they understand those issues and risks;

- all the clients have given informed consent in writing to you acting;

- you are satisfied that it is reasonable for you to act for all the clients and that it is in their best interests; and

- you are satisfied that the benefits to the clients of you doing so outweigh the risks.

Similarly, in Outcome 3.7 where the clients are competing for the same objective, you can only act if:

- you have explained the relevant issues and risks to the clients and you have a reasonable belief that they understand those issues and risks;

- the clients have confirmed in writing that they want you to act, in the knowledge that you act, or may act, for one or more other clients who are competing for the same objective;

- there is no other client conflict in relation to that matter;

- unless the clients specifically agree, no individual acts for, or is responsible for the supervision of work done for, more than one of the clients in that matter; and

- you are satisfied that it is reasonable for you to act for all the clients and that the benefits to the clients of you doing so outweigh the risks.

The code shows examples of where you can show that you have complied with the above principles. One set of circumstances is where you decline to act where there is unequal bargaining power between the clients. An example of this would be where a mother and son instruct you to transfer the mother's house in which they both live into the son's sole name. You should only act for one of the parties and only then when all the risks have been explained in detail to that client.

Another example is where you hold a power of attorney for a client using that power to gain a benefit for yourself which in your professional capacity you would not have been prepared to allow to a third party. Clearly this would demonstrate that the principles of the code have not been followed.

Confidentiality and Disclosure

The rules relating to disclosure of documents relating to clients regulate both what you may disclose to a third party and what third parties may disclose to you. The issues are further complicated by separate rules governing what may be disclosed on behalf of a mentally incapacitated client and who can make that disclosure. It is very often the case that paperwork needs to be disclosed in order to, for example, take a best interests decision on behalf of your client. Ensuring that they have the most appropriate care or making a claim for continuing NHS care are two cases where this needs to be considered.

There is an abundance of rules here and the interplay between them needs to be considered. There is, for example:

- the common law duty of confidentiality;
- professional codes of conduct – for example the Solicitors Regulation Authority (SRA), NHS, etc;
- Data Protection Act 1998;
- Human Rights Act 1998; and
- European Convention on Human Rights, Art 8 right to private life.

There is also guidance provided in chapter 16 of the Code of Practice to the MCA 2005.

There are two aspects to this area. Firstly, there is the duty to maintain confidential information relating to your client and secondly, as to what are your duties and obligations regarding disclosure of information about your client to a third party.

Common law duty

This duty ensures that an individual's consent is required before information concerning them is to be disclosed to another person or authority.

The conflict between this right to privacy and the public interest was illustrated in *R(S) v Plymouth City Council* [2002] EWCA Civ 388. Here the court had to consider the balance between a mother's wish to secure disclosure of documents relating to her son's guardianship order in the council's favour and the council's wish to maintain confidentiality. It also considered the impact of Art 8 of the ECHR which confers a right to private life.

Hale LJ commented:

> 'both the common law and the Convention require that a balance be struck between the various interests involved. These are the confidentiality of the information sought; the proper administration of justice; the mother's right of access to legal advice to enable her to decide whether or not to exercise a right which is likely to lead to legal proceedings against her if she does so; the rights of both C and his mother to respect for their family life and adequate involvement in decision-making processes about it; C's right to respect for his private life; and the protection of C's health and welfare. In some cases there might also be an interest in the protection of other people, but that has not been seriously suggested here.

> 'C's interest in protecting the confidentiality of personal information about himself must not be under-estimated. It is all too easy for professionals and parents to regard children and incapacitated adults as having no independent interests of their own: as objects rather than subjects. But we are not concerned here with the publication of information to the whole wide world. There is a clear distinction between disclosure to the media with a view to publication to all and sundry and disclosure in confidence to those with a proper interest in having the information in question. We are concerned here only with the latter. The issue is only whether the circle should be widened from those professionals with whom this information has already been shared (possibly without much conscious thought being given to the balance of interests involved) to include the person who is probably closest to him in fact as well as in law and who has a statutory role in his future and to those professionally advising her. C also has an interest in having his own wishes and feelings respected. It would be different in this case if he had the capacity to give or withhold consent to the disclosure: any objection from him would have to be weighed in the balance against the other interests, although as *W v Edgell* shows, it would not be decisive. C also has an interest in being protected from a risk of harm to his health or welfare which would stem from disclosure; but it is important not to confuse a possible risk of harm to his health or welfare from being discharged from guardianship with a possible risk of harm from disclosing the information sought. As *Re D* shows, he also has an interest in decisions about his future being properly informed.'

In the context of financial decisions all financial information about a mentally incapacitated client must be disclosed to their attorney or deputy so that they can carry out decisions in their best interests. In some respects the rules are clear. Firstly does P have capacity? If so, their consent is required. As we have seen in chapter 3 problems can certainly arise where the client is vulnerable but not mentally incapable. If they refuse to disclose important information then this may create problems. However, it is their right to withhold that information. Where the client has lost their mental capacity then their attorney or deputy may have the authority to obtain release of information about them.

It is important to firstly make sure that your powers as attorney or deputy are sufficient. Check the terms of the LPA or the Order appointing the deputy. Someone appointed for financial decisions needs to be able to access all financial details about P's estate. This includes property information, bank statements, passbooks and investment managers' reports, amongst others. Each financial institution will have their own rules that need to be complied with as regards the disclosure of confidential information to a third-party attorney or deputy rather than the bank's customer themselves. See below for steps to take if a financial institution refuses to release information.

The LPA for financial decisions makes the following statement in section 9 as regards the donor: 'I agree to the information I've provided being used by the Office of the Public Guardian in carrying out its duties.' For example, this allows the OPG to use its investigatory powers on the donor's behalf, when incapable, to investigate any allegations of abuse.

This area of conflicting rules can be confusing and the MCA Code of Practice provides the following helpful checklist to assist clients and practitioners

(1) Questions to ask when requesting personal information about someone who may lack capacity

- Am I acting under a LPA or as a deputy with specific authority?
- Does the person have capacity to agree that information can be disclosed?
- Have they previously agreed to disclose the information?
- What information do I need?
- What rules govern access to information about a person who lacks capacity?
- Why do I need it?
- Who has the information?
- Can I show that I need the information to make a decision that is in the best interests of the person I am acting for, and the person does not have the capacity to act for themselves?
- Do I need to share the information with anyone else to make a decision that is in the best interests of the person who lacks capacity?
- Should I keep a record of my decision or action?
- How long should I keep the information for?
- Do I have the right to request the information under DPA 1998, s 7?

(2) Questions to ask when considering whether to disclose information

- Is the request covered by DPA 1998, s 7?

- Is the request being made by a formally authorised representative? If not is the disclosure legal, and is the disclosure justified having balanced the person's best interests and the public interest against the person's right to privacy?

(3) Questions to ask in deciding whether the disclosure is legal or justified

- Do I (or does my organisation) have the information?

- Am I satisfied that the person concerned lacks capacity to agree to disclosure?

- Does the person requesting the information have any formal authority to act on behalf of the person who lacks capacity?

- Am I satisfied that the person making the request is acting in the best interests of the person concerned; needs the information to act properly; will respect confidentiality; and will keep the information for no longer than necessary?

- Should I get written confirmation of these things?

- What laws and regulations affect access to information?

- People caring for, or managing the finances of, someone who lacks capacity may need information to: assess the person's capacity to make a specific decision; determine the person's best interests; and make appropriate decisions on the person's behalf.

Clearly the information required will vary according to the circumstances.

Underlying all the above rules are the provisions of the Data Protection Act 1998 (DPA 1998). Penalties will apply if the DPA 1998 provisions are breached.

Data Protection Act 1998

DPA 1998 gives everyone the right to see personal information that an organisation holds about them. In particular, it provides in s 7 that a person has a right to know whether personal data about them is being processed by or on behalf of a 'data controller'. If so then that individual has a right to ask that data controller for the following information:

(i) the personal data of which that individual is the subject,

(ii) the purposes for which the data is being or are to be processed, and

(iii) the recipients or classes of recipients to whom the data is being or may be disclosed,

(c) to have communicated to him in an intelligible form

(i)   the information constituting any personal data of which that individual is the data subject, and

(ii) any information available to the data controller as to the source of those data, and

Such information should be requested in writing and released within 40 days of that request. If there is a failure to comply with such a request then a complaint can be made to the Information Commissioner's Office.

Judgements in the Court of Protection often refer to Art 8 of the ECHR. It is one of the considerations that needs to be balanced against society's need to protect the vulnerable. It provides a right to respect for private and family life:

(1) Everyone has the right to respect for his private and family life, his home and his correspondence.

(2) There shall be no interference by a public authority with the exercise of this right except such as is in accordance with the law and is necessary in a democratic society in the interests of national security, public safety or the economic wellbeing of the country, for the prevention of disorder or crime, for the protection of health or morals, or for the protection of the rights and freedoms of others.

What does this mean in practice? The ECHR has been incorporated into UK law by the HRA 1998. This means that there are remedies available under domestic law as well as to the European Court of Human Rights in Strasbourg. By way of illustration, the OPG will balance disclosure of information against the Art 8 right to private life.

The concept of a right to a private life encompasses the importance of personal dignity and autonomy and the interaction a person has with others, both in private or in public.

Respect for one's private life includes:

- the right to personal autonomy and physical and psychological integrity, ie the right not to be physically interfered with;

- respect for private and confidential information, particularly the storing and sharing of such information;

- respect for privacy when one has a reasonable expectation of privacy; and

- the right to control the dissemination of information about one's private life, including photographs taken covertly.

Family life

Article 8 also provides the right to respect for one's established family life. This includes close family ties, although there is no predetermined model of a family or family life. It includes any stable relationship, be it married, engaged, or de facto; between parents and children; siblings; grandparents and grandchildren etc. This right is often engaged, for example, when measures are taken by the state to separate family members (by removing a vulnerable person into care).

Respect for the home

Right to respect for the home includes a right not to have one's home life interfered with, including by unlawful surveillance, unlawful entry, arbitrary evictions, etc.

Limitations

There are limits to Art 8 so, for example, that right might conflict with the rights and freedoms of others.

Examples of where there could be a breach of Art 8 include:

● being treated badly in a care home;

● if personal information is disclosed to other people without consent.

There are also professional codes of conduct which regulate, for example, how clinicians and solicitors treat confidential information.

(1) NHS Code of Practice on confidentiality (November 2003)

A duty of confidence arises when one person discloses information to another (eg patient to clinician) in circumstances where it is reasonable to expect that the information will be held in confidence.

The main requirements are:

(a) PROTECT – look after the patient's information;

(b) INFORM – ensure that patients are aware of how their information is used;

(c) PROVIDE CHOICE – allow patients to decide whether their information can be disclosed or used in particular ways.

(2) SRA code of conduct

Solicitors must abide by their code of conduct which provides that protection of confidential information is a fundamental feature of your relationship with clients.

The duty of confidentiality to all clients has to be reconciled with the duty of disclosure to clients.

This involves the solicitor ensuring that:

4.1 – you keep the affairs of clients confidential unless disclosure is required or permitted by law or the client consents;

4.2 – any individual who is advising a client makes that client aware of all information material to that retainer of which the individual has personal knowledge;

4.3 – you ensure that where your duty of confidentiality to one client comes into conflict with your duty of disclosure to another client, your duty of confidentiality takes precedence.

If, for example, you disclose the content of a will on the death of a client without the consent of the personal representatives you will not have complied with the above principles:

Banks' duty of confidentiality

The Financial Services Ombudsman set out the banker's duty of confidentiality to the customer in April 2005 in the following terms:

'It is an implied term of the contract between customers and their banks and building societies that these firms will keep their customers' information confidential. This confidentiality is not just confined to account transactions – it extends to all the information that the bank has about the customer.'

Sometimes such breaches can have major consequences and other times they be technical breaches of that duty.

A banker's duty of confidentiality is not absolute. The 1924 case of *Tournier v National Provincial and Union Bank of England* [1924] 1 KB 461 set out four areas where a bank can legally disclose information about its customer. These principles still apply and are:

- where the bank is compelled by law to disclose the information;
- if the bank has a public duty to disclose the information;
- if the bank's own interests require disclosure; and
- where the customer has agreed to the information being disclosed.

Liability

If a bank discloses information about a customer in any circumstances other than those described above, then it has acted wrongly and should, as a general rule, be held liable for the reasonably foreseeable consequences of its action. Usually the information is released by accident.

Loss

The FCA states that a bank should generally be liable for losses that it could reasonably have foreseen when it disclosed the information.

The banker's duty of confidentiality to the customer

The Ombudsman cited the following cases it has dealt with:

Mr N was barely on speaking terms with his sister, Mrs G, because of their differing views as to how they should look after their elderly widowed mother. Mr N wanted his mother to move to an expensive nursing home, while Mrs G wanted to leave their mother at home and to arrange for a neighbour to call in each day to check on things.

Eventually, Mr N decided to go ahead and move his mother to the nursing home. Mrs G refused to pay when he asked her to contribute half of the costs, so Mr N and his wife arranged to go to a solicitor to try to force her hand.

Mrs G had a savings account at the branch of the building society where Mrs N worked. Mrs N decided to check how much money Mrs G had in this account. She then told the solicitor – who used the information in correspondence. When Mrs G discovered what the solicitor knew, she challenged her sister-in-law – who admitted how she had obtained the information.

Miss G complained to the building society about what her sister-in-law had done. However, the society said this was a private family matter. Mrs G then referred the complaint to the Ombudsman. The society accepted that Mrs N's actions had breached Mrs G's confidentiality. Mrs N had also broken her contract of employment.

Banks and the release of information to an attorney or deputy

If you encounter difficulties with a bank releasing information to you as the attorney or deputy ask them on what grounds they are refusing release of information. There are three categories of persons who can consent to release of the information:

- client who has capacity;
- attorney under property and financial affairs LPA;
- deputy for property and financial affairs.

You therefore have sufficient authority to request info in order to act in P's best interests.

Office of the Public Guardian

Information available to the public

As we have seen in Chapter 6, the OPG maintains a public register which has certain key information about a donor, attorney, deputy and their powers to act.

The question as to what information should be available brings into the focus the tension between the Art 10 freedom of expression versus Art 8 right to private and family life. It begs the question whether it is truly in the public interest for the public to be able to search the register freely.

The OPG holds detailed information about other parties, such as families, attorneys, deputies and whistleblowers, as well as the patients or donors themselves. The OPG has various data-sharing agreements with police, the SRA, the DWP and other agencies. This enables them to carry out their safeguarding and investigatory functions under the MCA 2005.

Suitability to be an attorney or deputy or a carer: Disclosure and Barring Service

Consider how the Disclosure and Barring Service (DBS) can help you here.

It may be that you need to check whether your client is employing someone who needs a DBS check carried out. Alternatively, there may be questions you need to ask of a care agency or care home provider as to the checks made in respect of an employee.

It is a criminal offence for a barred person to seek to work, or work in, activities from which they are barred. It is also a criminal offence for employers or voluntary organisations to knowingly employ a barred person in a regulated activity. The definition of 'regulated activity' (adults) is defined in the Safeguarding Vulnerable Groups Act 2006, which applied from 10 September 2012.

This provides that:

'(1) regulated activity continues to exclude any activity carried out in the course of family relationships, and personal, non-commercial relationships

(a) Family relationships involve close family (eg parents, siblings, grandparents) and relationships between two people who live in the same household and treat each other as family.

(b) Personal, non-commercial relationships are arrangements where either no money changes hands, or any money that does change hands is not part of a commercial relationship (for example, gifting a friend money for petrol after they have driven you to the hospital), and the arrangement is made between friends or family friends.

(2) An adult is a person aged 18 years or over.

(3) A person whose role includes the day to day management or supervision of any person who is engaging in regulated activity, is also in regulated activity.'

It includes the following activities which are in obvious caring roles:

- provision of health care;
- provision of personal care;
- providing social work.

It also extends to the following activities:

Assistance with household matters:

(1) A volunteer who collects shopping lists and the cash to pay for the shopping from older adults' homes, who then does the shopping on their behalf, would be engaging in a regulated activity.

(2) A befriender who helps a disabled person compile their weekly shopping list is not in a regulated activity.

Assistance in the conduct of a person's own affairs:

Anyone who provides assistance in the conduct of an adult's own affairs by virtue of LPA or an EPA.

Conveying:

(1) A person who volunteers to take an adult to and from their GP appointment on behalf of a community group is in regulated activity. It would not matter if that person knows, or is friends with, the adult they were taking to the appointment if the conveying is on behalf of the group.

(2) A friend who takes their neighbour to a hospital appointment would not be in regulated activity, as this is a personal relationship.

These checks were previously called the Criminal Records Bureau checks. There is useful guidance on their website at www.gov.uk/disclosure-barring-service-check/overview

You may need to check someone's criminal record if they apply for certain jobs or voluntary work, eg working with children or in healthcare.

These rules apply to England and Wales. Note that there are different rules for requesting a criminal record check in Scotland and Northern Ireland.

Who can ask for a DBS check?

Only employers and licensing bodies can request a DBS check.

Personal applications by job applicants

If you are a job applicant and you are asked to provide disclosure then a request for a basic disclosure from Disclosure Scotland can be applied for and obtained by the applicant themselves. See www.disclosurescotland.co.uk/disclosureinformation/index.htm for details.

What does a standard disclosure show?

A standard disclosure contains certain conviction information. This will include all unspent conviction information, including unspent cautions and relevant spent convictions. A standard disclosure application can only be completed in paper format and must be countersigned by an organisation authorised by Disclosure Scotland, known as a registered body. A Standard Disclosure certificate contains all unspent conviction information (including unspent cautions) and relevant spent convictions.

Different checks available

A standard disclosure costs £26 and checks for spent and unspent convictions, cautions, reprimands and final warnings. There are also enhanced checks costing £44 which provide more detailed police information and a check of the DBS barred lists.

Volunteers

Checks for eligible volunteers are free of charge. This includes anyone who spends time helping people and is not being paid (apart from for travel and other approved out-of-pocket expenses) and not only looking after a close relative.

This mostly concerns volunteering roles dealing with children, for example, as a scout leader. As you will note those working unpaid in a caring role for a close relative are not regarded as eligible volunteers for these purposes.

Chapter 9

Protection of the Individual and Recovery of Assets

9A

Protection of the Individual

A theme running through all the discussions of financial abuse is how do we respect a client's autonomy but at the same time allow intervention to protect them? As we have seen, the main perpetrators of abuse are those often closest to the victim: the middle-aged sons and daughters who perhaps are seeing their expected inheritance dwindle as their parents' life expectancy increases. There will be those instances where the adult child lives with the elderly parent as their only carer. The victim will feel dependent upon them. The thought that an external agency can step in and either remove the carer from the home or remove the victim to a place of safety, even if temporarily, will be resisted by the victim. The reality is that however bad the abuse, whether financial, physical or emotional, the victim will have a strong bond with the perpetrator. It is because of this deep conflict of interest that it could be argued that protective measures need to be put in place even without the consent of the victim. Only a third party can act dispassionately to protect the victim, who will recognise the behaviour being perpetrated as abusive.

The victim must be consulted and their views reported and considered. Article 8 of the European Convention on Human Rights gives them the right to respect for private and family life. As we have seen in cases like *Re DL v A Local Authority* [2012] EWCA Civ 253 the courts will step in and support a local authority acting to protect vulnerable adults. In that case, DL's mother did not agree with the intervention, which was designed to safeguard her and her husband from further abuse from their son, DL. The court ordered: an interim ex parte injunction restraining the son in various ways; a *Harbin v Masterman* order requesting the Official Solicitor to investigate the parents' true wishes and to ascertain whether they are operating under the influence of DL in relation to the contact that they had with him; and an expert report by a social worker.

Involve agencies to assist and safeguard

Police

Involving the police in cases of financial abuse is an important step but essential if evidence of abuse is clear. It is very often a third party who will make such a report. Only by bringing the matter to the attention of the police can the abuse be stopped and prevent the perpetrator repeating the offence.

Some police forces are now recording safeguarding concerns where a person has a reasonable cause to think that an adult with care and support needs, who is unable to protect themselves because of those needs, is experiencing, or is at risk of, abuse or neglect. Each local authority has a safeguarding adults board (SAB), which should be endorsing the safeguarding adults policy and procedures. The police are represented on each of those safeguarding boards.

However a safeguarding concern is raised, the police ought to ensure that the relevant local authority is made aware of any safeguarding concern as soon as possible and any subsequent police investigation should form part of the multi-agency response.

The police will complete a vulnerable adult at risk form, which is then sent for investigation and to the local authority SAB. The form details:

- the vulnerable adult's accommodation type, circumstances and vulnerability;
- any existing care arrangements or networks of support and contact details, if known;
- details of the risk to the vulnerable adult;
- details of current and any previous police involvement;
- the vulnerable adult's relationship with the abuser;
- the vulnerable adult's views of what they would like to happen and whether they know about the referral;
- details about the vulnerable adult's care provider and any previous or associated incidents which may indicate institutional abuse.

The local authority will gather information in order to evaluate any immediate risk to the adult and make a decision as to whether a care assessment or enquiry under the Care Act 2014, s 42 is required.

Office of the Public Guardian

Where a victim has lost their mental capacity and has an attorney or attorneys acting for them under a registered EPA or LPA, or a deputy appointed by the Court of Protection, the OPG will be the body to which safeguarding concerns should be raised. The OPG will also consider what further steps are required to protect the victim's estate. Such steps will include revocation of the appointment of the attorney or deputy, recovery of assets by any joint attorney, or new deputy appointed by the court, and/or calling in of the surety bond by the court.

Care Quality Commission

Where the financial abuse has been perpetrated by a member of staff at a care home and you are concerned about a child or a vulnerable adult the Care Quality

Commission (CQC) recommends that in the first instance you should contact the social care department at the appropriate local authority. If you can't get through to the local council, you can call the CQC on 03000 616161 or email them at enquiries@cqc.org.uk

The CQC's primary responsibilities for safeguarding are stated to be:

'(1) Ensuring providers have the right systems and processes in place to make sure children and adults are protected from abuse and neglect. We do this through our inspection regime. We publish ratings and inspection reports, so people who use services can understand if providers have effective systems to safeguard people.

(2) Working with other inspectorates (Ofsted, HMI Probation, HMI Constabulary, HMI Prisons) to review how health, education, police, and probation services work in partnership to help and protect children and young people and adults from significant harm.

(3) Holding providers to account and securing improvements by taking enforcement action.

(4) Using intelligent monitoring, where we collect and analyse information about services, and responding to identified risks to help keep children and adults safe.

(5) Working with local partners to share information about safeguarding.'

Care homes and other providers are responsible for keeping people in their care safe from harm or abuse at all times. Providers are required by the Care Quality Commission (Registration) Regulations 2009, SI 2009/3112 to notify the CQC of serious incidents that occur to people in their care, including the death of a child or adult using their service, abuse or allegations of abuse in relation to a child or adult using their service, or any incident that is reported to, or investigated by, the police. In addition, the CQC recommends that providers inform the CQC when a serious case review or safeguarding adults review is opened by a local authority regarding an adult cared for in one of their homes.

The CQC has a range of enforcement powers that can be used to hold providers and individuals to account for failures in protecting adults from abuse and neglect. These aim to protect people who use regulated services from harm and the risk of harm, and ensure they receive health and social care services of an appropriate standard. There is, therefore, a clear and direct link between safeguarding and enforcement powers.

The starting point in considering using enforcement powers is to assess the harm or risk of harm to adults using the service. The action the CQC may take corresponds to the severity of the risk posed to the individual(s) and evidence of multiple or persistent breaches. They will only take action that if it is proportionate. For instance, where an adult is exposed to harm (whether physical or psychological), or where that harm has occurred, the CQC will consider using their powers of prosecution – they can do this in certain circumstances without first having to issue a warning notice. For example, breaches of the fundamental standard on safeguarding are prosecutable.

Abuse helplines

The charity Action on Elder Abuse runs a helpline which offers confidential help and advice on all aspects elder abuse (telephone 080 8808 8141).

9B

What Does the Client Want to Do?

When we talk about remedies, we are not just considering recovery of missing funds or assets, but also how the victims can recover from the shame, trauma and embarrassment of having succumbed to the abuse in the first place. What is clear is that it takes its toll on the victim and anything that we as practitioners can do to recover not only their money but also their dignity and the status quo is time well spent. This will not be possible in many cases. The victim may well not recover from the loss and – even more pertinently – it may be only after their death that knowledge of the abuse or the extent of the financial abuse comes to light. We can, though, do all we can to recover the assets for their estate.

As we saw earlier, the first steps to be taken are to understand what has gone on. The first indication we usually have is of a concerned family member contacting us with information suggesting that (typically) another family member is misappropriating funds from the elderly relative. The first steps should be to ask the following questions:

(1) Does the elderly person have mental capacity?

(2) If they do, they need to be approached directly and asked what is happening and told that you have information to suggest funds are being taken. It is likely that the elderly person will either be unaware that this is happening, not believe what you are saying, or say that they do not want you to get involved. However, they may well have their capacity but be vulnerable due to reduced physical powers; they may have hearing, eye-sight or mobility problems that mean they are dependent on a third party to get cash from the bank. It is right for you to raise your concerns with them and ask them to check their bank statements, ask for receipts for cash withdrawals, make sure that their debit card is always returned to them with a receipt after use and all withdrawals explained. Bank statements should be checked every month and unexplained debits or transfers all accounted for.

(3) If they do not want you to get involved it is right that you remain concerned and vigilant so that if other incidents come to light you can then take steps and suggest that the elderly person should appoint an independent person to act at their attorney. Suggest this as a safeguard which can continue after they lose their capacity.

(4) If the incidents continue and you have firm evidence that funds are being taken which are unauthorised then report this to the police. See Chapter 6D for the different offences that could be committed.

You should also be aware that occasionally executors who have discovered missing funds from an estate have approached the recipients and asked them to repay the funds to the victims' estate or treat the funds as outstanding loans. It is understandable that this approach may be adopted, but if a crime has been committed then it should be reported. My personal view is that if funds have been taken then there is a clear responsibility on the executors to inform the police. The definition of theft (see above) is quite clear. There seems to be far too much blurring of lines between what is another person's money and a possible future inheritance. Note that the OPG no longer has jurisdiction once P has died.

It is important that if the victim has their capacity and the perpetrator has control of their finances then any power of attorney, third-party mandate or appointeeship should be revoked immediately. A registered LPA can be revoked by a deed of revocation. This must be sent to the OPG for the registration of the LPA to be ended. The LPA could be partially revoked if there are more than one attorney and the client only wants to revoke one of the appointments.

The client will need help to do this and inevitably they may be reluctant to take this step if the perpetrator is a close relative. The attorney will have to be informed of the revocation and asked to return any papers or copy powers of attorney. Informing social services would be sensible if there is any fear of repercussions. Any financial institution, for example, the banks or pension authorities who have received copies of the power of attorney, should also be informed of the revocation. Note that there is a difference between revocation of a registered LPA and a registered EPA. In the case of a registered EPA the revocation must be carried out by the Court of Protection as the donor will be mentally incapable of revoking the EPA.

The exercise of the High Court's inherent jurisdiction may also be used to obtain appropriate orders, where the person is vulnerable, even if not incapacitated by mental disorder or mental illness, or is reasonably believed to be, either:

- under constraint; or

- subject to coercion or undue influence; or

- for some other reason deprived of the capacity to make the relevant decision, or disabled from making a free choice, or incapacitated or disabled from giving or expressing a real and genuine consent.

Munby J has described a vulnerable adult as 'someone who, whether or not mentally incapacitated, and whether or not suffering from any mental illness or mental disorder, was or might be unable to take care of him or herself, or unable to protect him or herself against significant harm or exploitation, or who was substantially handicapped by illness, injury or congenital deformity'. See Chapter 3 on vulnerable but mentally capable clients and the cases of *DL v A Local Authority*

[2012] EWCA Civ 253 and *A (Vulnerable Adult with Capacity: Marriage)* [2006] 1 FLR 867.

Victim has lost their capacity

If the victim has lost their mental capacity, the OPG should be informed as well as the police. The OPG will, however, only have jurisdiction if an attorney or deputy has been appointed to act for the elderly person and provided that the power of attorney appointing the attorney has been registered. It may well be that there is an EPA in existence but not registered as it should have been if the donor has now lost their capacity. A concerned third party could apply to be the donor's deputy for financial affairs and in the application draw to the court's attention the fact that there is an EPA in existence but the attorney has failed in their duty to register the instrument and therefore ask the court to revoke their appointment.

The OPG's contact details are as follows:

Office of the Public Guardian

PO Box 16185

Birmingham

B2 2WH

opg.safeguardingunit@publicguardian.gsi.gov.uk

Telephone: 0115 934 2777

Or see www.gov.uk/report-concern-about-attorney-deputy

If there is no attorney or deputy appointed then a call to the local social services team for any care or safeguarding issues would be sensible. If the financial abuse occurred in a care home, a report to the care home manager or the Care Quality Commission would be advisable. If someone's benefits are being taken the Department for Work and Pensions should be contacted.

The Court of Protection has wide powers not only to remove an attorney or deputy and revocation of a power of attorney, but also the following in MCA 2005, s 18:

- the control and management of the patient's property;
- the sale, exchange, charging, gift or other disposition of the patient's property;
- the acquisition of property in the patient's name or on the patient's behalf;
- the carrying on, on the patient's behalf, of any profession, trade or business;
- the taking of a decision which will have the effect of dissolving a partnership of which the patient is a member;
- the carrying out of any contract entered into by the patient;

- the discharge of the patient's debts and of any of the patient's obligations, whether legally enforceable or not;

- the settlement of any of the patient's property, whether for the patient's benefit or for the benefit of others;

- the execution for the patient of a will;

- the exercise of any power (including a power to consent) vested in the patient whether beneficially or as trustee or otherwise;

- the conduct of legal proceedings in the patient's name or on the patient's behalf.

The OPG investigation unit is empowered by The Lasting Powers of Attorney, Enduring Powers of Attorney and Public Guardian Regulations 2007, SI 2007/1253 to investigate. In Reg 46 it has the power to require information from donees of lasting power of attorney. This regulation has as associated Explanatory Memorandum note. Where there are circumstances suggesting that the donee of a lasting power of attorney may:

- have behaved, or may be behaving, in a way that contravenes his authority or is not in the best interests of the donor of the power;

- be proposing to behave in a way that would contravene that authority or would not be in the donor's best interests; or

- have failed to comply with the requirements of an order made, or directions given, by the court.

The Public Guardian has the power to require the donee to provide information and produce specified documents. Regulation 47 has similar powers in respect of the the donee of an EPA where it appears to the Public Guardian that there are circumstances suggesting that, having regard to all the circumstances (and in particular the attorney's relationship to or connection with the donor) the attorney under a registered enduring power of attorney may be unsuitable to be the donor's attorney.

Visitors

Under Reg 48 the Public Guardian has power to:

- direct a Court of Protection visitor:

    (i) to visit an attorney under a registered enduring power of attorney; or

    (ii) to visit the donor of a registered enduring power of attorney, and to make a report to the Public Guardian on such matters as he may direct;

- dealing with representations (including complaints) about the way in which an attorney under a registered enduring power of attorney is exercising his powers.

Breaches of duty as an attorney or deputy

The Code of Practice to the MCA 2005 sets out the various duties on those who manage the finances of another person by way of attorney ship or deputyship. It provides as follows:

Breach of fiduciary duty

A fiduciary duty means attorneys must not take advantage of their position. They should not put themselves in a position where their personal interests conflict with their duties. They also must not allow any other influences to affect the way in which they act as an attorney. Decisions should always benefit the donor, and not the attorney. Attorneys must not profit or get any personal benefit from their position, apart from receiving gifts where the Act allows it, whether or not it is at the donor's expense.

Duty to keep accounts

Property and affairs attorneys must keep accounts of transactions carried out on the donor's behalf. Sometimes the Court of Protection will ask to see accounts. If the attorney is not a financial professional and the donor's affairs are relatively straightforward, a record of the donor's income and expenditure (for example, through bank statements) may be enough. The more complicated the donor's affairs, the more detailed the accounts may need to be.

Duty to keep the donor's money and property separate

Property and affairs attorneys should usually keep the donor's money and property separate from their own or anyone else's. There may be occasions where donors and attorneys have agreed in the past to keep their money in a joint bank account (for example, if a husband is acting as his wife's attorney). It might be possible to continue this under the LPA. But in most circumstances, attorneys must keep finances separate to avoid any possibility of mistakes or confusion.

In the case of *Re DWA* [2015] EWCOP 72, the LPA was revoked due to the attorney's breach of fiduciary duty to the donor (her mother) taking advantage of her position to obtain a personal benefit from it. She also failed to account for all the transactions carried out on her donor's behalf and she contravened the duty to keep her money separate from the donor's.

In the case of *Bashir v Bashir* [2013] EWHC 1043, the claimant sought a declaration in respect of funds removed by the deputy where some 80% of funds totalling £1.77 m had been left unaccounted for. As deputy she was a trustee of those funds and the declaration included an application for an order for an account and enquiry on account of the deputy's breach of trust and breach of fiduciary duty.

Where such breaches of duty are proved, these will be grounds for removal of the attorney or deputy by the Court of Protection. If there is no suitable joint or replacement attorney then a panel deputy may be appointed in their place.

9C

Investigation and Recovery of Assets

The Office of the Public Guardian

The Lasting Powers of Attorney, Enduring Powers of Attorney and Public Guardian Regulations 2007, SI 2007/1253, Regs 46–48 empowers the Office of the Public Guardian (OPG) to investigate activities of registered attorneys and deputies.

In the year 2015/16 the OPG annual report reported that Court of Protection visitors completed 9,829 visits during the year supporting the Public Guardian's supervision and investigations activity. Cases involving suspected abuse were prioritised with 97.3% of commissions issued to a visitor within 24 hours.

The OPG administers the panel of deputies, which the Court of Protection draws on in cases where no one is able or willing to act as deputy. In 2015/16, the court made 366 panel deputy referrals and the OPG made 186 panel deputy referrals. Twenty-nine assurance visits were made to panel deputies, along with visits to their clients.

The Public Guardian may commission a report by a Court of Protection visitor as part of his supervision of deputies, or investigations into concerns about the actions of a deputy or attorney. Reg 44 of the Lasting Powers of Attorney, Enduring Powers of Attorney and Public Guardian Regulations allows the Public Guardian, if he considers it appropriate to do so, to release a visitor's report to any person interviewed in the course of preparing a report, and invite him/her to comment on it. This could include the deputy, client, donor, attorney or any third party interviewed by the visitor such as a relative or carer.

Investigation unit

The first contact from the OPG investigation unit where a complaint has been made will be a notice confirming that the attorney or deputy is under investigation. The complainant's name will not be supplied to the attorney/deputy and sometimes the actual allegations but simply that the Public Guardian is investigating concerns raised about the management of X's Property and Financial Affairs. They will have to supply answers to questions and paperwork. It is important to ensure that whether you are an attorney or deputy you must keep full paperwork for all financial decisions and be in a position to explain all financial decisions, payments and transactions.

The OPG released statistics showing the source of the referrals received by the Unit. These were as follows:

- 38% were received from concerned relatives or friends;

- 24% from local authorities;

- 9% from solicitors;

- 9% received from attorneys and deputies (usually to report concerns about a co-deputy/attorney or about a third party);

- 20% were received from banks, doctors, advocates, carers and the police.

The OPG's Annual Report and Accounts 2014–15 reported that it had received a total of 1,970 new safeguarding referrals during 2014/15, down from 2,200 in 2013/14.

Following risk assessment, 743 cases were progressed to full investigation, an increase of 18% from the previous year. 695 cases were concluded in that year. Where cases were not suitable for investigation, advice was offered or they were signposted to the appropriate agency such as the local authority or police.

Aspect investigations

The OPG introduced a pilot fast-track procedure called 'aspect investigations' aimed to progress investigations of suspected abuse more quickly in non-complex cases. Out of 50 cases in the pilot, 25 were concluded in an average of 42 working days, well within the target of 75 days for full investigations. Seven of the 25 concluded cases needed further enquiries beyond the original scope.

Mediation pilot scheme

A key objective carried forward from previous years was to develop the approach to resolving issues with deputies and attorneys, without the need for recourse to the Court of Protection, by building an in-house mediation capacity. A pilot scheme ran between December 2013 and March 2015. Fifty-six cases were identified where mediation would benefit parties. Mediation was eventually successful in nine of these cases, and in each of these a satisfactory formal agreement was reached. This avoided the need for the OPG to undertake further investigations or make a referral to the Court of Protection, so there was benefit to all parties. They plan to launch the mediation service in 2016/17.

Investigation and Recovery of Assets

2015/16

The OPG Annual Report for 2015/16 reported:

'Safeguarding referrals came from a number of sources, including relatives, local authorities, care homes and financial institutions. We continue to work very closely with our external partners – including the CoP, security bond providers, local authorities and the police – to protect and safeguard our clients.

'OPG received a total of 2,681 new safeguarding referrals during 2015/16, an increase of 26.5% from the previous year. This year we investigated 876 cases, an increase of 15.2% from the previous year, of which 151 cases resulted in an application to the CoP. All of our investigations were concluded within 69 days on average, exceeding our target of 70 days. Where cases were not appropriate for us to investigate, we offered advice or directed referrals to the right agency such as the local authority or police.'

In 2014/15 fast-track investigations were introduced by the OPG. These were investigations centred on singular aspects or concerns, such as cases where the investigation is focused on solitary allegations of financial or welfare related abuse.

Typical examples of cases considered during the year included:

- undervalued house sales;
- the client's home being sold to the attorney;
- large financial sums transferred from the client's bank account to another bank account;
- creating fraudulent LPAs.

Sharing information with other agencies

The OPG report also stated:

'... in July 2015 we put in place a memorandum of understanding with the Department for Work and Pensions so we can share information to jointly protect adults at risk. In December we agreed an information sharing protocol with the National Police Chiefs' Council. This is to ensure we apply best practice to referrals made to the police where any criminal activity is suspected.'

In its annual report for 2015/16 the OPG reported that it had been involved in over 300 unreported cases involving action against misbehaving attorneys and deputies. They also assisted judges under MCA 2005, s 49 in over 200 cases, instigating new inquiries and investigations where needed.

Court of Protection

Recovery of assets

As can be seen above, the OPG is introducing a mediation service as part of their tools to assist the Public Guardian in resolving disputes. If funds and assets can be recovered as part of that process then this is to be welcomed.

Alternatively, very often a panel deputy will be appointed by the court and they will have to consider, following financial abuse of the patient, taking proceedings to recover assets for P. They will have to weigh up the cost of taking proceedings against the likelihood of recovery of those assets.

Calling in of surety bond

As we will see in Chapter 9E they are designed to provide financial security if a deputy falls foul of the rules. It is clear, however, that the court rarely enforces the calling in of the bond. What would make more sense is that they were called in as a matter of course where funds have been misappropriated and also to introduce bonds where attorneys actively acting under a financial affairs LPA or an EPA to protect and secure the patient's funds. This would be a simple security measure to reassure clients that their estate has a safety net if their appointed attorney or the court-appointed deputy removes assets from their estate.

Statutory wills

The Court of Protection (see MCA 2005, ss 16 and 18) provides that a will can be executed on behalf of the patient by the court. This can be a useful device to put right any financial abuse and provides a remedy for the patient's intended beneficiaries. It can be used to provide a new will where the patient would otherwise die intestate or it can be used to amend an inadequate will.

Accounts

There is a common law duty to account, but there is no statutory requirement.

Attorneys

An attorney taking up his or her appointment under an LPA in the 2013 version had to sign a declaration that included the following:

> 'I have a duty to keep accounts and financial records and produce them to the Office of the Public Guardian and/or to the Court of Protection on request.'

Unfortunately – and, it could be said, to the detriment of the donor's protection – this wording no longer appears in the attorney's declaration in the later versions of the LPA. It is hard to understand the reasoning behind this. Surely it is so important to stress to attorneys the need to keep the fullest possible accounts. It is certainly worth reminding them at this important point and not simply leaving it to accompanying notes to provide details of this important obligation.

Code of Practice paragraph 7.49 provides that 'All attorneys should keep records of their dealings with the donor's affairs ... The court can order attorneys to produce records (for example, financial accounts) and to provide specific reports, information or documentation. If somebody has concerns about an attorney's payment or expenses, the court could resolve the matter.'

Paragraph 7.67 states that property and affairs attorneys must keep accounts of transactions carried out on the donor's behalf. Sometimes the Court of Protection will ask to see accounts. If the attorney is not a financial expert and the donor's affairs are relatively straightforward, a record of the donor's income and expenditure (for example, through bank statements) may be enough. The more complicated the donor's affairs, the more detailed the accounts may need to be.

In respect of EPAs the Court of Protection has jurisdiction under MCA 2005, Sch 4, para 16(2)(b)(iii) in respect of the keeping of accounts and records by EPA attorneys.

Deputies

MCA 2005, s 19(9)(b) provides that the court may require a deputy:

- to give to the Public Guardian such security as the court thinks fit for the due discharge of his functions; and

- to submit to the Public Guardian such reports at such times or at such intervals as the court may direct.

Para 8.66 of the Code of Practice is a duty to keep accounts in the following terms:

> 'A deputy appointed to manage property and affairs is expected to keep, and periodically submit to the Public Guardian, correct accounts of all their dealings and transactions on the person's behalf.'

In practice, annual accounts are required from deputies on the anniversary of their appointment.

Deputy's annual report for property and financial decisions will cover the following details:

- decisions made over the reporting period;
- people you consulted;
- safeguarding including contact with the client and care arrangements;
- care arrangements;
- client's accounts and assets;
- client's money paid out – including gifts and professional and other expenses;
- client's assets and debts – including whether you have taken independent financial advice on behalf of the client and who occupies the client's property;
- decisions in the next reporting period – including whether significant financial decisions & whether you have any concerns about your deputyship.

Case law shows that one of the early indicators that funds are being misappropriated is when accounts are not produced to the court in accordance with the rules. Similarly, another indicator is when care home fees are left unpaid but the client seemingly has sufficient funds to pay these. The accounts rules are an important tool in both helping deputies to regulate their patient's affairs but also in showing the OPG that management of the patient's affairs are getting out of hand or even that funds have gone missing without adequate explanation.

In the case of *Re AFR* [2015] EWCOP 73 the court heard that the deputies annual report referred to loans made to the deputies themselves. When asked for further details the deputies responded by saying they were paying the loans back and that one of the loan payments had been to fund the legal fees for her divorce. The deputies here also made payments to themselves and had shopping and restaurant bills debited from the patient's accounts even though the patient was resident in a care home. The deputies' appointment was revoked and a panel deputy appointed in their place. That new deputy would then need to recover the funds

Duty to keep the donor's money and property separate

Para 7.68 of the Code of Practice states:

> 'Property and affairs attorneys should usually keep the donor's money and property separate from their own or anyone else's. There may be occasions where donors and attorneys have agreed in the past to keep their money in a joint bank account (for example, if a husband is acting as his wife's attorney). It might be possible to continue this under the LPA. But in most circumstances, attorneys must keep finances separate to avoid any possibility of mistakes or confusion.'

In *Re DWA* [2015] EWCOP 72 the LPA was revoked due to the attorney's breach of fiduciary duty to the donor, her mother, taking advantage of her position, obtaining a personal benefit from her position. She also failed to account for all the transactions carried out on her donor's behalf and she contravened the duty to keep her money separate from the donor's.

Where such breaches of duty are proved these will be grounds for removal of the attorney or deputy by the Court of Protection. If there is no suitable joint or replacement attorney then a panel deputy may be appointed in their place.

Action by attorneys, deputies or executors to recover assets

What steps can be taken to recover assets for the donor or patient or their estate?

Evidence required

The remaining joint attorney or new deputy or executor needs firstly to collate all necessary evidence including bank statements, cheque book stubs, bills and all other financial records. A best interests assessment should be carried out to show that the patient does not have capacity to revoke any power of attorney themselves or to litigate to recover misappropriated funds and property on their own behalf.

- handwriting expert evidence: evidence may not be conclusive but that the forged signatures suggest that the defendant was responsible;
- check dates for when bank transfers were made;
- medical evidence as to capacity of victim at the date of transfer of funds;
- bank's/NSI fraud unit's assistance;
- Social Services safeguarding unit assessment;
- paperwork – including copy of care home registers, wills, paperwork, bank statements, cheque stubs, computer records, property details, share contract notes and investment manager's statements. DWP evidence concerning benefit applications.

The post-death investigation into accounting for the patient will usually be through the Chancery Division as the Court of Protection's jurisdiction will have ended. It is only likely to be successful if fraud or misrepresentation can be established.

Negotiations

It may well be that an OPG investigation coupled with a visitor report will assist in recovery of assets. If not then negotiations and mediation will assist. It is not always sensible to initiate court proceedings where the cost of those proceedings will outweigh the benefits.

Declaration for an order for an account and enquiry

In the case of *Bashir v Bashir* [2013] EWHC 1043 the claimant sought a declaration in respect of funds removed by the deputy where some 80% of funds totalling £1.77m had been left unaccounted for. As deputy she was a trustee of those funds and the declaration included an application for an order for an account and enquiry on account of the deputy's breach of trust and breach of fiduciary duty.

Freezing injunctions

The High Court can make freezing injunctions to prevent money or property being disposed of, and search orders to allow access to the perpetrator's home or workplace to locate documents. Injunctions can also be obtained to prevent the perpetrator from leaving the country. The donor with capacity or a person acting as litigation friend for the mentally incapacitated donor can also apply to the High Court for recovery of funds and setting aside a transfer of an asset, procured by undue influence, duress or fraud.

An application for such an injunction should include a request that the respondent does not remove from England and Wales or in any way dispose of deal or diminish the value of any of their assets in England and Wales up to the value of a certain amount depending on what evidence you have as to funds missing. Specify any known property or bank accounts in the respondent's names. If further funds are found to be missing then return to court and have the amount of the freezing injunction amended upwards. Request the court to provide for your costs.

The injunction application should apply to all the respondents' assets whether in their sole or joint names. There should also be a request that the respondent provides you with information about all their assets within the jurisdiction within 24 hours giving the value, location and details of all such assets.

Request also that the respondents preserve and deliver up within three working days after service of the order, all documents in their possession or control belonging to the victim.

Witness statement

You will need to set out full details in witness statement form as to what is missing, what evidence you have and why you think the respondents have taken this.

Case law illustrations

In *Hammond v Osborn* [2002] EWCA Civ 885 the respondents argued that the deceased Mr Pritler had made gifts to Mrs Osborn. Mr Pritler was 72 years old and lived alone and became dependent on others, including Mrs Osborn, a neighbour, to help him. It transpired that he wrote out cheques in her favour totalling £297,005 and these represented some 91.6% of her liquid assets. A further consequence of the realisation of his investments was that he became prospectively liable for charges for capital gains tax and higher rate tax amounting to £49,670.92.

The judge found that on no occasion did Mrs Osborn specifically draw to Mr Pritler's attention the size, even in approximate terms, of the gift he was making her. Nor did she draw his attention either to the proportion of his liquid assets that it represented or to the relatively small amount that was left to him. Nor did she discuss with him the possible fiscal consequences of the realisations.

Mr Pritler died intestate, leaving as his next of kin three first cousins including the claimant, Margaret Betina Hammond. On 5 June 2000 letters of administration were granted to Mrs Hammond, who, on 19 July 2000, obtained a freezing order against Mrs Osborn and Mr Francis, the claim form in the action being issued in the Queen's Bench Division on the following day. On 2 August 2000 the freezing orders were continued, with minor modifications, until the trial. The court ruled in favour of the appellant Mrs Hammond on the grounds of presumed undue influence.

In *Bashir v Bashir* [2013] EWHC 1043 (Ch) the claimant applied for summary judgement on his claim. It involved a declaration that the defendant, the claimant's elder sister, was a trustee of all amounts paid out to her from the Court of Protection funds. These funds were held for the claimant by the court as a result of compensation of £1,773,611 awarded to him following a serious injury from an assault. He also asked for an order for an account and enquiry as to the application of such funds and for immediate payment to him of the whole amount received by the defendant. This was on the basis of breach of trust and breach of fiduciary duty in relation to all such amounts.

In this case, as Tim Polli of Tanfield Chambers has written, the Court of Protection suspended Ms Bashir's deputyship and made an interim appointment of a professional deputy. The OPG arranged a visitor to visit and report back. Ms Bashir was ordered to provide detailed accounts. An application was made for a freezing order and a proprietary injunction on the basis that it was needed to preserve property in which the applicant had an interest. Ms Bashir argued that the payments included payments for a cousin's wedding, a payment to Mr Bashir's wife to allow her to buy a house for him and regular cash payments for living expenses for the family. The court ordered an account, summary judgement for £550,000, Order for costs to be assessed and an order for a payment on account of costs. It is understood that a criminal trial is still awaited.

9D

Practical Steps to Safeguard against Abuse

In reflecting on what is involved in financial abuse of the elderly it seems that there are some simple steps we can all adopt to give us protection for the future for ourselves, our elderly relatives and friends.

First of all, how do we envisage the future when we are less able to shop and care for ourselves, less mobile, more forgetful and less able to see and hear? We would presumably want someone close to us to be our carer. To carry out all those tasks that we will be unable to do. We want to trust them to care for us in a loving way with compassion and patience. What should we do if we do not have the benefit of an adult child who has the time, energy and ability to carry out this role? If we have a spouse or a partner then we have a carer ready and able to do this. What if we are bereaved and have lost our partner? The problem is just as significant for those in large families as for those with no family at all. In a large family will there be one or more individuals who can share this role? Is it a role that can be shared? We live longer but will also be postponing retirement from work to a later date. How do we reconcile this problem?

There are various steps we can take to protect our finances and estates from an abuser. Many people would recognise that most abusers come from within their own families and are often those closest to them and who are ostensibly there to care for them. What is suggested is that, as we do not know if this problem will affect us in later years and especially when dementia takes hold, some simple protective measures seem sensible.

(1) Identify who you would like to look after you in the future:

(a) your partner or spouse;

(b) other family member;

(c) close friend;

(d) professionally qualified carer;

(e) no one.

(2) Ask yourself the following questions:

(a) How well do you understand their financial management skills?

(b) Will they treat your finances and assets with respect and as your own rather than general family funds?

(c) Have they ever had financial problems or have they been declared bankrupt?

(d) Does anyone have influence over them and could therefore influence them in the management of your finances and property?

(e) What will happen if they can no longer act for you?

(f) Have you taken independent legal advice and discussed all details with your solicitor?

(3) Appoint an attorney under a lasting power of attorney:

(a) incorporate safeguards into that document;

(b) annual audit of your finances and property;

(c) prohibit any powers of gifting your property unless the court has authorised this;

(d) prohibit loans to anyone. Those who need loans should make their own commercial arrangements. Remind them you are not the family bank;

(e) limit the care allowances or expenses allowed by your attorney and have them agreed by a professional third party.

(4) If appointing a live-in carer:

(a) avoid employing a carer directly unless they come recommended from a trusted source;

(b) use a reputable carer's agency who can monitor and supervise the carer and change them as required;

(c) ask the appointed person to provide you with a criminal records check (see www.disclosurescotland.co.uk for details). This will provide the employer with details of any convictions or confirmation that there have been no convictions.

(5) Ensure no social isolation:

(a) prepare a statement of wishes and values so that these are available to any carer or care agency when you are no longer able to communicate these (see example in Appendix A);

(b) ensure regular contact with:

(i) family;

(ii) friends;

(iii) GP;

(iv) solicitor.

(c) key-holders;

(d) careline call services;

(e) call the Silver Line helpline on 0800 4 70 80 90 (this is the only national confidential and free helpline for older people open every day and night of the year);

(f) Consider very carefully whether you want someone to be a live-in carer when you grow old and how they can be monitored. Remember your ability to be rational and focused will diminish if you are bereaved and lonely.

(6) Banking arrangements:

(a) consider how you will pay for services as you get older. Set up direct debits and standing orders. Insist that all services are paid for through your account and not by cash. Retain a cheque book for this purpose or ask the bank to arrange payment;

(b) introduce your trusted carer to the bank so that they can recognise them and allow them to talk to the bank on your behalf if you are unable to do so;

(c) arrange a limited-spend cash card and ensure that a third party can verify expenditure on this. See above about annual accounting of expenditure.

(7) Ensure that your trusted third parties can recognise financial abuse warning signs – see Appendix B.

(8) Give your solicitor a full family tree so they know at a glance what the family relationships are. It will not tell them who is in favour or not, but it is a really helpful starting point. It also leads to discussions about other non-family members who feature prominently in their lives and who should be considered in discussions with the solicitor.

Surety Bonds

One of the ways in which a person's estate can be protected against unauthorised use or abuse is by the provision of a security or surety bond. Whenever a deputy is appointed by the Court of Protection the order appointing the deputy will require the deputy to take out a bond before the order is issued. Under MCA 2005, s 19(9)(a) the court may require a deputy to give such security as the court thinks fit for the discharge of his functions. The giving of security is governed by rule 200 of the Court of Protection Rules 2007 and in the Lasting Powers of Attorney, Enduring Powers of Attorney and Public Guardian Regulations 2007, SI 2007/1253 as amended by the Lasting Powers of Attorney, Enduring Powers of Attorney and Public Guardian (Amendment) Regulations 2010, SI 2010/1063.

The regulations provide that security must be given by means of a bond in accordance with the regulations or in such other manner as the court may direct. The applicant only complies with this if the bond has been endorsed in accordance with the regulations and that person has notified the OPG of that fact. A bond is only entered into if it has been endorsed by an authorised insurance company or authorised deposit-taker. Such companies may be those already authorised by the OPG or the person may make other arrangements which the OPG will then authorise.

In practice this means that most deputy applicants will take up the bond with an existing authorised provider through Howden Group UK Ltd who won the contract from 1 October 2016. Formerly surety bonds were provided by Marsh Ltd and then Deputy Bond Services. The contract is usually reviewed every two to four years.

Bond providers' expectations

In March 2012 the OPG issued a statement of expectations of the Public Guardian. This note was issued by the OPG to explain what was required by bond providers where deputies wanted to move outside the scheme. They would need:

- to understand the unique nature of deputy bonds;
- meet the requirements of the Regulations; and
- provide the requisite protection for the patient.

Those providers who can meet the requirements of the scheme are placed on a list maintained by the OPG and made available to the Court of Protection. The OPG reviews the way the providers are meeting those requirements on an annual basis. The providers are in addition be expected to maintain full membership of the British Insurers Brokers' Association. They must also understand that the bond is solely put in place for P's protection and not the protection of the deputy.

The OPG note also required providers to understand the following:

- the amount of security required is set by the court and cannot be varied by the bond provider or the OPG;

- neither the OPG or the court are party to the bond, which is between the deputy and the bond provider;

- once entered into, the bond cannot be cancelled by either party for any reason;

- the bond can only be discharged by the court;

- upon cessation of the deputyship the bond will lapse in line with the timescales in SI 2007/1253, Reg 37(3) as amended;

- to discharge a bond outside these timescales will require one of the parties to make an application to the court.

Where a deputy wishes to change providers, the new provider must not only comply with these regulations but also ensure that it will accept retrospective liability for any loss during the deputyship no matter when it occurred. If this is not accepted, the deputy will need to understand he will be liable to pay premiums for both bonds.

Level of premiums and amount of security

The level of security is set by the Court of Protection. The level depends on various factors including the size of the estate, and the extent to which the deputy will have access to that estate. It will also take into account where there is a professional deputy the existence of professional indemnity insurance.

The court will consider various options including that security be given:

- to cover the entire value of the estate under administration;

- proportionate to the value of the estate (income and/or capital) over which the deputy will have direct control (where the court restricts access to funds and property);

- through a single premium bond of generic value designed to provide lifetime cover for estates of limited value.

On 1 October 2016 a new provider was appointed. The tender process documents request that management information is provided in relation to the provision of suretys. This will include volumes of bonds, amount of security provided, claims, size of premiums, trends and issues. Existing bonds continue to with the existing insurance brokers.

The usual level of the bond set by the OPG will be 0.2% of the assets of the patient. £100,000 is the average security and therefore the premium at this level is £200 per annum. Most deputyship last on average 3.5 years and therefore the the payment required for the period of the deputyship at £700 for £100,000 of cover is not too high a price to pay for that level of security. The bond cover is limited to £1,000,000. Accordingly, for very high-value estates further consideration needs to be given for protection; for example, the appointment of a professional deputy who has the benefit of professional indemnity insurance.

SI 2007/1253, Reg 35 provides that the OPG must be satisfied that the premiums have been paid. This is usually confirmed in the annual accounts. It is possible to replace the security during the currency of the deputyship order. Again, the OPG must be satisfied that that is sufficient and that the requirements of the regulations have been met.

Changes to the amount of security

The court can make stipulations that the bond should be increased. This could happen where the deputy makes an application to increase access to funds. For example, if a house is sold and the deputy then controls the proceeds of sale. This increases the level of risk that funds could be lost through abuse, unauthorised gifts or poor investment. In such cases the bond level will be reviewed and increased. In such instances no further paperwork is required, but the level of security is increased and the premiums rise as a result (see also Public Guardian's Practice Note SD15 issued in September 2016).

Case law

In *Baker v H* [2009] EWHC B31 (Fam), H was born on 18 January 2001. He suffered from severe dystonic quadriplegic cerebral palsy and was unable to move or support himself unassisted. He required 24-hour care. He lives with and is cared for by his parents.

A claim was made on H's behalf against the local NHS Trust. In anticipation of a structured settlement Mr Baker was appointed with very wide general powers to manage H's funds, for the benefit of him, and his family and anyone else for whom H might be expected to provide.

Initially the Court of Protection exercised its power to set security, and did so in the sum of £15,000 at an annual premium of £47.50. There was then a settlement under which H received a lump sum of £1,211,714 and annual periodical payments commencing at £25,000, rising to £32,000 at age 11 and £85,000 at age 18.

He applied for permission to apply £819,274 out of H's capital to purchase a property to be held in the names of his parents as trustees. This was to secure an appropriate house for H, with subsequent arrangements to be made to replace at least part of H's capital when the then family house could be sold.

On 25 June 2008, DJ Jackson made an order without a hearing to include the following: 'The deputy is required forthwith to obtain and maintain security in the sum of £750,000 in accordance with the standard requirements as to the giving of security.'

The annual premium for Mr Baker to post security of £750,000 under the standard Master Bond scheme was £1,875.00 per annum. Comparison was made with the previous premium of £47.50, in respect of £15,000 security, and this caused considerable concern amongst the profession. Furthermore, the damages settlement agreed on behalf of H had included an estimate for the anticipated costs of providing security under the new regime, but this was only £765 per annum, which would provide security of £300,000.

The deputy argued firstly that the level of security ordered was way above the amount of the funds to which he had effective access – some £445,000 of capital, and only £25,000 a year of income. Secondly, as a solicitor he had professional indemnity cover set at many times the value of H's whole estate (in fact £105m per claim in his firm's case) and 18 years' experience in this field, holding many professional receiverships and deputyships, and had never had any claim made against him. All these points show, he submitted, that security of £750,000 was excessive, unnecessary and wasteful.

He also showed that the problem was more widespread, referring to two cases involving lay deputies who had been ordered to give security of the whole value of the estate (respectively £750,000 and £1m) when the deputyship orders under which they operated restrict their access to funds of £60,000 in any one year.

Summary of general guidance

Her Honour Judge Hazel Marshall stated as follows:

'(1) If the court has real doubts about whether a deputy can be trusted with P's assets, then it must consider not appointing him as a deputy. Alternatively (if this will largely allay such doubts), the court can and should consider imposing limits on the funds under the deputy's control and, in particular, should consider whether the general words of the order appointing the deputy should be narrowed to prevent his having any authority to deal with any property occupied by P as his home, (or any interest of P therein) without further order of the court.

(2) The court should then consider the amount of funds that are to be placed in the deputy's hands or under his control, and envisage the costs and/or loss to P if there were to be a total default by the deputy.

245

(3) The court should then consider whether the deputy carries professional indemnity insurance which would be effective to replace P's assets in his hands in the event of such a total default. This will include reviewing such matters as the level of aggregation of assets in the hands of a single deputy relative to his insurance.

(4) In the absence of adequate insurance cover then the starting point will be the value of the assets in or passing through the deputy's hands. This consideration may lead back to a review of the terms of the deputyship order with a view to limiting the value of the vulnerable assets.

(5) Where the deputy apparently has adequate and effective professional indemnity insurance, then the court:

    (i) should require him to deposit a copy of this with the OPG and inform the OPG/court immediately if its level is reduced; and

    (ii) should aim to set a level of security which will provide adequate resources to meet P's immediate expenditure needs for a period related to the time it may take to settle the insurance claim (perhaps up to two to three years), the costs of making such a claim, and an allowance in case immediate debts of P may have been left unpaid, applying a suitable margin for error.

[(6)] Having formed the above provisional view as to the appropriate level of security, the court should finally consider the level of premium and whether this would cause P undue financial hardship, or would otherwise in all the circumstances (including the apparent status of the deputy) appear to be an unjustifiable or wasteful use of P's resources, when balanced against the benefit of having that security. Special circumstances (eg husband/wife deputyships, or lay deputies of obvious stature, or situations in which the real risk would appear to be merely negligence rather than total default) may mitigate this, but must provide some real justification for taking the view that such a level of security is not reasonably necessary. The court will then decide whether it is in P's best interests to maintain the level of security originally assessed, or to reduce it to any extent.'

How is the security bond enforced?

Under SI 2007/1253, Reg 36 the court must order the enforcement of the security and the Public Guardian must notify any person who endorsed the security of the contents of the order and notify the court when payment has been made of the amount secured. In the OPG's Practice Note 03/2012 it explained what providers must understand about enforcement as follows:

• the court can call in all or part of the bond up to the limit secured. There is no requirement to prove fraud and the loss may not be quantifiable;

• the court may order an interim payment, ie that part of the bond is called in pending quantification of the loss;

- the insurer must pay on demand without further investigation;
- notification will be via a court order;
- it is expected that insurers will have the right to recover the amount they have paid out, plus their expenses, from the deputy. This is a matter for the insurer and in which the Public Guardian or court play no part.

Surprisingly there is very little case law on when the court calls in the security bond. The leading case here was *Re GM, MJ and JM v The Public Guardian* [2013] COPLR 290 handed down by the Court on 22 April 2013.

This was an application by the property and affairs deputy for an order calling in the £275,000 security bond of the two former deputies. The they had engaged in a course of conduct involving gifts to themselves, members of their families and charities. They had bought themselves cars, computers and luxury items and involved large transfers of cash. They had then made an application for retrospective approval of the gifts and transfers. Senior Judge Lush commented on his reasons for his judgement at paragraphs 95–99:

'95. I do not accept that the gifts were made in GM's best interests. They are completely out of character with any gifts she had made before the onset of dementia. There was no consultation with her before they were made and there was no attempt to permit and encourage her to participate in the decision-making process, or to ascertain her present wishes and feelings.

96. Nor do I accept the applicants' argument that they believed that the order appointing them allowed them to make gifts on such an extensive scale. They should have been aware of the law regarding their role and responsibilities. Ignorance is no excuse.

97. The fact that GM's remaining assets were in the names of one or other of the applicants, rather than in GM's name, is a further example of what is, at best, ignorance, and, at worst, stealth.

98. I realise that MJ and JM are the only visitors that GM receives, but this does not give them a licence to loot, and I was unimpressed by the veiled threat that, if the court were to remove them as deputies, they would find it difficult to continue seeing GM.

99. If they had made a proper application for the prospective of approval of gifts, I would possibly have allowed them to make gifts to themselves and their families to mitigate the incidence of Inheritance Tax on GM's death, but only if they had been the residuary beneficiaries under her will.'

The judge ordered their removal as GM's deputies and considered that a statutory will application was required to determine who would be entitled to GM's estate on her death and whether any of the gifts should be authorised.

The case of *Re Meek* [2014] EWCOP 1 was the subsequent application by the new deputy before HH Judge Henry Hodge QC for the following:

'(i) authority pursuant to section 18(1)(i) of the Mental Capacity Act 2005 to execute a statutory will on behalf of Mrs Meek; and

(ii) consequential directions in relation to Mrs Meek's property and affairs, and in particular:

(a) an order calling in the £275,000 security bond of Mrs Meek's two former property and affairs deputies, Mrs Janet Miller and Mrs Margaret Phyllis Johnson; and

(b) a direction as to whether the deputy should refer the conduct of Mrs Miller and Mrs Johnson to the police.'

The deputy suggested that it would not be in Mrs Meek's best interests for him to be required to bring recovery proceedings and he wanted the court to take a broad-brush approach calling in the security bond in the sum of £250,000. The judge referred to the case of *Baker v H* as above and summarised the position as follows:

'Effectively, the bond scheme offers an alternative to a deputy bringing an action against a previous defaulting deputy to recover lost or stolen funds. It provides an immediate, and straightforward, mechanism by which the court can ensure that an incapacitous person is compensated for losses that have been incurred through the default of his deputy. It avoids the delay and expense which the incapacitous person would otherwise face in bringing proceedings against a defaulting deputy, who may be of questionable solvency, and enforcing any judgment obtained within those proceedings. The defaulting deputy does not get off scot-free, but he is instead likely to face proceedings brought by the bond provider.'

There was then a review as to whether calling in the bond was in accordance with the 'best interests' principle laid down by MCA 2005, s 1(5). It was suggested that it would be rare event for the court not to ratify the gifts made by the deputies and not call in the security bond. Calling in the bond would ensure that P's estate would be recompensed without having to go to the expense of taking civil proceedings for the recovery of the loss suffered. If the court did not act in the case such as this, it was pointed out, it would undermine the whole basis of the security bond system.

The barrister for the former deputies argued that her clients should have an opportunity to repay half of the agreed amount outstanding of £250,000 within three months. She also argued that the balance should be called in during P's lifetime if she requires any further sums to meet the annual shortfall in income. The balance could be satisfied out of the presumptive entitlement of her clients under her proposed statutory will. However, it was unlikely that those arguments would sway the court and they were rejected.

The judge called in the whole security bond so that there was an effective and speedy source to remedy the default of the deputies.

Another case where the security bond was called in was *Re Joan Treadwell (Deceased), Public Guardian and Lutz* [2013] COPLR 587. Colin Lutz became the receiver (and subsequently deputy) for his mother, Mrs Treadwell. He was required to take out security in the sum of £200,000. There were five children from her first marriage and two step-daughters from her second. Colin Lutz was one of the children of the first marriage. It transpired that he made a series of unauthorised gifts whilst acting as deputy. These were discovered when he had to submit annual deputyship accounts to the OPG. He was invited by the OPG to apply for retrospective approval. There had been a great number of gifts to his own siblings and their children, but none to his step-sisters or their children despite the fact that his mother had wanted them to benefit under the terms of her will.

An investigation by the OPG investigations officer and a report by the senior legal adviser resulted in the Public Guardian applying to the Court of Protection to enforce the security bond. An analysis of the gifts made resulted in some which could be described as made on customary occasions and those within the principle that they were 'not unreasonable having regard to all the circumstances and, in particular, the size of the estate'. Having excluded the total of those gifts that it would have authorised the Public Guardian asked the court to call in the bond in the sum of £44,300 which represented the loss to Mrs Treadwell's estate.

The court had looked at the amount and type of gifts made. For example, it was not prepared to agree to the following gifts:

- housewarming gift of £1,800;
- graduation gift of £2,500;
- housewarming gift of £2,500;
- christening gift of £1,500.

These were respectively reduced to £50 for the housewarming gifts and £100 for the other gifts. These sums were much more reasonable. Furthermore, it was noted that his daughter Emily graduated some four years before the gift for her graduation was given.

The case is also an example of where the court will act even where the patient has died before the hearing had taken place. The court has residual jurisdiction in such an event concerning the deputy's final report and the transfer and delivery of funds.

Discharge of the surety bond

Under SI 2007/1253, Reg 37 the bond will be discharged if the court makes an order discharging it. Otherwise, under Reg 37(3) it will be discharged on the expiry of two years from the date of death of the patient or in any cases where the patient died before 1 May 2010 then the period was seven years from the date of death.

If the order discharging the deputy does not also discharge the surety bond then the seven-year period runs from the date of that order. Similarly, if the deputy otherwise ceases to be under a duty to discharge the functions in which he was ordered to give security, the period of seven years runs from the date on which that duty ceased.

If anyone takes any action with a view to discharging the security before the end of the period, the security will be treated as though it has not been discharged.

An application for the discharge of a security bond should be made by filing a COP9 application notice in accordance with the procedure set out in the Court of Protection Rules 2007, SI 2007/1744, Part 10.

Calling in of the bond

The terms of the guarantee bond taken out through Howden Group UK Ltd (or as otherwise agreed with the OPG or the Court of Protection), is that the company will guarantee that upon payment of the premiums due it will pay, as directed by the court or the OPG, to the patient or patient's personal representatives the amount of the loss not exceeding the amount of the security should the deputy fail to carry out their deputyship duties. The deputy and their personal representatives and estates will remain liable to the surety company should the bond be forfeited, and the surety company may take such action as is appropriate against the deputy personally to recover any loss.

OPG Practice Note 03/2012 states that bond-holders are required to understand the following points:

- the court can call in all or part of the bond up to the limit secured. There is no requirement to prove fraud and the loss may not be quantifiable;
- the court may order an interim payment, ie that part of the bond is called in pending quantification of the loss;
- the insurer must pay on demand without further investigation;
- notification will be via a court order;
- it is expected that insurers will have the right to recover the amount they have paid out, plus their expenses, from the deputy. This is a matter for the insurer and in which the Public Guardian or court play no part.

When the bond is enforced the sum claimed must be paid on first demand and there must be no onus on the Public Guardian or the court to prove fraud. The payment usually happens within two weeks. The bond provider then can take steps to recover from the defaulting deputy.

Chapter 10

Foreign Aspects

What can we learn from safeguarding and protection from other countries?

Eire

A body comparable to the Eire Government's HSE Elder Abuse Service established in 2007 would assist in this process. The Health Services Executive runs the National Centre for the Protection of Older People (NCPOP). The centre is funded by the Health Service Executive to undertake a programme of research into elder abuse in Ireland. Its website (www.ncpop.ie) is a useful resource for all those working with or having contact with older people in areas such as health and social care, legal and financial services, as well as for older people themselves.

More specifically, at its inception the committee set objectives to:

- develop a training programme for senior case workers and dedicated officers;
- expand on the agreed dataset for use nationally;
- ensure that appropriate work plans and targets are developed by individual local health offices to support the National Service Plan;
- ensure appropriate integration and communication between the four area steering groups on elder abuse and the national steering group;
- develop a public awareness campaign in relation to elder abuse;
- develop an implementation plan for the roll-out of HSE policy;
- implement a process for the collation and analysis of emerging data and review data collection processes;
- ensure linkage with vulnerable adults' policy;
- develop best practice guidelines for voluntary/private sector and for the wider public;
- participate in the review of 'Protecting our Future';
- develop a training programme for staff;
- ensure consistency in the dissemination and application of HSE policy and procedures in relation to elder abuse;

- ensure that the learning from investigations/complaints, etc, is applied appropriately in future policy.

This committee has a multi-agency and multi-disciplinary membership to enable it to address specific and complex issues relating to elder abuse.

A 2010 report by NCPOP, 'Abuse and Neglect of Older People in Ireland', provided the first national prevalence statistics on the extent of elder abuse and neglect amongst community-dwelling older people. The overall prevalence of elder abuse and neglect in the previous 12 months was 2.2%. This suggests that over 10,000 people over the age of 65 years experienced mistreatment in the past year. Financial abuse was the most common type reported at 1.3%, followed by psychological abuse (1.2%), physical abuse (0.5%), neglect (0.3%) and sexual abuse (0.05%). Approximately 4% of older people living in the community have experienced some form of abuse since turning 65 years of age.

In their 2014 report the service noted that they had received over 2,590 referrals of alleged elder abuse that year. Psychological abuse was the most frequently reported at 29% followed by financial abuse at 21% (see the report at www. ncpop.ie/whatiselderabuse).

What they recognise is that having an effective government-backed research and advice service is a first step towards countering the problem of elder abuse. It brings together academics and health professionals to investigate the levels and types of abuse, offers training and advice. It also links to the website for older people's services in Ireland. This in turn links directly to the safeguarding officer allocated to a particular area. It is an extremely helpful resource and what is refreshing is that it sets out the information in such a clear format.

USA

In the United States, the Senate has a Special Committee on Ageing (www.aging. senate.gov). The Senate Special Committee on Aging was first established in 1961 as a temporary committee. It was granted permanent status in 1977. While special committees have no legislative authority, they can study issues, conduct oversight of programmes, and investigate reports of fraud. Throughout its existence, the Special Committee on Aging has served as a focal point in the Senate for discussion and debate on matters relating to older Americans. Often, the Committee will submit its findings and recommendations for legislation to the Senate. In addition, the Committee publishes materials of assistance to those interested in public policies which relate to the elderly.

In March 2011, the Government Accountability Office (GAO) produced a report to the above Committee entitled 'Stronger Federal Leadership Could Enhance National Response to Elder Abuse'. This provided information on:

- existing estimates of the extent of elder abuse and their quality;

- factors associated with elder abuse and its impact on victims;

- characteristics and challenges of state Adult Protective Services (APS) responsible for addressing elder abuse; and

- federal support and leadership in this area.

They reviewed relevant research; visited six states and surveyed state APS programs; analysed budgetary and other federal documents; reviewed federal laws and regulations; and interviewed federal officials, researchers, and elder abuse experts. The report recommended that the Secretary of Health and Human Services (HHS) should determine the feasibility of providing APS dedicated guidance, and, in coordination with the Attorney General, facilitate the development and implementation of a nationwide APS data system. Also, Congress should consider requiring HHS to conduct a periodic study to estimate elder abuse's extent. HHS indicated that it will review options for implementing GAO's recommendations.

The Special Committee on Ageing holds hearings into the extent of elder abuse. Testimony by the GAO, including 'Elder Abuse: The Extent of Abuse by Guardians Is Unknown, but Some Measures Are Being Taken to Help Protect Older Adults', shows that the US faces similar problems to those evidenced by cases heard by our Court of Protection and the abuse carried out by attorneys. The Committee's resources are listed at www.aging.senate.gov/resources and show the depth of organisations and work being carried out in this area.

Passage of the Elder Justice Act in 2010 has the potential to bring to bear more attention to this crime and resources to better understand, educate about, and prevent elder financial abuse among the expanding older population. In addition, a new Office of Financial Protection for Older Americans was established in 2010 as part of the new Financial Regulatory Reform Bill. Congressional activity on the Elder Abuse Victims Act (s 462) and the expected introduction of the Senior Financial Empowerment Act indicate that Congressional attention will continue to be focused on the issue of elder financial abuse. This last Act had been 'to prevent mail, telemarketing, and Internet fraud targeting seniors in the United States, to promote efforts to increase public awareness of the enormous impact that mail, telemarketing, and Internet fraud have on seniors, to educate the public, seniors, their families, and their caregivers about how to identify and combat fraudulent activity, and for other purposes.' Unfortunately, this was not enacted by the previous Congress.

A National Institute of Justice study in July 2012 showed that nearly 11% of Americans aged 60 years or older faced some type of elder abuse in the past 12 months. The Elder Justice Act was signed into law in March 2010, as part of the Patient Protection and Affordable Care Act. It provides federal resources to 'prevent, detect, treat, understand, intervene in and, where appropriate, prosecute elder abuse, neglect and exploitation'.

The Act requires that the Department of Health and Human Services oversee the development and management of federal resources for protecting the elderly from elder abuse. The Act requires the following:

- establishment of the Elder Justice Coordinating Council;

- establishment of an Advisory Board on Elder Abuse;

- establishment of Elder Abuse, Neglect, and Exploitation Forensic Centers;

- enhancement of long-term care;

- funding to state and local adult protective service offices;

- grants for long-term care ombudsmen programs and for evaluation of programmes;

- programmes to provide training;

- grants to state agencies to perform surveys of care and nursing facilities.

The Act also directs the US Department of Justice (DOJ) toward actions to prevent elder abuse. The prosecution of abusers has been a challenge. As part of the Elder Justice Act, the DOJ is tasked with dedicating resources, studying and evaluating existing laws, and providing grants to local and state agencies. Their directives include:

- developing objectives, priorities, policies and long-term plans for elder justice programmes;

- conducting a study of state laws and practices relating to elder abuse, neglect and exploitation;

- making available grants to develop training and support programs for law enforcement and other first responders, prosecutors, judges, court personnel and victim advocates;

- ensuring that the DOJ dedicates sufficient resources to the investigation and prosecution of cases relating to elder justice.

The Elder Justice Act creates a nationwide database and programme for background checks for the employees of care facilities. It also requires that any elder abuse perpetrated in a long-term care facility be reported immediately to law enforcement.

The Act also provides grants to state and community agencies to create and promote awareness programmes that focus on scams, online fraud and abuse. Before the Act was passed, federal funding for programmes and justice regulations was not available. Now, community education, awareness campaigns, training for law enforcement personnel, and Adult Protective Services are available to millions of elderly across the USA.

Elder financial abuse continues to decimate incomes both great and small, engenders health care inequities, fractures families, reduces available healthcare options, and increases rates of mental health issues among elders. Elder financial abuse invariably results in losses of human rights and dignity. Despite growing public awareness from a parade of high-profile financial abuse victims, it remains underreported, under-recognised, and under-prosecuted.

Elderly law practitioners hope that the conviction of Anthony D Marshall on charges of financially abusing his mother, legendary New York socialite and philanthropist Brooke Astor, will give a boost to the prosecution of similar but lower-profile cases around the US. Marshall, 85, was convicted of stealing from his mother as her capacity to make decisions deteriorated due to Alzheimer's disease. She died in 2007 at age 105. He was found guilty of 14 of the 16 counts against him, including persuading his mother to make changes to her will that greatly benefited him, and abusing his power of attorney by giving himself an additional $1 million. Her lawyer, who did estate planning work for her, was also convicted on multiple counts, including forging Astor's signature on a codicil to her will.

A 2009 study by MetLife (www.metlife.com/mmi/research/elder-financial-abuse.html) in the US found that up to one million older Americans are targeted by financial abuse yearly, and family members and caregivers are most often the culprits. Craig Reaves, past president of the National Academy of Elder Law Attorneys, termed Marshall's conviction on nearly all the charges 'a huge victory'.

Scotland

The Office of the Public Guardian in Scotland website (www.publicguardian-scotland.gov.uk) provides a single information point about financial provisions contained in the Adults with Incapacity (Scotland) Act 2000. That office has a statutory responsibility in Scotland to supervise people appointed by the court to make financial or property decisions on behalf of an incapable adult. They supervise those granted authority to access an agreed amount of an incapable adult's funds to pay for their day-to-day needs. In addition to their supervisory function they register continuing and/or welfare powers of attorney under the terms of that Act.

The website contains some interesting case studies to assist families and elderly clients in understanding when something is going wrong. (The English OPG could usefully add this to their website.) See, for example, www.publicguardian-scotland.gov.uk/investigations/our-stories/case-study-a.

The passing of the Adult Support and Protection (Scotland) Act 2007 (the Act) is designed to protect adults vulnerable to harm or abuse. Section 1 of the Act provides the general principle on intervention in an adult's affairs , ie that a person may intervene, or authorise an intervention, only if satisfied that the intervention: (a) will provide benefit to the adult which could not reasonably be provided without intervening in the adult's affairs; and (b) is, of the range of options likely to fulfil the object of the intervention, the least restrictive to the adult's freedom (see www.actagainstharm.org). As we have seen in Chapter 6C the English Parliament missed an opportunity with the Care Act 2014 to include similar powers for England and Wales.

Wales

The Welsh Government's challenge in its Strategy for Older People 2013–2023 is as follows:

'the Welsh Government's challenge for the next ten years is:

- to create a Wales where full participation is within the reach of all older people and their contribution is recognised and valued;

- to develop communities that are age-friendly while ensuring older people have the resources they need to live;

- to ensure that future generations of older people are well equipped for later life by encouraging recognition of the changes and demands that may be faced and taking action early in preparation.'

The Older People's Commissioner for Wales is an independent voice and champion for older people across Wales, standing up and speaking out on their behalf. It:

- promotes awareness of the rights and interests of older people in Wales;

- challenges discrimination against older people in Wales;

- encourages best practice in the treatment of older people in Wales;

- reviews the law affecting the interests of older people in Wales.

The Commissioner has a wide range of legal powers to support her in delivering the change that older people want and need to see. The Commissioner's role and statutory powers are defined by the Commissioner for Older People (Wales) Act 2006 and Regulations. See www.olderpeoplewales.com/en for more details.

By way of example, the powers available to the Commissioner include the following:

- May review the way in which the interests of older people are safeguarded and promoted when public bodies discharge their functions, propose to discharge their functions or fail to discharge their functions. This includes those who are discharging functions on behalf of public bodies.

- Has legal authority to enter premises other than private homes to interview older people (with their consent).

- Carry out a review of advocacy, whistleblowing or complaints arrangements. This is focused on whether, and to what extent, the arrangements of certain bodies' advocacy, whistleblowing and complaints arrangements are effective in safeguarding and promoting the interests of relevant older people in Wales.

- May assist a person who is, or has been, an older person in Wales in making a complaint about or representation to public bodies. Assistance includes financial assistance or arranging for a person to advise, represent or assist an older person.

- May examine the case of an older person in relation to a matter which affects the interests of a wider group of older people and not just the individual concerned. Following an examination, the Commissioner must produce a report and may make recommendations.

- May produce guidance on best practice in connection with any matter relating to the interests of older people in Wales. The Commissioner must consult with such persons as she thinks appropriate when producing the guidance.

It is clear from the above that the English Parliament has some way to go to match the work carried out by the Scottish and Welsh Governments. The English system needs to learn from their experiences and improve representation for the elderly.

Northern Ireland

Northern Ireland established a Commissioner for Older People in Northern Ireland by the Commissioner for Older People Act (Northern Ireland) 2011. This is a non-departmental public body with a responsibility to advise and influence Government, focusing on the rights and interests of older people. Due to a shortage of funding the Commissioner has had to refine how it uses its resources.

In respect of protecting older people the commissioner has stated his protection aims as follows:

- 'look at the strategic approach to the provision of services and support for dementia in Northern Ireland;

- examine the role of the health and social care regulator and make recommendations to improve its effectiveness;

- identify the scale of financial abuse against older people, raise awareness of the issue and challenge relevant organisations to make required changes;

- work with criminal justice agencies to better support older people who are victims of crime;

- press government for the introduction of an Adult Safeguarding Bill for Northern Ireland.'

The Commissioner's website sets out the legal powers at his or her disposal:

- make arrangements for research or educational activities concerning the interests of older people;

- issue guidance on best practice in relation to any matter concerning the interests of older people;

- conduct investigations for the purpose of any of his functions;

- compile and publish information concerning the interests of older people;

- provide advice or information on any matter concerning the interests of older people.

The website goes on to expand on those legal duties. Their aim is to

- promote awareness of the interests of older people in Northern Ireland;
- keep under review the adequacy and effectiveness of the law as it affects the interests of older people;
- keep under review effectiveness of services provided to older people by relevant authorities;
- promote provision of opportunities for, and elimination of discrimination against, older people;
- encourage best practice in the treatment of older people;
- promote positive attitudes towards older people and encourage participation by older people in public life;
- advise the Assembly, Secretary of State and any relevant authority on matters concerning the interests of older people.

The Commissioner for Older People for Northern Ireland, Eddie Lynch, launched research in September 2016 that revealed that 21% of older people in Northern Ireland are likely to be experiencing some form of financial abuse. This comes from the Commissioner's research report 'Financial Abuse of Older People in Northern Ireland: The Unsettling Truth'.

Over 1,000 older people across Northern Ireland were surveyed in relation to financial abuse. They were asked 29 direct questions in relation to their personal finances, money-management and decision-making in the last 12 months. The survey (carried out by Perceptive Insight) showed clear evidence that some respondents have experienced a range of financial abuses. The survey sample was representative of Northern Ireland's older population and indicates that over 75,000 older people are experiencing some form of financial abuse in Northern Ireland.

The survey produced the following statistics:

- issues relating to money and possessions 7% (25,061);
- buying and selling goods 6% (21,480);
- issues relating to charity contributions 4% (14,320);
- coercion to sign and fraudulent use of signatures 3% (10,740);
- changes to legal and financial documents and investments 3% (10,740);
- experience of coercion 3% (10,740);
- bank account activity 2% (7,160);
- deception and misuse of money 2% (7,160);

- issues relating to inheritance and power of attorney 2% (7,160).

Speaking about the figures, the Commissioner for Older People, Eddie Lynch said:

'I was both shocked and saddened that 1 in 5 older people in Northern Ireland are experiencing some form of financial abuse. In my role as Commissioner for Older People I have seen the devastating impact that financial abuse can have on older people. Aside from the financial loss itself, this crime affects the emotional wellbeing of older people, bringing with it feelings of betrayal, embarrassment and fear.

'In November last year, my office organised a discussion with a wide range of organisations, professionals, academics and others working on the issue. It became clear that whilst everyone acknowledged that financial abuse is a problem, there was much confusion around the scale and scope of the problem. To date, there has been no region-wide study examining the prevalence of financial abuse against older people. I undertook this research so that for the very first time in Northern Ireland, we can capture the scale of the problem.

'21% of older people surveyed confirmed they had experienced issues indicating financial abuse, ranging from feeling pressured into buying something to family trying to prevent spending in order to maximise their inheritance. This figure is even more alarming when you consider that underreporting is common with financial abuse. This is because it is often difficult and painful for older people to report the crime, especially when the perpetrator is a trusted person. However, I must stress that most older people are loved and valued by their neighbours, friends and relatives who care for them, with their best interests at heart.'

Statistics on adult protection referrals to Health and Social Care Trusts in Northern Ireland, available through the Northern Ireland Adult Safeguarding Partnership (NIASP), shows that in 2014/15 there were 609 cases where the alleged financial abuse of older people was the primary reason for referral. 20% of cases of alleged abuse committed against older people were financial abuse cases. The research also indicated that the problem of financial abuse is widely under-reported. 30% of victims tell no one about their abuse.

The conclusions drawn from the 2016 report were that:

- more than 75,000 older people in Northern Ireland are experiencing some type of financial abuse;
- the overall prevalence of financial abuse of older people in Northern Ireland is an alarming 21%;
- organisations must now target their responses to this crime;
- responsibility for protecting older people from financial abuse lies across the public, private, independent, voluntary and community sectors, as well as with families and with Northern Ireland society as a whole;

- increasing public awareness and educating older people about financial abuse could lead to an increase in the detection of abuse and give older people more confidence to report it;

- it is also important that staff working with older people are trained to recognise when financial abuse is taking place, and that they are informed about the need to ensure good practice when selling goods and services so that older people are informed about what they are purchasing;

- the introduction of an Adult Safeguarding Bill for Northern Ireland, incorporating a clear definition of financial abuse, would also help those working in this area to prosecute offenders, deterring potential abusers and offering greater redress for older victims.

It concludes with this call for action:

'This report needs to change how organisations work together, as well as raising awareness. The data within this report should enable those dealing with the prevention or effects of financial abuse to better identify older people who are at risk, or who may be 'silently' experiencing financial abuse. It should help organisations to recognise behaviours and transactions which are indicators that financial abuse is happening. This report must underpin action to tackle financial abuse across Northern Ireland and should help guide organisational collaboration. It should enable organisations to work together to combat financial abuse, combining their collective resources to do so.'

On a limited budget the North Ireland Commissioner is attempting to influence the North Ireland Government to take account of the older person and how legislation and policies affect this important section of the community. The English Government could well fund a similar office in Whitehall.

Chapter 11

Reforms

11A

Reforms

Parliamentary oversight

In 2015 a House of Lords committee was established to look at the workings of the MCA 2005, ten years after it came into force. As the website proclaims:

'The Committee was appointed to consider and report on the Mental Capacity Act 2005.

'Status: A debate on the report took place on Tuesday 10 March. The Committee ceased to exist on the publication of its report.'

This was surely a missed opportunity to continue that work and to have a permanent oversight into legislation that affects the elderly.

A co-ordinated approach

What is apparent from the England and Wales provision of services is that we have no co-ordinated approach to this issue. If your client has lost their mental capacity then the OPG is the body responsible for investigating financial abuse. Surely it is time for a co-ordinated multi-disciplinary approach? At the very least a resource along the Irish lines pulling together research in this area, offering training and advice would be a start. There is no doubt that the more that is done to raise public awareness here, the more elderly and vulnerable people will be protected. Only by giving the elderly a voice to express their concerns in a co-ordinated manner can any real progress be made towards tackling the abuse or at the very least identifying it at a much earlier stage. A more caring and inclusive approach to the elderly that demonstrably values them and their opinions would begin to shift the balance away from the younger and able-bodied in society.

Visit www.gov.uk/government/organisations/office-of-the-public-guardian. It sets out the legal decisions you can make and how the OPG is run. Neither elder abuse nor financial abuse is mentioned. The only connection to such abuse is where it says 'Report a concern about an attorney or deputy'. There may not be an attorney or deputy in place. It may simply be that your adult son or daughter is helping themselves to your money and you are powerless to do anything about it.

If you search on the web for details about financial abuse in England you will find references to AgeUK, the Law Society and Citizens Advice, but no reference to the OPG, NHS or Action on Elder Abuse.

Action on Elder Abuse is a charity that has over many years used its helplines to respond to concerns. Its website (https://elderabuse.org.uk) is a first port of call for many suffering abuse. It runs an important helpline and courses for practitioners, and undertakes policy work. At present the charity is campaigning for a criminal charge of elder abuse. They report that many countries have specific legislation in place to protect older people from abuse, including all the states in the USA, Canada, Japan, South Korea, Israel and Slovenia. By March 2015 they had received 21,267 calls to their helpline as compared with 10,013 to March 2014. This significant increase illustrates the depth of the problem of elder abuse generally in society. What is apparent, though, is that this charity is undertaking such an important role whilst at the same time having to fund raise to fund its activities. Surely this should be wholly funded by government?

The ongoing process of using web-based services for much of Government activity accelerates by the day. As Alan Eccles, the Public Guardian, said in October 2013:

> 'More and more people are taking the important decision to apply for Lasting Power of Attorney and it is right they receive the best possible service.

> 'We are continually looking to improve our service. By creating a fully digital process for creating and registering Lasting Powers of Attorney we will make it simpler, clearer and faster for the public.'

The Law Society and other professional bodies have expressed alarm at this process. However, Helen Clarke, former chair of the Law Society's wills and equity committee, disagreed with Eccles' vision. She stated that:

> 'I am utterly opposed to digital LPAs. Without the need for a witness or wet signature, there will be no forensic evidence that an elderly or vulnerable person had really entered into an LPA agreement with someone they trusted. There is a huge risk of being cheated.'

Online LPAs are part of the policy to make all public services 'digital by default'. It is clear to practitioners in this field that this denies the vulnerable in society much needed safeguards.

Not surprisingly, online production of LPAs have already reached the Court of Protection. In *Public Guardian v Marvin* [2014] EWCOP 47, CS did not take legal advice regarding the powers of attorney and it emerged at the hearing that the family had downloaded the prescribed forms from the Internet and decided that CS's son, Marvin, should be the attorney, because MM was already his appointee for social security purposes. They assumed erroneously that she could not act as both attorney and appointee. The attorney then delegated powers to the attorney's mother and at some point the donor's house was transferred from the donor to the son and his mother's names.

In *JL (Revocation of Lasting Power of Attorney)* [2014] EWCOP 36 the court heard that she executed a digital LPA for property and financial affairs. The LPA was drawn up by JL's daughter (AS) online. JL appointed AS to be her sole attorney. She did not receive any independent advice about the creation of the LPA, though AS claims that she fully explained the document to her mother before she signed it. The court found that AS has behaved in a way that contravened her authority and is not in JL's best interests. The attorney admitted that she failed to keep proper accounts and financial records. Her explanation for the dramatic increase in JL's expenditure was 'there is no point in her being the wealthiest woman in the graveyard'.

Recommended safeguards

A tightening up of rules to prevent abuse would help to reassure the public that steps are being taken to prevent abuse and safeguard the vulnerable elderly population. A few suggestions as follows would assist in this process:

Lasting powers of attorney

- LPA certificate providers should always see the donor alone without anyone else present;
- statement of the capacity in which certificate providers are signing;
- only professionals should act as certificate providers;
- all attorneys actively managing a donor's finances and property should always keep annual accounts which can be shown to concerned parties as required;
- random checks on attorneys by the OPG;
- random calling in of accounts for attorneys;
- care allowances to be only agreed if authorised by the OPG or the Court of Protection;
- no loans, equity release or expenses for other members of the family or friends to be permitted unless authorised in advance;
- if annual accounts are not mandatory then consider whether certain transactions should trigger audit of attorney's accounts: equity release, sale of properties, cashing in investments over a certain value.

Lifetime gifts

No gifts of any sort to be allowed by attorneys or deputies unless authorised by the Court of Protection. It is clear from the cases that there is confusion about what gifts attorneys and deputies can make. It would be far better to have a blanket ban on gifts unless the court has approved them.

Surety bonds

To be extended to attorneys acting under an active registered EPA or LPA. This would give protection to the donor and their estate beneficiaries that if their estate has been dissipated by the action of their appointed attorney or attorneys then the surety bond could be called in to recompense the estate.

Separate appointments of attorneys and executors

One of the problems with detecting financial abuse is that if the attorneys are also the appointed executors of the victim's estate then there will be no independent oversight into past instances of lifetime financial abuse. For this reason, it seems sensible to have separate appointments. The OPG will not have any jurisdiction to investigate financial abuse once a donor of a power of attorney has died. The only persons with the authority to do so will be the nominated executors.

Training

More training for frontline staff in banks, GPs, solicitors, investment managers and other professionals dealing with the elderly and vulnerable is an important part of raising awareness of the problem.

There should be a legal duty to report wherever financial abuse is suspected.

Statistics should be collated to find the real level of abuse. This would ensure that a full record of incidents, the action taken and whether any report was made to the OPG and or the Police.

It is Time for a Minister for the Elderly?

In writing a book about financial abuse of the elderly it has been clear that the issue is not being given the attention and priority in Government that should be expected. At present there are some 10 million people in the UK over the age of 65 and by 2030 this is expected to have risen by 5.5 million. The elderly command a large proportion of the population's wealth and increasingly are seemingly the victims of an unstoppable wave of financial abuse.

According to the Office of National Statistics, since mid-2005 the UK population aged 65 and over has increased by 21%, and the population aged 85 and over has increased by 31%. The number of males aged 85 and over has increased by 54% since mid-2005, compared to a 21% increase for females. Currently, the Government minister responsible for our older population is based in the Department of Health, which begs the question as to how a minister surrounded by health officials can set policy, deal with legislation and take an overview of what the elderly population require when there is so much more to the role than simply health alone.

The minister responsible is titled the Minister of State for Community and Social Care. They have the following responsibilities:

- adult social care;
- autism;
- integration;
- local government;
- mental health;
- older people;
- physical and learning disabilities;
- allied health professions;
- primary care, including dentistry and ophthalmic services:
  - GP contract;
  - out-of-hours care;

- ○ pharmacy;
- ○ primary care commissioning policy.

According to his own website the announcements made by the minister since February 2015 have no mention of the elderly. You would be hard-pressed to find anything about the elderly aside from policies for carers' health, dementia and end-of life care. The elderly are also invisible on the Ministry of Justice's website.

We have commissioners for the police and crime, an information commissioner, and now a victims commissioner. At the very least we should have a Commissioner for the Elderly speaking up for the elderly and overseeing policy. There is no voice at present and no one taking an overview on what the different agencies are doing and what they should be doing.

By way of comparison, in New Zealand there is a Minister for Seniors. Her office is an information source for the elderly and their carers, but also has a role in helping 'government and communities keep up to date with the needs of seniors'. Her work includes the following:

- positive ageing;
- age-friendly communities;
- social isolation;
- the business of ageing;
- elder abuse and neglect;
- protecting your future with an EPA.

This looks like a good starting point. In the US the Administration on Aging, an agency of the Department of Health and Human Services, carries out the provisions of the Older Americans Act 1965. It also 'promotes the well-being of older individuals by providing services and programs designed to help them live independently in their homes and communities. The Act also empowers the federal government to distribute funds to the states for supportive services for individuals over the age of 60'.

Many other countries have now recognised the economic and cultural value of their elderly populations. It seems so short-sighted that this and earlier governments again miss the opportunity to co-ordinate policy and provide a voice in Government for such a key part of the population. By comparison, we have a minister responsible for children and families in the Department for Education. Their responsibilities include:

- adoption, fostering and residential care home reform;
- child protection;
- special educational needs and disability;
- family law and justice;

- children's and young people's services;
- school sport;
- Cafcass;
- Office of Children's Commissioner.

In respect of financial abuse generally, two major charities have been calling for such a voice. AgeUK in a September 2013 press release called 'more collaboration between health, social services and financial sectors to recognise and report signs of financial abuse'. They said:

> 'Tens of thousands of older people are at risk of financial abuse, with those with dementia or reduced cognitive function the most vulnerable.

> 'The warning comes as the latest figures show that at least 130,000 older people have suffered some form of financial abuse from someone known to them since turning 65. The figures also show that women are twice as likely as men to be victims of financial abuse in later life, with the majority being women aged 80 to 89 and living on their own, single or widowed. Disability and cognitive decline are also factors that increase the risk of financial abuse.'

In 2013 Age UK said: 'The ageing population is a challenge for any government, and what we need is someone who will draw attention to the issues that affect older people and work to find the best way to make later life better for all.' The charity Action on Elder Abuse has called for a crime of elder abuse to be enacted. A minister with responsibility for the elderly could promote this.

It is clear that there is real need to address this problem and create a voice for the specific needs of the elderly. Their contribution and experience to the wider society could also be championed.

Appendix A

Lasting Powers of Attorney

Donor's Statement of Wishes and Values

Name:

Address:

Date of birth:

LPA dated:

Attorney's duties

Attorneys have a duty to:

- apply certain standards of care and skill (duty of care) when making decisions;
- carry out the donor's instructions;
- not take advantage of their position and not benefit themselves, but benefit the donor (fiduciary duty);
- not delegate decisions, unless authorised to do so;
- act in good faith;
- respect confidentiality;
- comply with the directions of the Court of Protection;
- not give up the role without telling the donor and the court;
- keep accounts;
- keep the donor's money and property separate from their own.

OPG guidance on how an attorney should act

Attorneys can only make gifts on the following occasions:

- births or birthdays;

- weddings or wedding anniversaries;

- civil partnership ceremonies or anniversaries; or

- any other occasion when families, friends or associates usually give presents.

If the donor previously made donations to any charity regularly or from time to time, the attorney can make donations from the person's funds.

But the value of any gift or donation must be reasonable and take into account the size of the donor's estate.

Safeguards

(1) Joint decisions:

- eg sale of property, investment decisions with a value exceeding £10,000, taking out equity release plans;

- joint and several decisions.

(2) Accounts to be audited once a year by an independent third party.

Donor's specific wishes:

Signed:

Dated:

Financial Abuse Warning Card for Professionals

Characteristics of potential victims

- advanced age;
- stroke;
- dementia or other cognitive impairment;
- physical, mental or emotional distress;
- depression;
- recent loss of spouse or divorce;
- social isolation;
- middle or upper income bracket;
- taking multiple medications;
- frailty.

Indicators of irregularities

Financial
- missing belongings or property;
- missing paperwork;
- evasive or implausible explanations;
- unawareness or confusion by the victim of a recent transaction;
- the victim being afraid or worried about talking about finances;
- unpaid bills;
- eviction notices.

Lack of care

- evidence of lack of care, eg lack of clothing, food other necessities;
- unkempt home where the victim used to be house-proud;
- untreated medical problems;
- provision of unnecessary services.

Social isolation

- discontinued relationships with friends and family;
- increased dependence on others;
- sudden heavy traffic in and out of the home;
- new acquaintances;
- caregivers or family members having an excessive interest in amount of money being spent on the elderly person;
- mutual dependence on another;
- family members addicted to alcohol or drugs.

Conduct of banking transactions

- unexplained transfers out of or between accounts;
- unusual or unexplained sudden activity;
- large withdrawals when the elderly person is accompanied by another;
- frequent transfers or ATM withdrawals;
- change of address for statements and cheque books;
- suspicious signatures;
- inclusion of other names on bank card;
- suspicious credit card activity;
- ATM withdrawals by housebound person;
- online banking by person with no internet-enabled device or IT experience;
- person with no awareness of personal financial affairs, eg become in debt but not sure why;
- unusual number of cheques written to cash.

Legal transactions

- execution of powers of attorney who is confused or does not understand or remember the transaction;
- forged signatures;
- changes in their property wills or other documents where they are unexpected, sudden or in favour of new acquaintances;
- sudden appearance of previously uninvolved relatives claiming rights to the victim's affairs and possessions.

Visits to healthcare providers

- unmet physical needs;
- missed medical appointments;
- dropping out of treatment;
- declining physical and psychological health;
- defensiveness by caregiver during visits or on telephone and unwillingness by caregiver to leave the victim alone during appointments.

Immediate action to be taken

- speak to the victim;
- speak to non-involved family or trusted friends if consent from victim has been obtained;
- protect finances and property if at all possible against further misappropriation;
- if there is real evidence of a criminal offence having taken place, call the police;
- if the victim has lost their mental capacity and their affairs are managed by an attorney under a registered power or a deputy, speak to the attorney or deputy if the abuse is by another;
- if the abuse is by the attorney or deputy call the OPG;
- call the adult safeguarding team at the relevant social services department responsible for the area;
- if unsure call the Action on Elder Abuse hotline.

Appendix C

Statistics from Court of Protection Cases 2014–16

Years	2014	2015	2016
Sex of victims	Male = 25%	Male = 25%	Male nil
	Female = 75%	Female = 75%	Female = 100%
Sex of abusers	Male =55%	Male = 65%	Male = 100%
	Female = 45%	Female = 35%	Female nil
Deputies	20% of cases	15% of cases	
Attorneys	80% of cases	85% of cases	100% of cases
Age range of victims	80–95 = 85%	80–95 = 10/18 = 55%	80–95 = 2/2 = 100%
	Less than 80 = 2 =15%	Less than 80 = 8/18= 45%	
Age range of abusers	50–60 years = 55%	50–60 years = 55%	50–60 years = 100%
	60–70 years = 45%	Under 50 years = 45%	
Abuser as child of the victim	45% of cases	95% of cases	50% of cases
Unpaid care home fees	20% of cases	40% of cases	50% of cases

Notes

Sample sizes of Court of Protection cases where financial abuse has taken place:

2014 = 12

2015 = 13

2016 = 2

Index